THIRST

JB JOSSEY-BASS

THIRST

FIGHTING THE CORPORATE **THEFT** OF OUR WATER

Alan Snitow
Deborah Kaufman
with Michael Fox

John Wiley & Sons, Inc.

Published by Jossey-Bass
A Wiley Imprint
989 Market Street, San Francisco, CA 94103-1741   www.josseybass.com

Jossey-Bass books and products are available through most bookstores. To contact Jossey-Bass directly call our Customer Care Department within the U.S. at 800-956-7739, outside the U.S. at 317-572-3986, or fax 317-572-4002.

Jossey-Bass also publishes its books in a variety of electronic formats. Some content that appears in print may not be available in electronic books.

Library of Congress Cataloging-in-Publication Data

Snitow, Alan.
  Thirst: fighting the corporate theft of our water/Alan Snitow,
Deborah Kaufman; with Michael Fox.
    p. cm.
  Includes bibliographical references and index.
  ISBN 978-0-7879-8458-8 (cloth)
1. Water resources development—Social aspects. 2. Privatization—
Social aspects. I. Kaufmann, Deborah, date. II. Fox, Michael, date.
III. Title.
  HD1691.S625 2007
  333.9100973—dc22   2007003997

Printed in the United States of America
FIRST EDITION
HB Printing   10 9 8 7 6 5 4 3 2 1

Contents

Preface

The event that started us on the journey to our 2004 documentary film—also called *Thirst*—and later to this book took place not far from where we live in the San Francisco Bay Area. A bearded Alaskan named Ric Davidge arrived one day in Northern California with a seemingly ingenious plan to reduce what he called "the waste" of river water that flows unused into the sea. Why not lay some pipe up the river bottoms, tap the flow into giant water bags moored off the coast, and drag the bags off to sell the water in drier climes? Because fresh water is lighter than salt water, the bags float near the surface, so a person can stand on top and appear to walk on water. The inventor of the technology, Terry Spragg, does just that in a promotional photo, dancing joyfully on the waves off the Pacific coast. Californians have fought water wars for 150 years, so at first they greeted Davidge's idea with amused disbelief, especially after the eight hundred-foot-long water bags were referred to as "bladders" or even "giant condoms."[1]

For us, the visual possibilities of a film about this effort seemed almost too good to be true. Walking on water, giant condoms . . . what a wealth of imagery! But it was not to be. Because Northern California's rivers already supply much of arid Southern California's water, people in the north are rabid about protecting the water that remains. So when Davidge applied for permits to carry out his scheme, amusement quickly turned to outrage. "Not here. Not ever." The water-bag plan was scuttled before we could even point our cameras.

Many people look back at the incident with laughter, but Davidge was by no means some isolated crackpot. He had been water adviser to Interior Secretary James Watt in the Reagan administration, and his company had powerful backers: the multi-billion-dollar empire of a Saudi prince and Japan's NYK Lines, one of the world's largest shipping companies. It suddenly became clear to us that the once-staid world of pipes and pumps was changing. Water was becoming a global business, with entrepreneurs and multinationals competing to take over water sources and services.

As we began to focus on water as a subject for a film, another event swept the headlines. Enron and other energy companies had taken advantage of California's disastrous deregulation of electricity to "game" the system, driving up prices and reaping windfall profits. At the end of 2001, Enron went bankrupt, its employees lost their jobs and pensions, its top officials were forced to make "perp walks" like common criminals, and it had to sell its assets, even its crooked "E" logo. One of those assets was Azurix, a subsidiary that had become one of the world's largest water corporations. It turned out that Enron had planned to do with water what it had done with electricity—sell the resource to the highest bidder and the public be damned.[2] Soon, we were noticing efforts to privatize and commodify water everywhere we looked, and we started asking questions. How come a six-pack of bottled water costs more than a gallon of gasoline? Why doesn't anybody fix the broken water fountains in our public high schools? What's this about shipping water out of the Great Lakes to Asia? Why is the Bechtel Corporation managing water in occupied Iraq?

Our curiosity was growing, but, in the end, we were driven to make our documentary film because of our amazement at how intensely people responded to perceived threats to their water. We eventually focused on three stories that captured the spirit of this grassroots rebellion. In Cochabamba, Bolivia, the citizens carried out a full-scale insurrection against privatization of their water by a global consortium led by Bechtel. In Rajasthan, India, rural women took on the World Bank and their own government to stop companies like Coca-Cola from taking control of precious water sources. In Stockton, California, a citizens' coalition fought the mayor's proposal to hand over the public water system to a multinational consortium led by Rheinisch-Westfälisches Elektrizitätswerk Aktiengesellschaft (RWE), hardly a household name, but one of the hundred largest corporations in the world.[3]

The 3rd World Water Forum, Kyoto

We continued to film as activists from each of our stories traveled to Kyoto for the 3rd World Water Forum in 2003. The Forum was sponsored by the World Water Council, a group whose goal is to improve water management worldwide but whose political agenda often seems to be to promote privatization as the best means to achieve that goal.[4] The World Bank played a major role in driving that agenda. Before the Forum, the World Bank had been widely criticized for its controversial practice of requiring the privatization of public services, including water, as a condition for providing loans to developing countries.[5] At the Forum, the World Bank and the private water industry generally dismissed their critics and claimed "a consensus" for privatization.

Water activists from dozens of countries came to Kyoto to shatter that consensus. In their view, making water a private commodity to be bought and sold in the marketplace was morally wrong, unjust to the poor, and environmentally dangerous. The "water warriors," as they called themselves, hoped to overturn resolutions from the previous World Water Forum in The Hague (2000), which had defined water as a "basic need" and "economic good." Instead, the activists called for formal recognition that access to water is a basic "human right."[6]

The Kyoto Forum, attended by almost twenty thousand people from around the world, displayed a startling clash of cultures—dark-suited industrialists and bankers on the dais challenged at panel after panel by colorful international activists who pummeled them with pointed questions and personal case histories of corporate abuse. After days of increasing acrimony, the conference was disrupted at the final plenary when activists stormed the stage in a demonstration that was confrontational in spirit and surprisingly minimalist in message: they chanted a slogan and held banners that simply proclaimed, "There is no consensus."

Filming a Movement

Our documentaries take shape slowly as we film and edit our material. This process allows for many changes of direction and new insights at any stage. In the case of *Thirst*, while filming in Stockton we suddenly encountered a new theme in that town's ongoing water battle. In his annual State of the City address before a crowd of almost a thousand people, the mayor called on the City Council to approve privatization of city water services. "It's time that Stockton enter the 21st Century in its delivery of services," he said, "and think of our citizens as customers."[7]

The comment struck us as a remarkable one-sentence summary of an entire worldview about the role of the citizen in the new millennium. That once-proud, self-conscious, entitled participant in the life of the community had now become a mere consumer. The mayor also argued that public participation in decision making should be limited to quadrennial elections, when voters choose the leaders who will make decisions on their behalf.[8] But as we worked on the film, time and again we were amazed to see multinational water companies and their allies in government try to prevent citizens from voting on, or even knowing about, decisions that would affect their lives.

Two million people saw *Thirst* when it was nationally broadcast on PBS in 2004 as part of the documentary series *P.O.V.* As we traveled to film festivals and community screenings in the United States and Canada, people we met told us about local water battles where they lived and asked us to tell their stories.

Inspired by those encounters, *Thirst*, the book, is a chronicle of an exciting new movement that is challenging old political alignments and new economic hierarchies in the United States. In fighting for their water, people are relearning old strategies and developing new ones. They are experiencing victories and defeats. They are reasserting democratic values in a world where citizens are being reduced to customers.

Often, it's not until the end of writing or film editing that we can see the shape of the story, what our film or book is really about. With *Thirst* we came to see that the conflicts over water are really about fundamental questions of democracy itself: Who will make the decisions that affect our future, and who will be excluded? And if citizens no longer control their most basic resource, their water, do they really control anything at all?

Berkeley, California   Alan Snitow
January 2007   Deborah Kaufman

Acknowledgments

Our friend, co-writer Michael Fox, joined us as we developed the stories for this book. Together, we followed the backroom deals, the public debates, and some inspiring new leaders who have emerged in the cities, towns, and rural communities that have become ground zero for the new politics of water. A longtime film critic, Michael has now joined the growing number of "water people" as we spread across our blue planet. Thank you, Michael, for joining us on this journey.

We have many people and organizations to thank for their support. For their significant funding for the film, we are grateful to the John D. and Catherine T. MacArthur Foundation. For their support of additional research for the book, we thank the Panta Rhea Foundation and the Park Foundation.

For ongoing feedback we acknowledge the Pacific Institute for Studies in Development, Environment, and Security, Food & Water Watch, and the Council of Canadians—three organizations that have provided much of the brains, brawn, and inspiration for our work.

We also wish to thank the individuals who read a draft of this book and provided discerning criticisms and important advice: Peter Gleick, Jill Hannum, Wenonah Hauter, Simeon Herskovits, Jacques Leslie, and Alan Ramo. However, their willingness to engage in dialogue with us should not be construed in any way as agreement with the views expressed in this book. For those, we bear sole responsibility.

We are grateful to our editors at Jossey-Bass and Wiley, particularly Dorothy Hearst, who planted the seeds for this project, and Jesse Wiley, who shepherded the book through publication.

We are also indebted to PBS' *P.O.V.* series for recognizing the importance of independent film and of this subject early on and to the distributors of our film, Bullfrog Films, especially John Hoskyns-Abrahall and Winifred Scherrer, for their commitment to social-change media.

We have countless others to thank, including the dozens of people who agreed to be interviewed, especially Michael McDonald, Dale Stocking, Diane Park, and Sylvia Kothe in Stockton; Jim Graham in Felton; Chetan Talwalkar in Lexington; Deidre Consolati in Lee; Mark Lubold and Carolyn Toll Oppenheim in Holyoke; Hiroshi and Arlene Kanno in Wisconsin Dells; and Terry Swier in Mecosta County. We also want to thank Juliette Beck, formerly with Public Citizen; Ruth Caplan of the Sierra Club Water Privatization Task Force; Jonathan Leavitt of Massachusetts Global Action; and Anil Naidoo of the Council of Canadians' Blue Planet Project. Many other individuals too numerous to thank contributed to our research and to our growing appreciation of the magnitude of this new struggle.

We are grateful for the ongoing research and activism of the Polaris Institute, the Sierra Club, Public Services International, Corporate Europe Observatory, Corporate Accountability International, the Alliance for Democracy, and the World Development Movement, which have all played an important role in protecting our water rights.

Many international leaders and institutions are fighting to protect public access to water. In particular, we continue to be inspired by the brilliant work of water advocates Maude Barlow and Tony Clarke in Canada, Oscar Olivera in Bolivia, and Rajendra Singh and V. Suresh in India. We have been honored to meet them and see them in action in the course of our research.

Many other individuals encouraged the writing of this book from the beginning. Many thanks in particular go to Pam Troy, Jill Hannum, and Janet Traub. Our families have provided encouragement, ideas, and love: Bernard Kaufman, Shirley Kaufman Daleski, Bill Daleski, Sharon Kaufman, Rabia Van Hattum, and Ann Snitow. We dedicate the book to our children, Adam and Tania, and to their generation—the future is yours to shape.

—A. S. and D. K.

Let justice well up like waters, and righteousness as a mighty stream.

—Amos 5:24

1

Water: Commodity or Human Right?

A new kind of citizens' revolt has broken out in towns and cities across the United States. It's not made up of "the usual suspects," it has no focused ideology, and it's not the stuff of major headlines. The revolt often starts as a "not-in-my-backyard" movement to defend the character of a community or to assert a desire for local control. But quickly, almost spontaneously, the revolt expands its horizon to encompass issues of global economic justice, and its constituency grows to include people across party, class, and racial lines.

A number of issues have sparked local activism—the arrival of big-box stores like Wal-Mart, factory shutdowns, unwanted real estate development—but the new movement against the corporate takeover of water is shaped uniquely by its subject. Water is a necessity of life that touches everyone in their own homes. Because each community has only one supplier, the transformation of water from public asset to private commodity raises unavoidable questions about affordability, environmental impact, and local control. When a multinational water company comes to town, citizens are forced to recognize the arrival of globalization on their doorsteps.

This emerging citizens' movement coincides with the recognition that society faces the ticking clock of global warming. Scientists expect climate change to reduce available water supplies, especially in areas dependent on winter snowpacks. The clean, reliable, and cheap water we have taken for granted for decades is now threatened. Water scarcity, already a crisis in much of the world, is a coming reality in the United States.

An environmental crisis cannot be dealt with ad hoc. It demands concerted action from citizens through government. But, over the years, national, state, and local governments have been weakened by those ideologically opposed to a strong public sector. They are against government intervention in economic affairs and against populist movements that aim to reassert values of environmental stewardship and public service.

This book describes how citizens and communities across the United States are fighting to defend their water and take back their government at the same time. These activists often have no idea what they are getting into when they start. But, ready or not, they are thrust into a battle that takes them far from their initial concerns about their personal water supply or their local government. They must confront an elaborate array of ideas that seductively meld the traditional utopian impulse of Manifest Destiny with a corporate project of global economic integration. They must grapple, first, with an almost religious belief in the marketplace as the route to a more perfect society and, second, with the unmatched financial and political power of multinational corporations.

Nevertheless, these people and communities have shown that when it comes to water, the ideologues and practitioners of globalization may have overreached. Water is what makes life possible on this planet. It is "of the body" and essential. Our reaction to it is visceral, and when we suddenly find we can no longer take it for granted, we react very rapidly. The unanswered question is whether the struggles for control of water described in this book are simply a last stand against a corporatized future—or the beginnings of a revolt that will redefine how people interact with the environment and how citizens define democracy.

A Limited and Defining Resource

More than food, guns, or energy, the control of water has defined the structure of civilizations. Ruling classes have always been water rulers, and cities and farms can exist only to the extent that they control their water resources. For thousands of years, the conflicts between towns and countries have been defined by the battle over who gets to use the stream. The words *rival* and *river* have the same root.

Water is not merely a medium of conflict, it is also a purifying, regenerative, and hallowed element. The essential nature of water is sanctified in Christian baptism, the Jewish *mikvah*, and Hindu submersion in the holy waters of the Ganges River. Muslims and Hopis have their sacred water rituals, as does virtually every spiritual group.

Water itself isn't just a substance, it's a flow—the hydrologic cycle—from cloud to rain to river to sea and back to cloud. Until recently, this marvelous circulation has blinded us to the very real limits of water. Whether we believe in a Creator or not, no one is making more water. We have only the amount that we've always had. We drink the tears of Leonardo da Vinci and wash in the saliva of dinosaurs. Fresh water is a finite resource that is quickly dwindling compared with the world's growing human population and the rate at which we are polluting the water we have.

Although the majority of the earth is covered by water, most of it is in the oceans—salty, undrinkable, and unusable for growing food. Much of the remainder is in polar ice caps and glaciers, leaving less than 1 percent for human use in rivers, lakes, streams, and aquifers. The plenty we imagine as we look at satellite photos of a blue planet dwindles quickly to those thin blue capillaries on the map.

Scarcity is the soul of profit—if profit can be said to have a soul. The water crisis is already here, and that means clean, fresh water can command ever higher prices. Eager investors are bidding up water-industry stocks and lining up at industry-sponsored forums to get into the "water business." But because governments own most water services, investors have few choices. "How do we take some of the market share away from the government?" asked the vice chair of Southwest Water at an investors' conference. The water industry's answer is to ally with the financial industry, which also wants to open up the market. "It sounds like an exciting opportunity," an investment adviser told *Bloomberg News*, "but you have to have viable vehicles with which people can buy into the asset."[1]

Corporations hope to fill that void primarily by privatizing urban water systems, either by outright purchase or by operating them under long-term contracts euphemistically called "public-private partnerships." The aim in both cases is to siphon profits from the flow.

Water is fast becoming a commodity to be bought and sold, rather than the medium through which a community maintains its identity and asserts its values. But for most people in the United States water is still just water—not the stuff of profit or politics. We don't give it a second thought until the tap runs dry or brown or we flush and it doesn't go away.

Public Water in the United States

In the past, most conflicts over control of water have been local, typically confined to a single watershed, the area drained by a stream or river. It's difficult to see great national political trends or global corporate strategies at work when local politicians, technical consultants, and engineers personify the arcane power relations of our plumbing. Although hidden out of sight and scent, even sewers have a history. In the United States in the nineteenth century, water ownership and management were largely in private hands. River or well water was tapped for local needs by individuals and, as the country grew, by small private companies.

Historian Norris Hundley, author of *The Great Thirst*, has written about a chaotic period in the late nineteenth century when "entrepreneurs promised clean, bountiful, reasonably priced water supplies" in return for a chance to make a profit. "These dream deals soon became nightmares of diversion facilities ripped out by floods, wooden pipes leaking more water than they carried, mud holes pitting the streets, pollution exceeding anything witnessed in the past, and an escalating fire threat."[2] Across the country the pattern was repeated: private water management often meant leaky pipes, pollution, and disease.

In New York City, Aaron Burr's early-nineteenth-century Manhattan Company (later to become Chase Manhattan Bank) was one of the most corrupt, incompetent, and disastrous experiments in water privatization on record. As the city grew, access to clean drinking water was uncertain at best. People drank beer rather than risk disease and death from fetid waters. Some customers received no water at all, and many fire hydrants failed to work. It took the devastating cholera epidemic in 1832 and the Great Fire of 1835—so huge it was seen as far away as Philadelphia—to push the devastated commercial center of the United States into taking its water future into its own hands.[3]

The story was similar in cities across the United States and Canada. As populations grew, private water companies did not have the resources to meet the need. Citizens demanded and eventually won modern public water systems, financed through bonds, operated by reliable engineers and experts, and accountable to local governments.[4] The nation built a dazzling system of community waterworks, which provide clean, reasonably priced water and sewer systems that still rank among the best in the world. Approximately 85 percent of Americans are presently served by the thousands of publicly owned and locally operated water systems. For several generations, water has been a public trust.[5]

But the country's once dependable public water systems now face a worsening crisis. In a survey of water professionals released in 2006 by the American Water Works Association, many utility managers chose the adjective *failing* to describe their water infrastructure rather than choosing the word *aging* as they had in previous years.[6]

The growing crisis arises not just from scarcity but also from the failure of politicians at all levels of government to invest in water and sewage works. Federal cutbacks, in particular, have devastated city budgets, forcing elected officials to choose which programs to cut. Water services have been high on their lists. Wenonah Hauter of the national consumer-rights organization Food & Water Watch warned of this danger in a 2005 letter to the U.S. Conference of Mayors: "The more financially troubled a city's water system, the more receptive city leaders will be to ceding control over that system to a private operator in a long-term monopoly contract or through an outright sale." A 2005 survey indicated that the mayors of two hundred cities, large and small, would "consider" a privatization contract "if they could save money."[7] In addition, local politicians have often raided profitable public water systems to pay for other programs, stripping local water departments of resources needed for maintenance or new equipment. And many rural water companies, public and private, are too small to afford the large investments necessary to upgrade their systems to meet environmental regulations.

In spite of these problems, public utilities in the United States are considered a model in many parts of the world. Public operation ensures transparency and documentation. It provides the opportunity for communities to work for positive outcomes through public hearings, citizen action, and elections.

Nevertheless, there's lots of work to do. Industry and government studies calculate that water utilities need to invest enormous sums over the coming years to fix the aging network of pipes under every street and the outdated plants that clean drinking water or treat sewage. A report issued by the Congressional Budget Office estimates the cost at $500 to $800 billion through the early-2020s.[8] Much of that investment is necessary to meet new federal clean-water mandates handed down without the funding needed to fulfill them.

In the past, meeting such challenges was a sign of national pride and purpose, but those days now seem like distant history. U.S. government spending for water infrastructure is being reduced, even slashed, year after year. Everywhere, we hear instead the language of private markets. "In recent years, what we have seen is a kind of theft of the commons," says Maude Barlow, chair of the Council of Canadians, an independent, nonpartisan citizens' group. "The notion [is] that absolutely everything should be commodified and put on the open market, and it is happening very, very fast. Basically, we see this as an issue of human rights versus corporate rights."[9]

The conservative agenda of small government, deregulation, and privatization has given big business an opening to create a private water market to replace a public service. Repeating promises made by nineteenth-century entrepreneurs, the private water lobby praises the efficiency of corporate enterprise and demands that water become like other industries that are run for profit. The potential market is huge and extends beyond municipal drinking water and sewage systems to include the bulk transport of water, bottled water, and new technologies like desalination.

The Players

If you've seen Roman Polanski's *Chinatown*, the classic film about obsession and corruption in a mythical, drought-stricken Los Angeles, or if you've read Marc Reisner's brilliant *Cadillac Desert*, a study of the savage billion-dollar battles over western water rights, you know there have always been ruthless and colorful players in the water business. However, today's corporate water executives are hardly the Horatio Algers, risk-taking moguls, and colorful scoundrels of the past. There's an entitled seediness rather than unbridled optimism to their efforts. Their wealth typically comes from buying and selling businesses rather than building them.

The railroad moguls' crude collusion with corrupt government bosses in the nineteenth century has become Halliburton and Bechtel's polished "public-private partnership" of the twenty-first. Close ties to the George W. Bush administration won both companies big

contracts in occupied Iraq in 2003. Bechtel was awarded what the
New York Times called an "unacceptable" deal to fix and run Iraq's
ruined water systems: "The award of a contract worth up to $680
million to the Bechtel Group of San Francisco in a competition limited to a handful of American companies can only add to the impression that the United States seeks to profit from the war it waged."[10]

Old notions of public service seem to evaporate when water
becomes a business and profit becomes the motive. Seeking to con-
solidate market share, private water companies are merging or buying other companies, creating a volatile and unpredictable
market—hardly the kind of stability required for a life-and-death
resource like water. The turmoil continues as control of this most
basic resource has become as volatile as ownership in a game of
Monopoly.

Three corporate players have controlled the water game—Suez
and Veolia, based in France, and the German utility corporation
RWE, which in 2006 announced plans to sell its major water
assets.[11] Few Americans have heard of them, but the Big Three have
dominated the global water business and are among the world's
largest corporations. Together they control subsidiaries in more than
one hundred countries. When the Center for Public Integrity issued
a report on these powerful companies in 2003, their rapid growth
had already triggered "concerns that a handful of private companies
could soon control a large chunk of the world's most vital resource."
The title of the report was *The Water Barons*.[12]

Each of the Big Three bought subsidiaries in the United States
after a 1997 Bill Clinton administration decision to change an Internal Revenue Service regulation that limited the potential market.[13]
Previously, municipal utility contracts with private companies were
limited to five years. Now, such public-private partnerships could
extend for twenty years. The rule change unleashed a wave of industry euphoria with predictions that private companies would soon be
running much of what is now a public service. With 85 percent of
water services still in public hands, "there's a tremendous market

out there," said Peter Cook, head of the National Association of Water Companies, an industry trade group.[14] Eager to get in on the predicted boom, Veolia purchased U.S. Filter in 1999, and Suez acquired United Water. Two years later, RWE subsidiary Thames Water purchased American Water Works, the largest U.S.-based private company, taking on $3 billion in debt in the process.

The companies moved quickly to gain market share. Between 1997 and 2002, the number of municipal water contracts with private industry tripled. The companies avoid the red-flag term *privatization,* calling the contracts public-private partnerships (or PPPs) because the contracts leave cities as the owners of the underlying pipes and treatment plants. The distinction is real, but it is also academic. Once a city goes down this path, especially for a twenty-year period, it becomes increasingly difficult to reverse course because long-term contracts undermine local governments' in-house capacity to reclaim public control should things go wrong. Such PPPs are still considered the industry's growth area in the United States.

Despite the speed and pervasiveness of privatization, few citizens knew about the changes, even in their own cities. Local officials often presented the deals as mere technical changes to save money. As a result, it took several years for Americans to begin recognizing the names Suez, Veolia, and RWE. Sometimes, this recognition occurred when ratepayers called customer service and found themselves talking to someone in another state. In other cases, the understanding dawned when residents noticed increased rates, poor water quality, and slower service than in the past.

While Suez, Veolia, and RWE have dominated the water industry, a different Big Three dominate the retail side, the exploding bottled-water business, which rakes in more than $10 billion a year in the United States alone. Swiss-based Nestlé is the top-selling water bottler in North America, followed by U.S. multinationals Coca-Cola and PepsiCo.[15]

Water scarcity has also created an opening for a cadre of smaller water entrepreneurs, who are reminiscent of old-time salesmen of sure-fire remedies. They've proposed schemes to harvest glacier water, drag icebergs to deserts, store water in underground aquifers, float giant water bags across the seas, and convert old oil tankers for the water trade.

Public vs. Private

Two parallel debates are being conducted over whether water services should remain public or go private. One is concerned with practical issues of efficiency and economics, and the other is about principle. In the first case, both advocates and opponents of privatization point to successes and failures that allegedly prove their case. The debate over principle is more fundamental and involves questions of ethics and moral values.

Privatizing water in the United States has often been a hard sell on both counts. Opponents such as Barlow of the Council of Canadians and Tony Clarke of Canada's Polaris Institute are against privatization in principle. They believe private companies can reasonably be involved in limited areas of infrastructure development but not in the ownership, control, or delivery of the basic service. "The commodification of water is wrong—ethically, environmentally and socially," they write. "It insures that decisions regarding the allocation of water would center on commercial, not environmental or social justice considerations. Privatization means that the management of water resources is based on principles of scarcity and profit maximization rather than long-term sustainability."[16]

Peter Cook of the National Association of Water Companies believes that if market principles are sound for other products, why not for water? "There's certainly nothing unethical about making a profit because investors' money is being used to benefit customers and provide them with services," he told us in an interview. "I never remember seeing anything in the Ten Commandments that said making a profit is a sin. . . . It really comes down to a philosophical difference between the municipal sector and the private sector. We believe utilities should be operated as enterprises."[17]

The practical debate over who can provide water better focuses on the issues of transparency, efficiency, rates, and sustainability. In public systems, major decisions must go through a deliberative process that not only is conducted in public but also involves the public. Such transparency gives citizens' groups and individuals access to the information they need to understand the workings of their utility and to follow the money. The same cannot be said for private water companies. Yes, wholly-owned water systems are regulated by state public utilities commissions and public-private partnerships are overseen by city councils, but getting information out of a giant corporation—even information required by contract—is often a difficult and contested process. In addition, it is nearly impossible to audit the money flows between a local subsidiary and its parent multinational based abroad.

More than money is at stake. Lack of transparency can endanger lives. In 2006, two top managers at a Suez/United Water plant in New Jersey were indicted for covering up high radium levels in the drinking water. Prolonged exposure to radium is linked to cancer, and the communities served by the plant had a history of unusually high rates of childhood cancers. The two United Water officials face up to thirteen years in prison, and the city is now trying to revoke the contract because of nonperformance.[18]

The industry responds to such incidents by pointing to the many mayors who express satisfaction with their contracts and the money they save. For example, a 2006 Los Angeles Times exposé of private water industry "ethics scandals, violations, and irate consumers" quotes Mayor Dean Mazzarella of Leominster, Massachusetts, who praises Veolia's U.S. Filter subsidiary for solving water-leak problems. "We've got nothing but good things to say," he told a reporter. "They're such a big company, they have the ability to tap into a larger talent pool, to reach for people on the cutting edge of technology and understanding."[19]

Such economies of scale are one of the industry's biggest selling points, but many of the suggested economies can and are being realized by the public sector as well. Some also question how significant size is for a local service like water. A study of England's private water industry did not find significant benefits from economies of scale.[20] Even RWE's CEO Henry Roels admitted, "It's a very local business," in which a global water giant "just doesn't have outstanding advantages."[21]

The frequently made case for marketplace competition also doesn't apply in the water sector because sewage and water services are by nature a monopoly. Competition occurs only at bidding time for a contract. After that, for up to twenty years, competition is over. There is only one set of pipes in town.

The major challenge for companies that do win contracts is providing good service while making sufficient profit to satisfy corporate headquarters and shareholders. Like any other enterprise, a private water company ultimately has two ways to do that: cut costs or raise prices. Private companies are under heavy pressure to do both. The industry cites these pressures as an advantage. The need to cut costs "incentivizes" efficiency, but all too often that efficiency is achieved through service cutbacks, staff layoffs, and failure to invest in the preventive maintenance necessary to avoid deterioration of the underlying infrastructure. In Stockton, California, a citizens' watchdog group reported that water leakage doubled in the first year after OMI/Thames took over system operations. In Indianapolis, customer complaints nearly tripled in the first year of Veolia's contract, and inadequate maintenance resulted in hundreds of fire hydrants freezing in the winter. In Milwaukee, Suez subsidiary United Water discharged more than a million gallons of untreated sewage into Lake Michigan because it had shut down pumps to reduce its electricity bills.[22]

As for rates, private systems usually charge more than public systems right next door. In Lexington, Kentucky, a study found that the city's privatized water rates were higher than those in ten nearby cities. In Connecticut, the attorney general stated that a private water company's proposed rate increases were "outlandishly excessive" and ordered a rate reduction instead. The company had been charging nearly twice the rate of nearby public systems. In California, similar complaints have been made in Felton and Thousand Oaks.[23]

Although most public systems cover their day-to-day costs through rates, the private industry complains that rate comparisons are unfair because public systems can issue tax-exempt bonds and apply for low-interest federal loans for new infrastructure. That helps keep the cost of public water low. Public water departments also don't pay taxes and don't have to make a profit. The private water industry says these factors make for an uneven playing field. "The water industry should be financially self-supporting just like every other utility industry in this country is," said Peter Cook. "We don't subsidize telephone costs. We do not subsidize gas costs or electricity costs in general. Why should the federal government be providing large amounts of money to the water utilities to help pay for the costs of replacing infrastructure and pay for the maintenance of their systems? We believe that customers should pay through their rates the full cost of this service being provided."[24] As a result, industry lobbyists oppose proposals to provide federal grants or additional low-interest loans for public water infrastructure because doing so would undermine a key rationale for privatization.

Conservation may be one of the most decisive arguments for public systems. Profit-making enterprises want you to use more water, not less, in order to maximize profit for their shareholders. The Pacific Institute for Studies in Development, Environment and Security concludes, "One of the greatest concerns of privatization watchdogs is that [water-conservation] efficiency programs are typically ignored or even cancelled after authority for managing public systems is turned over to private entities."[25]

There are other critical differences between public and private water services. Public utilities are not against large-scale real estate developments, but they are not inherently for them either. Private companies, however, are eager to expand their customer base and thus their profits. The result has been a close alliance of big developers and private water companies against citizens' groups trying to limit growth, preserve agricultural land, or establish greenbelts. In addition, there is another powerful argument for maintaining water as a public trust: climate change is a warning that uncontrolled abuse of the earth's natural resources is leading toward planetary catastrophe. Who is to set the necessary limits to the abuse of the environment? Private companies fighting for market share are incapable of doing so.

Strategies of Corporate Control

Billions of dollars and the future of our water resources may be at stake in the debate over public versus private control, but for the most part public water agencies aren't active participants in the debate. They don't have significant advertising budgets, and they are required to stay out of politics. Private companies, however, are aggressive in shaping public opinion and influencing elected officials. They employ teams of publicists, lobbyists, lawyers, and political-campaign consultants as part of a concerted effort to expand and maintain their control of the water market.

Indeed, one of the industry's key strategies in winning or keeping contracts is the aggressive use of sophisticated public relations campaigns. In Chapter Five we tell how a private water company in Lexington used four public relations firms to fight the city's attempt to take over the utility. Their efforts even included the creation and funding of a pro-company "grassroots" coalition. In American Water Works's company history, A *Dynasty of Water*, author Gilbert Cross called the public relations process "a kind of 'magic money machine' that spent the customers' money to persuade the customers that it was all right to charge the customers still more money."[26]

The calculated use of language is a key part of these campaigns. The companies insist that they don't control or "own" the water.

They simply "manage" systems. They are correct from a legal standpoint. No one really "owns" water. Legal rights to use water are generally either the right to reasonable use in the eastern United States or the right of prior appropriation (first come, first served) in the West. But it is disingenuous to assert that operation and management of an essential and monopoly resource for twenty years does not mean de facto control.

Local politics is the key arena for winning water contracts, and the bulk of industry political spending takes place locally. However, the wheels of national campaigns are also greased. Since the mid-1990s, water firms have contributed more than $4 million to federal campaigns, according to the nonpartisan Center for Responsive Politics.[27] Although companies usually can't give directly to candidates, their employees have made large donations to help swing elections in towns where contracts are at stake. However, even though community groups that have put privatization on the ballot in cities like Felton, Stockton, and Monterey have been outspent many times over, they often still win.

Another important strategy has been to finance and influence key national associations of city officials. As we'll see in the chapters that follow, the U.S. Conference of Mayors has become an engine of water privatization through its Urban Water Council (UWC). One mayor described a Conference of Mayors session he attended as a kind of feeding frenzy, with companies bidding to take over everything from his city's school-lunch program to its traffic lights to its water services. Financed by the private water industry and staffed by former industry officials, the UWC works hard to give its corporate sponsors "face time" with mayors. Peter Gleick, director of the Pacific Institute for Studies in Development, Environment and Security, said, "The advice mayors are receiving from the Urban Water Council is heavily biased toward the interests of the private water sector, which funds and supports the Council."[28]

Communities Take Action

Citizen reaction to the challenge of water privatization has been swift and strong. Both in the United States and around the world, privatization efforts have galvanized citizens to assert not only that water should be a human right and a public trust but also that they themselves must be involved in the reform of public water services. These tenacious movements have become catalysts for a broad agenda to reclaim local government and the political process from corporate influence.

Although this book focuses on the United States, many domestic coalitions have found models or inspiration in the conflicts that have driven global water companies out of a growing number of cities and countries in the developing world. One of the key international leaders of this effort is Oscar Olivera from Cochabamba, Bolivia's third largest city. A shoemaker and union leader, he led a citizens' coalition against heavy odds, taking on Bechtel and the Bolivian army in what became known as the first of the new global "water wars" in the spring of 2000.

After the World Bank had pressured that impoverished country to accept loans conditioned on water privatization, an international consortium led by Bechtel imposed enormous price hikes—even for water in residents' own backyard wells. Everyone from farmers to hotel owners opposed the privatization, and even the World Bank pulled out. But only when Olivera's coalition organized massive strikes and, finally, a virtual insurrection did the Bolivian government throw out Bechtel and hand the utility to a community-based organization accountable to the residents. To put the scale of this event in perspective, at the time Bechtel took over Cochabamba's water system, the company's annual receipts were larger than Bolivia's gross national product.[29]

The popular victory reverberated around the world as a symbol of communities' ability to overcome vast disparities in power with persistence and militancy. Despite their governments' dependence on World Bank loans, communities in the global South became the real founders of the movement against water privatization. In South America, they formed a continent-wide coalition called Red Vida to coordinate and support antiprivatization campaigns, and Olivera has toured the world to spread his message of self-reliance and the human right to water.

Worldwide, public water companies still provide more than 90 percent of water and wastewater services, but privatization has increased dramatically since the mid-1980s. Private companies provided service to fifty million people in 1990. By 2002, they were servicing more than three hundred million.[30] They were also eyeing new opportunities in spite of successful grassroots efforts to stop water privatization in Argentina, India, Tanzania, Germany, and France, among many other places. As they encounter increasing resistance in the developing world, the global water companies have turned to new, perhaps less militant regions: Eastern Europe, China, and North America.

With its aging infrastructure, often-uninformed public, and conservative political leadership, the United States—the supposed architect of corporate globalization—has become one of globalization's favored targets. Olivera's message of resistance has been slow to reach the United States. Many major environmental organizations are only now beginning to see the connection between their traditional issues of wildlife preservation and pollution and larger political issues, including corporate privatization. "It's just too much outside of what we've ever worked on," said one veteran environmentalist. "I hadn't connected the dots."[31]

But our huge country has a history of grassroots, democratic rebellion that runs counter to the move toward corporate privatization. The Boston Tea Party, the movement for the abolition of slavery, the Vietnam War protests—each revolt against authority has deepened our national character and furthered our understanding of global politics. In the same way, local fights over water in the United States are alerting participants to the concerns of people in faraway places like Cochabamba. As Dale Stocking, a water activist in Stockton, told us, "One of the things that I'm being exposed to is the web, the global web that is developing. This privatization here in Stockton could be part of an overall puzzle."[32]

Resistance to the commodification of water is also percolating through North American culture with books, videos, Internet satires, and even standup comedy. Edgy comic Lewis Black took on the bottled-water craze in his 2004 HBO special *Black on Broadway*. "Try to go through this logic," he shouts. "Our country had water coming to our homes . . . . clean water. And we said, 'No! Fuck you! I don't want it to be that goddamned convenient. I want to drive and drive and drive and look for water like my ancestors did!'"

In 2005, Varda Burstyn, a Canadian environmental activist, published *Water Inc.*, a thriller about a plan by corporate moguls to pipe Canadian water to developers in the United States. It's fiction, but not farfetched. Unlike the behemoth to the south, Canada has vast freshwater resources, making it a prime target for speculators who believe that U.S. demand will eventually overwhelm what Burstyn's scheming moguls consider to be Canada's pitiful pretense of sovereignty.

North American entrepreneurs have long floated ideas about changing major features of Canada's topography to quench the U.S. thirst. One such plan involved siphoning water from Alaskan and British Columbian rivers into the Rocky Mountain Trench, creating a five-hundred-mile-long reservoir to serve thirty-five states. Another proposal called for a giant dike across Quebec's James Bay and a string of nuclear power plants across Canada to pump the water into Lake Superior and then down to the arid Southwest or to midwestern farmers in danger of exhausting the giant Ogallala Aquifer. Other plans aim directly at the Great Lakes, which hold 20 percent of the earth's fresh water and are already threatened by withdrawals, pollution, and border disagreements between Canada and the United States.[33]

Some version of these plans for bulk water transport reappears regularly. Whenever there is a drought, the arid South jealously eyes the water-rich North. Perhaps that's why some of the leading activist and intellectual opposition to privatization has come from Canada. Barlow of the Council of Canadians and Clarke of the Polaris Institute in Ottawa are pioneers in the fight for water as a human right. Their 2002 book, *Blue Gold*, was a landmark in the international campaign against water privatization.

Canada's lakes and rivers, as well as many U.S. rivers and streams, may be the ultimate stakes in the fight over privatization of water utilities. Once multinationals' control over local water reaches critical mass, their lobbyists will be in an even more powerful position than they are now to challenge the public sector for water rights and bulk delivery. It won't be an oddball Alaskan entrepreneur proposing to suck river water into offshore condoms anymore (see Preface). It will be oil-company-sized water conglomerates aligned with pipeline giants like Bechtel and Halliburton lobbying in international trade talks to define water as a product to be sold to the highest bidder.

Unexpected Coalitions

Serious challenges call for unusual alliances. When is the last time you saw conservative evangelicals on the same side of a political campaign as body-pierced antiglobalization activists? Or rowdy union activists strategizing with straight-laced advocates of good government? Or local-control Republicans allying with public sector Democrats? When it comes to water, such unlikely coalitions have spread like wildfire.

Across the country, the impulse to defend water has regularly produced election supermajorities for state water bonds and, in a recent poll, 85 percent support for the idea of a federal clean-water trust fund like those that exist for highway and airport construction.[34] In hamlets like Felton, California, and Lee, Massachusetts, hundreds of people show up at community meetings to protect their water rights. And in diverse cities like Lexington and Stockton citizens overflow city-council meetings to debate and oppose privatization. Lots of work goes into making grassroots action happen, but when an issue clicks with people, the rapid response may appear to be almost spontaneous. Dedicated organizers like Wenonah Hauter of Food & Water Watch and Ruth Caplan of the Sierra Club's Water Privatization Task Force have worked on this issue for years, but now they're hard put to keep up with the numerous community groups emerging to oppose water privatization in their hometowns.

It's not easy to define the spark that ignites local rebellion and transforms it into a national movement. It may be the widespread sense of frustration people feel about national politics in an era of conservative hegemony and globalization. Donations to progressive policy groups and letters to Congress seem like money and messages stuffed in bottles and tossed out to sea. Perhaps as a result, there's a renewed focus on issues at the local level, where having an effective voice seems possible and where the forces of globalization are more immediate and more easily confronted than they are on the national scene—whether those forces are developers, high-handed politicians, or distant multinationals that must beam down representatives to convince locals to let them in. At the local level, the grassroots has the potential to win. Stockton mayor Gary Podesto learned this lesson the hard way. He warned other supporters of privatization among his colleagues on the Urban Water Council, "Don't begin this process if you are fainthearted."[35] Podesto spent two terms battling for privatization, a bitter fight that contributed to his defeat when he ran for higher office.

The little-known coalitions like the one that opposed Podesto in Stockton are described in the following chapters. These groups and individuals are waging a kind of guerilla war against sophisticated political lobbying, huge campaign contributions, public relations SWAT teams, fake grassroots coalitions, and pro-privatization alliances of real estate developers and Chambers of Commerce. Despite the power imbalance, the hardball tactics of the corporate water industry have not deterred local activists, who have had to advance on a steep learning curve to confront the global reach and deep pockets of multinational companies.

Landscape of Battle

Scores of privatization battles are taking place in the United States today. We chose to tell the stories presented here because they provide an overview of the conflict. Together, the places in which these battles are occurring represent many regions and types of communities. The stories reveal the conditions of our drinking water and sewage systems under both public and private control, and they show the successes and failures of both community groups and corporations. Moreover, these stories have a compelling cast of characters, surprising twists and turns, and some shocking conclusions.

The next six chapters of this book deal with battles for control of drinking water and sewage in three different regions of the United States. They reveal company strategies, citizen initiatives, the rise of new coalitions, and the role of government in either protecting or selling off this resource.

In Chapters Two and Three, we tell of new water wars in the West. In Stockton, California, a strong mayor played hardball in an effort to win approval of the largest privatization contract in the West, while a grassroots coalition went to the ballot box and the courts to stop him. In tiny Felton, California, a creative and feisty citizens' group had to create not only a sense of community but also the structures of local democracy to buy the town's utility from corporate giant RWE.

We head to the South in Chapters Four and Five, first to look back at Suez's effort to privatize Atlanta's dilapidated water system. The largest such privatization in U.S. history, it was a major test of industry promises, which imploded in charges of corruption and incompetence. In Lexington, Kentucky, wealthy racehorse breeders and environmentalists united to take public control of the city's private water company after it was bought by a multinational giant.

In Chapters Six and Seven, we visit New England, where small towns are increasingly the focus of corporate attention. In Lee, Massachusetts, community and union activists used the tradition of town meetings to fight an imminent corporate takeover by Veolia. And in nearby Holyoke, elected officials got hoodwinked into giving up their right to vote on the mayor's plan to privatize.

Finally, in Chapters Eight and Nine, we examine the front lines of the new bottled-water controversy, which raises a different set of billion-dollar issues, including the commodification of water and the transport of bulk water. In Wisconsin, a tenacious citizens' movement took on Nestlé, the world's largest food and bottled-water company, to stop it from pumping a valuable spring. In Michigan, student antiglobalization activists and an Indian tribe joined with a rural community group to stop Nestlé; their actions led to a dramatic lawsuit in the state's highest court.

We are only at the beginning of this epic power struggle, which will spread to every corner of North America. Each side is testing tactics and strategies in an effort to control the most valuable natural resource we have. The courts, the streets, the media, and individual families are all part of the landscape of battle. So far each side has won some fights and lost some. The final outcome will depend not simply on access to money and connections but on the political skill, creativity, and tenacity of new citizens' coalitions. Most of all, for individual citizens, this is an existential fight that goes well beyond issues of efficiency and cost. Today, water is where we are taking a stand on our basic values as individuals and on who we are as a society.

Battles for Water in the West

2

Hardball vs. the High Road
Stockton, California

Mayor Gary Podesto has played baseball as long as he can remember. "I was pretty good-sized as a ten-year-old," he says. "Usually the biggest kid is the pitcher."[1] A compact sixty-one-year-old with a taste for silk ties, Podesto was still pitching in 2003, hoping to fulfill a long-term dream of bringing a minor league baseball team to his hometown. He'd need a new ballpark for that and the means to pay for it, but he wasn't daunted. His city of 260,000 was on an economic upswing; it was becoming not just an agricultural hub but also a bedroom community for the San Francisco Bay Area, sixty miles away. Real estate development was booming, and Podesto was confident about his ability to lead the city into the future. The baseball mounted on his desk sent that message loud and clear to anyone visiting. In bold letters across the stitches were the words: "Sometimes you just have to play hardball."

This philosophy had fueled Podesto's successful business career running big-box grocery stores, a pursuit that paid off fabulously when he sold out to a major chain store. He was able to retire comfortably, but his staying home without any major projects to channel his energy drove his wife crazy. She told him to get out of the house and get a job. "I had friends that encouraged me to run for political office," he recalled. Having dealt with government as a businessman, he felt no need to pay dues as a political novice. "The office I decided to run for was mayor."

Michael McDonald also grew up in Stockton playing baseball, but on the other side of the highway that splits the town. African Americans like McDonald lived on the south side. When he played ball, he was a catcher like his hero, Dodger Hall of Famer Roy Campanella. "I was always willing to take the punishment. That was the fun part." His mother was a civil rights activist in the late 1960s and pursued her own version of the Montgomery bus boycott. Fed up with having to stand while waiting for the bus, she successfully sued the city to install benches on the south side like the ones in white neighborhoods to the north.

After a stint in the Air Force, McDonald started work at Stockton's sewage-treatment plant, where he did almost every job over twenty-six years. "Just a great bunch of people," he said. "Not a glamorous job, but it's always something challenging and a lot of fun as well." A stylish, solidly built man with an easy smile, McDonald became a respected leader among the employees and was promoted to senior plant maintenance supervisor. A supportive boss, McDonald shared with a surprising number of his co-workers a passion for cigars—perhaps substituting that aroma for the less pleasing stench of the plant's raw materials.

In 2002, Podesto and McDonald met head-on in a different kind of game, each staking his job, his ideals, and his reputation on the future of the city's water department.

The Front Line of the California Water Wars

Water is a particularly sensitive issue in Stockton, as it is in many rapidly growing communities. Just ninety minutes northeast of San Francisco, Stockton lies in a beautiful landscape of trees, rivers, and fertile Central Valley farms. Add to those attractions Stockton's strategic location at the hub of California's complex hydrologic system. The San Joaquin River flows through the city's downtown, and the enormous pumps that quench Southern California's thirst are located just south in the nearby town of Tracy. That puts Stockton at the pivot of the California water wars. Whoever plays a major role in the local water system here is positioned to have a loud voice in water and development issues affecting the state's thirty-five million people and the world's fifth largest economy.

Stockton's attractions have rarely achieved the spotlight. Famed Hollywood director John Huston put the town in a different light in *Fat City*, based on Stockton native Leonard Gardner's acclaimed novel. A portrait of small-time prizefighters, the story is set in a run-down burg of seedy downtown bars and flophouses. It was an image proud Stocktonians detested even as they acknowledged its truth. Those mixed feelings of shame, anger, and pride were a driving force behind Podesto's mayoral campaign in 1996. "My goal was to change the image of our community," he declared. Along with the Chamber of Commerce and major real estate developers, Podesto was bullish about a new vision of downtown as a commercial and cultural center.

Skyrocketing real estate prices in the Bay Area have driven thousands of workers and their families east over the hills to Stockton and other Central Valley towns. Enormous gated housing developments have been built to accommodate them, and more are either under construction or in the planning stage. The housing market has also been growing tight in the working-class south side, where African Americans and Filipinos are now outnumbered by a rapidly growing Latino community that makes up one-third of the city's current population.

Podesto aimed to carry out his mission to remake Stockton by centralizing authority and streamlining government to make it resemble a business. He successfully pushed through a strong-mayor form of city government and then launched what was to be the defining battle of his tenure: the privatization of the city's water system. It was part of his master plan from the beginning. Even before he took office, he had visited facilities in Indianapolis and other cities that had privatized their water departments. Once in office, he wasted no time joining the Urban Water Council of the U.S.

Conference of Mayors, a task force that helps private water companies meet mayors and convince them to privatize their public water systems.

To his critics, the mayor's commitment to privatizing the water system was ideological, part of a hegemonic conservative antipathy toward government. In the mayor's view, the superiority of the profit motive was a straightforward conclusion drawn from his own experience. "If you're a for-profit company, you compete daily for profits," unlike government departments, which have no such "incentive to improve," he said. Such comments outraged employees like McDonald who took seriously the idea that they were public servants ensuring a basic human right to water. "We don't have to think about how we are going to make a profit. All we have to think about is how we're going to provide a good service to the citizens."

Podesto was beginning to take some heat for the privatization idea, and he learned quickly that one of the first battlegrounds would be language. It may have been a lesson he picked up at the Urban Water Council. "Privatization," he said, "you have to be careful with that word." The Urban Water Council and a host of conservative think tanks have created a more appealing public relations alternative: "public-private partnerships." The euphemism became all the rage during the 1990s as both conservative Republicans and Clinton Democrats competed to grant subsidies and concessions to business. Podesto argued that a private company running the water department would not be privatization because the city would still own the water and the facilities.

To his critics, this characterization was pure spin, a cover for the mayor's disdain for the public sector. "A public-private partnership is privatization because it's taking a municipal function that has municipal employees and turning it over to the private sector," said Dale Stocking, an orthodontist active with the government watchdog group the Concerned Citizens' Coalition of Stockton (CCCOS). "This idea that bringing a private business model into a municipal operation brings the benefits of competition is an oxymoron," argued Stocking. "The only competition is at the bidding over who is going to get the spoils."

The Coalition had formed in 2001 to monitor and challenge what its members called Podesto's "political-control machine." Fighting water privatization became its defining cause. The Coalition included locally-based environmental groups and labor unions, churches and the NAACP, police and firefighter organizations. It was a congenial group of like-minded, mostly middle-class Stocktonians, chaired by Sylvia Kothe, a bespectacled activist with the League of Women Voters whose grandparents were Christian missionaries in Brazil. She prided herself on her honesty and on the Coalition's commitment to taking the "high road" in politics. Others in the group included a stock analyst, the owner of a party-supply store, and a university professor. Several employees of the city's utility department were also active, and the Coalition received support from the local organizer for Public Citizen, the national consumer group that was making water privatization a major target of its efforts against the accumulation of corporate power.

The Coalition members' relaxed fashion sense was about as far from Podesto's silk ties and tailored jackets as it could get. Largely untouched by the radical cross-currents of political activism in the nearby Bay Area, they were unaccustomed to the militancy of new member Dezaraye Bagalayos, a young Filipina activist who encouraged the group to consider outreach to the Latino population and spoke about the merits of civil disobedience. Nevertheless, the group was unified by the conviction that the mayor was out to railroad the privatization plan through the City Council without a thorough public hearing and a citywide vote. The group members had a visceral sense that democracy itself was being hijacked by the mayor's machinations and that nothing was so wrong with their publicly run, award-winning municipal water utility that it couldn't be fixed.

The take-charge mayor wasn't waiting for a consensus; he issued a Request for Proposals to take over the Municipal Utilities Department

(MUD). Several multinational water companies were interested in taking up the challenge, and three proposals were submitted. For them, Stockton's increasing population and rapid development were major attractions. More people translates into more ratepayers and greater profits. It's an equation that has ensured alliances between private water companies and real estate developers. There was another lucrative incentive for the industry. An expanding city will outgrow its water and sewage-treatment plants and infrastructure and as a result will require large capital outlays to build a new plant or add to an existing one. Such construction projects are often the most profitable part of public-private partnerships.

Aside from rapid growth and the need for expanded water facilities, Stockton, like other cities, faced some serious water problems. New state guidelines required cities to treat storm runoff. The rains that cleanse the world do their job too well in a polluted society, picking up pesticides from farmland, oil from roads, fiberglass from roofs, and carrying the whole noxious mixture into rivers and streams. The California Environmental Protection Agency mandated that storm water be collected from sewers and treated before discharge. The new regulations and population growth put expansion of Stockton's water system at the top of the city's agenda, with an estimated price tag of $250 million.

The mayor brought in consultants who specialized in assisting privatizations. Their analysis claimed the city would save $175 million over twenty years by contracting out water services. The Coalition countered that independent research by an Oakland-based think tank, the Pacific Institute for Studies in Development, Environment, and Security, had concluded that possible savings from privatization were "greatly overstated" and that continued public operation would cost less than bringing in a private company.[2]

Mayor Podesto was unimpressed by such countervailing views, but he did have a problem on his hands. Morris Allen, director of the Municipal Utilities Department (MUD), was against privatization. A civil engineer with forty years of experience, sixteen of them in his current post, he was knowledgeable, respected, and a strong believer in the idea of water as a public service. That made him an impediment and a target for those who wished to ram through privatization. Very much the engineer, Allen expressed his reservations quietly behind the scenes without playing politics or media games. "I am a good soldier," he said. "I do what I'm told." With McDonald and other water-district supervisors, Allen had developed an alternative MUD plan to streamline operations and expand facilities. The reorganization was already saving the city substantial sums. Some City Council members thought the city should allow that process to continue, but Mayor Podesto would not consider keeping the utility public. It was time to play hardball.

Coalition members had been attending City Council meetings to raise objections and questions about the privatization plan, and the mayor was getting impatient. He limited comments and insisted that details of the various privatization proposals not be released until the winning bidder had been selected. Frustrated at the information and communication blockade, Coalition members decided the only way to gain a measure of input was to go to the voters. They began the arduous process of putting an initiative on the ballot that, if approved, would require a public vote on privatizing the city's water department. They had ninety days to gather the required signatures. It was a busy summer. With such a small window the Coalition relied on paid as well as volunteer signature gatherers, a decision derided by the mayor as contradicting the group's claim to be grassroots. Podesto was also annoyed by what he considered the Coalition's meddling in his basic responsibilities under the guise of wanting public participation. "To some people there's never enough," he complained. "They want to write the contract. If you want to be in that position, run for City Council and sit up here."

As the Coalition gathered signatures for its initiative, the mayor did appear to make a concession to his critics. He agreed to establish an ad hoc committee on water privatization with members from the community. Coalition member Stocking, the energetic orthodontist and past president of the local chapter of the Sierra Club, was appointed to the committee. His research convinced him that members of the City Council "were basically spoon-fed dog-and-pony shows from the consultants."

At first, Stocking was hopeful that the committee would consider his objections to a public-private partnership. "My concern," he said, "is when privatization happens, rates have been known to go up and services have been known to decline." But as Stocking immersed himself in City Council minutes going back a decade, he realized the ad hoc committee was stacked with Podesto allies from the business community who had long favored privatizing the water department. He concluded that the committee was just a Podesto maneuver to stall and block opposition to a contract.

Any notions that Podesto was softening in his attitude toward the Coalition were put to rest by one of the mayor's regular columns in the local newspaper, the *Stockton Record*. He dismissed public opposition to privatization as uninformed, characterizing his critics as "the butcher, the baker and the candlestick maker."[3] How, he asked, could the public be expected to evaluate the terms of a nine-hundred-page contract?

Podesto later regretted this momentary expression of anger, but the encounter with the Coalition was not like anything he had experienced in his business career. The Coalition, with no resources to speak of besides brains and tenacity, had raised public awareness and could block his plans. At the end of ninety days, the Coalition had gathered more than eighteen thousand signatures, well over the target. "Through the initiative process we were able to wrench our way to a seat at the table," Stocking says proudly.

It looked as though the citizens would have their say after all. The City Council scheduled the initiative to go before the voters of Stockton on March 4, 2003, more than six months away. The Coalition didn't fight the delay—perhaps a lack of killer instinct. The same could not be said of Podesto. The delay gave him breathing room to maneuver. The Coalition "could have played a harder game," said McDonald. "But then again, these are people respected in the community. I'm proud to be a part of it."

Round One: "Let Us Vote"

Events began to move quickly. In the fall of 2002, the multinational consortium of OMI and Thames Water was chosen over two other groups to negotiate a contract with the city. A subsidiary of construction giant CH2M Hill, OMI was a fast-growing Colorado-based utility-management firm specializing in the water business.[4] Thames Water was London's public water utility until privatized by Britain's conservative prime minister Margaret Thatcher in 1989. Twelve years later, Thames was caught up in the wave of corporate buy-outs sweeping the United States and Europe. One of the leading predators was Rheinisch-Westfälisches Elektrizitätswerk Aktiengesellschaft (RWE), a German energy conglomerate known as the Enron of Europe. RWE's top management was rapidly expanding its $50 billion, *Fortune* Global 500 empire, buying out Thames in 2001 and then buying the private U.S. company American Water Works in 2003. The deals made RWE/Thames the world's third largest corporate water company.[5]

For OMI and RWE/Thames, Stockton was a plum, a well-run, in-the-black municipal utility at the center of California's fierce water politics. For them, this was an opportunity to show California and the country what a private utility could do. It would be the largest water privatization in the western United States—a twenty-year, $600 million deal.

Allen, McDonald, and other employees reviewed the proposed contract, raising a number of uncomfortable questions and challenging the mayor's constantly repeated prediction of $175 million in cost savings. "Everybody knows you can do whatever you want with numbers," said McDonald. In addition, Allen disagreed with OMI/Thames's design plans for expanding the sewage plant. He thought he was acting as a principled public servant, looking out for the citizens' best interests. The city manager seemed to agree, going out of his way to tell Allen what a great job he was doing. But perhaps Allen was doing too good a job. He asked for time to complete a careful review of the nine-hundred-page contract, insisting that the city take the time to consider alternatives.

Podesto, however, was in a hurry. The Coalition initiative, if passed, could scuttle his plans not only for privatization but also, his critics suspected, for diverting MUD funds reserved for capital improvements to help finance the ballpark and downtown development so dear to his heart. Just a week after the city manager's fawning compliments to Allen, he stripped Allen of his director duties and exiled him to Boston to meet with privatization consultants. The local papers reported it as the "Friday Night Massacre."[6] Allen saw the writing on the wall and, shortly thereafter, retired. "I think Morris forced himself out by the way he conducted himself," Podesto commented, but the mayor denied a role in the purge. "It certainly wasn't an order I gave." Nevertheless, virtually everyone suspected that the mayor was behind the deed.

McDonald drew some personal conclusions from what had happened to his colleague. "My integrity is not for sale." He told his friends that he wouldn't work for the private company. "When OMI walks in the door, I'll walk out the other door headed to another job," he said. "It's not so much the concerns that I have for my job," McDonald said, "as the concerns that I have for the rates that I'm going to pay as a resident of this town and what's going to happen to the Delta that I go fishing in and water-skiing in. These people [OMI/Thames] aren't in here to do the people of Stockton a favor. They're in it to make money. And wherever they can cut costs and make money, they're going to make money."

OMI's vice-president Gary Miller had a different view. "It's a democratic society," he said, "and what makes America great is the ability for businesses to make a margin and a profit for taking on the risks that we'll be taking on." RWE/Thames vice-president Dreda Gaines, in from London, tried to be more reassuring. "You are always going to find controversy in these types of projects," she said. As for the employees, "they should have no concerns at all."

But the concerns wouldn't go away, and to the Coalition it was becoming increasingly clear that Council sessions on the privatization were not devoted to a serious investigation of the city's options but to a charade of public participation. With Allen now out of the way, water department employees were also cut out of the review process.

Podesto seemed back in control, but he needed to lock down a final crucial detail. He had to ensure that a majority of the City Council would vote to approve the contract before the March 4 referendum. Otherwise, the deal might be subject to the initiative's requirement of a citywide vote, and Podesto was not willing to risk a loss at the polls. Although details of the contract were still being worked on and the unions had not yet completed their own negotiations with OMI/Thames, Podesto went ahead and scheduled a City Council vote on the contract for February 19, just two weeks before the citywide vote.

The Coalition had been outmaneuvered, but it still hoped that it might eke out a victory on the City Council itself. Council members had been bombarded about the issue for months, but, of the seven members, only four had openly stated how they would vote, two for the contract (including the mayor), two against. The coalition had little hope to win over the vice mayor, also a City Council member. That left attorney Leslie Martin and Larry Ruhstaller, a restaurant owner with mayoral aspirations, as the potential swing votes.

The date of the vote was also the day Podesto was scheduled to give Stockton's annual State of the City address at the Port of Stockton. The Chamber of Commerce, statewide politicos, and assorted business leaders were among those crowding the festively decorated warehouse waiting to hear the mayor speak. When he finally took the stage, he was still campaigning for privatization, but he sounded confident. "I stand in front of you today very proud of the courageous path your city council is traveling in re-energizing this great city." It was a friendly crowd of his peers in the business community, and his confidence increased with each round of applause. Podesto went on to make a clear statement of his philosophy of government, an echo of the conservative zeitgeist trumpeted from Stockton to Washington, D.C.: "It's time that Stockton enter the 21st Century in its delivery of services and think of our citizens as customers."[7] This sentiment infuriated local activists, who felt they were fighting as citizens for their basic democratic right to vote on a major issue.

Stockton City Hall is a perfect setting for high political drama. Hollywood had used the building as a backdrop in the Oscar-winning 1949 film *All the King's Men*. With its wide flight of steps and neoclassical colonnade, City Hall stood in for Louisiana's state capitol in the climactic scene, when dictatorial populist governor and potential presidential candidate Huey Long steps out before a crowd on the stairs and is gunned down by an assassin.

Now, City Hall was again a place of pandemonium and charges of dictatorship, but this night's events were unstaged. The Coalition, union members, student activists, clergy, and interested townspeople all made their way to the city center amid cops on horseback and long lines of patrol cars. Angry sewage-plant workers and their supporters rallied on the steps before the meeting. Banners read "No to Privatization." A giant puppet mimed Mayor Podesto tearing up a ballot, and speakers worked the crowd with bullhorns and hopeful chants of "Let us vote" and "This is a democracy."

As the meeting began, the crowd poured inside City Hall, overflowing the second-floor Council chambers into the hallway and filling the downstairs lobby. McDonald couldn't bear to go in with them. After attending the demonstration, he went home to watch the meeting on cable television. Inside the chambers, speakers, the vast majority of them against privatization, addressed the council for two electrifying hours before the Council members were to pass judgment.

The details of the privatization deal itself had become secondary. Everyone at this meeting was debating the rights of citizens, the value of the ballot, the meaning of representative democracy, and the human right to water. The context had also broadened in another way. The meeting was taking place in the midst of the greatest wave of corporate misdeeds in U.S. history. Enron, World-Com, Tyco, and insider trading scandals were all in the background as Stockton debated whether to entrust two multinational corporations with responsibility for the city's most precious resource.

Kothe voiced the crux of the Coalition's objections to Podesto's authoritarian style. "It is clear that the decision to privatize has been made covertly without a public vote." Bagalayos spoke from the heart that a vote for privatization would be a betrayal of the citizenry. "You should not sign without the consent of the people whose life this will ultimately affect. Water for life, not for profit."

The mayor was clearly willing to have opponents blow off steam, but he didn't want to lose control of the meeting. He had his own list of speakers, and as opposition momentum was building, he called on the OMI president, Don Evans. "You have the absolute commitment of our company and you have the commitment of Thames Water to deliver this contract effectively," Evans told the Council. "We will safeguard the water of Stockton and we'll protect the environment of this community." He concluded by saying that this was not just the promise of a faceless corporation "but my personal commitment to you."

The public hearing was over. It was time for the City Councilors to weigh in. Thought to be a Coalition supporter, new Council member Steve Bestolarides was the first to speak, praising the mayor, but then questioning predictions of millions in savings over twenty years. "If the state government can't predict accurately what happens six months from now, how can we rely on twenty years of numbers?" He warned of "dire" consequences of preempting the public's right to vote.

One of the potential swing votes, Leslie Martin, spoke to the motion, and the Coalition's worst fears were realized. "We have not been elected to baby-sit and maintain the city until a vote can be taken by the citizens on major issues." Vice Mayor Gloria Nomura, a close Podesto ally, agreed with Martin. She told the crowd that, as a Christian, she had prayed for guidance on her decision to vote to privatize and added, "It says it in the Constitution that you will elect representatives to vote and to make decisions that are best for you."

Podesto recognized Coalition ally Dr. Richard "Doc" Nickerson to speak next. The elder of the Council, Nickerson lit into the idea that the public didn't know or didn't care enough to vote on this issue. "There were eighteen thousand people who were not too apathetic to sign a petition," he railed. "And you know the people who founded this republic obviously didn't think the people were too dumb to run it." The room burst into applause while the mayor grimaced and shook his head. Nickerson concluded with a warning. "I will tell you," he prophesied, "this is not the end. It's not even the beginning of the end."

Next up was the gregarious Ruhstaller, a fence-sitter throughout the long debate on privatization. A potential candidate for mayor, Ruhstaller wanted to please everyone in a situation that was totally polarized. "I agree with all of them," he joked. Expressing support for the contract with OMI/Thames, he ended up taking a position on principle. "There comes a time when the people become so involved in an issue that it is important that they be heard by way of the ballot."

It couldn't have been any closer, but old political hands doubted that Podesto would have called this meeting without having the needed four votes in hand. It was almost time to vote, but Council supporters of the mayor, now ready to finalize the deal, were eager to strike back at their critics. Martin asked to make a point of personal privilege, objecting to Nickerson's remarks. "No one on this council believes that the people are too dumb to resolve or to understand the issues . . ." The angry crowd instantly interrupted her with a chant that was picked up and echoed through the building. "Let us vote! Let us vote!"

Podesto stepped in to regain control, demanding quiet and ordering police officers to close the doors that led from the chamber to the overflow crowd outside and downstairs watching the debate on TV. It was finally his turn to speak just before the vote. "Do I believe that this should go to a vote of the people?" he asked. "Absolutely not." Calling the vote "a gut check," he asked Council members to cast their ballots in a silent room.

"The resolution carries, four to three," he announced. The contract had been approved, and with that the mayor quickly adjourned the meeting. Watching on TV at home, McDonald's heart dropped. "They're circumventing what people have fought and died for, the right to vote on these issues. And I for one will never give up my right to vote."

Two weeks later, the public vote on the citizens' initiative seemed like an anticlimax, but it renewed the Coalition's hopes. Almost 60 percent of voters approved the initiative to require public votes on major changes to their water system.

Round Two: The Referendum

The public vote fueled the Coalition's counterattack on two fronts. The Coalition and its allies in the League of Women Voters and the Sierra Club decided to challenge the privatization in court. The City Council resolution to approve the contract had included a unilateral declaration to exempt the decision from California environmental law, which requires an environmental-impact report on major water projects. The Coalition's lawyers believed that the declaration was clearly illegal and prepared to file suit.

The Coalition also decided to go back to the voters and gather signatures one more time for a citywide referendum to overturn the City Council decision. The group had to move quickly, however, for they had just thirty days to collect ten thousand signatures to place the referendum on the ballot. "It's an enormous undertaking," said Stocking. Each petition had to be attached to a copy of the complete water contract, all nine hundred pages. The cost of photocopying alone ran into thousands of dollars, but the city unions and Public Citizen helped out with office support and funds. It was a huge challenge for people with families, full time jobs, and small businesses. Coalition members devoted hours and hours to meetings, strategizing, making phone calls, writing letters to the newspaper, talking to neighbors and strangers, and fundraising to cover expenses.

OMI and RWE/Thames also mobilized, and their actions showed how the entrance of huge multinationals can change the political equation and torque a local political process. The two companies gave the antireferendum campaign $60,000, an enormous sum for Stockton.[8] Meanwhile, the Coalition's Sunday-morning pancake-breakfast fundraisers were barely making a dent in underwriting the Coalition's mounting legal costs.

Everything rode on getting the needed signatures for the referendum. The Coalition made a questionable strategic decision that made the difficult job even harder. They decided to rely only on volunteer signature gatherers, in part to save money and in part to answer Podesto's criticism of the Coalition's past use of paid signature gatherers. Stocking said the all-volunteer effort was "the proper way to go."

Podesto himself felt no such obligation, and the antireferendum campaign hired as many paid signature gatherers as it could find to ask people to sign petitions against the referendum. OMI and RWE/Thames took out full-page newspaper ads. Leaflets and mailers went out to homes across the city, and Podesto recorded automatic phone messages, warning voters against the "misinformation and sometimes downright lies" being spread by Coalition supporters.[9]

Nevertheless, Coalition organizers believed they could gather the necessary signatures quickly. At the first signature-gathering mobilization at the Operating Engineers union hall, they gave supporters the impression that the campaign was in the bag. McDonald and other sewer-plant employees joined the teams going door to door. But as the days counted down, the volunteer cadre dwindled dangerously. The Coalition's core activists were exhausted. Kothe and Stocking both came down with pneumonia. With the campaign in jeopardy a week before the deadline, a no-nonsense aide to the local state assemblywoman brought in paid signature gatherers to increase the total. They were able to help bring the number of signatures above the required ten thousand, but not by much.

The Coalition's decision to take the high road by using only volunteers proved to be a crucial miscalculation. A comfortable cushion is essential in any petition drive because some signatures are always disqualified. In this case, there was precious little room for error. As the Coalition brought hand trucks to City Hall to deliver the book-sized petitions to the city clerk, campaign leader Bill Loyko admitted he had never been involved in a project like this campaign before. "I feel good about what we've done," he said. "I wish our numbers could be a little bit higher."

Even as the signatures were counted, the Coalition met at the local Service Employees International Union (SEIU) hall to evaluate the campaign. There was a feeling of nervous dread but still hope that the effort had been successful. Kothe called the meeting to order, and members went around the room, first recognizing one another's hard work and accomplishments and then reluctantly admitting the campaign's faults and weaknesses. It was as if this voluntary civic group were putting itself on the couch for a therapy session, arguing over existential questions raised by virtually all local community groups, nonprofits, and social movements.

"We just didn't have enough committed people to go out and collect signatures," said Loyko, the signature campaign's tireless coordinator. Loyko had been bullish on the group's chances of gathering the signatures with volunteers, predicting early on that the process might not even take the full thirty days. Instead of keeping coalition members in feverish fear of defeat, the Coalition had projected complacency about the petitions. Instead of quickly shifting to add paid signature gatherers, the group had delayed, unable to evaluate its current signature totals accurately as volunteers often kept their partly filled petitions rather than turning them in each week.

To the Coalition, water as a public trust and informed citizen participation in governance were not abstractions but ideals embodied in real jobs at the sewer plant and a visible public process. *Process* was the essential word. Public water was about democracy, and civic action was about not only government process but also the internal democratic process of the Coalition itself. Susan Loyko, Bill's wife and a water-department employee, was passionate on this point. "I want to say that this group always took the high road," she told the meeting. "We refused to run in the mud with the rest of them, and I couldn't be prouder of being a member of this group." Almost everyone in the room applauded, although some with less enthusiasm than in the past.

John Boisa, the state Assembly aide who had hired the paid signature gatherers, was unimpressed. Dressed like a gunslinger, in a black suit, black shirt, and black tie, Boisa seemed to relish being the messenger from the land of political hardball. He reminded the group that his paid signature gatherers got the Coalition over the ten thousand mark. "I've heard a couple of comments about 'when this thing goes to an election,'" he said. "Maybe I'm the only one in this room that thinks it, but I don't think we've won." For Boisa, the Coalition's internal process was irrelevant if it resulted in the loss of public control of the city's water services. He wanted results and clear-eyed political analysis.

"I'm going to be blunt now and I may hurt a few people's feelings," said Boisa. "I don't want to spend more of my time just about making myself feel good." And then he launched into a critique common to sophisticated political operatives working with idealistic grassroots groups. "The fact is that when you talked about the high road and you worried about people's feelings, you ran this thing in a manner that would have failed. So the difference is, a winning campaign is one where you win. A losing campaign is one where you lose and then maybe a day later at least you can say, 'I feel good about myself.'" This classic debate is repeated in almost every community group that tries to affect government while trying also to keep its own independence and soul.

For Bagalayos, the youngest activist to regularly attend and participate in Coalition meetings, the only way to stop the companies' inexorable drive to privatize was to change the rules of the game. Bagalayos was just back from an international water conference where she had met antiprivatization activists from around the world. She felt the Coalition was not militant enough, limiting its attraction for younger and more radical activists. "I've talked to people engaged in these water struggles from around the world," she said, "and in each case, they never won without civil disobedience. We also failed to go into the poor sections of the city where people have a big stake in our winning." She also repeated her frequent calls for the Coalition to expand its education and outreach work to the growing Latino and other minority communities on the south side of town.

Coalition elder Ursula Meyer, a veteran of local politics, rolled her eyes about civil disobedience and quickly dismissed Bagalayos's idea about outreach to Latinos. "They don't vote," she said. That analysis became more questionable later on. The city's large Latino population was an important factor in the victory of Podesto's successor as mayor, Police Chief Edward Chavez.

Similar debates go on in every antiprivatization campaign and in most other grassroots political movements. Can such movements use different strategies and tactics without divisive internal disputes? How can an already-existing group expand its social base? How can it bring in activist-oriented young people and conservative church-going people at the same time? How can it win without making the political compromises that are often necessary?

On the other side, internal debates over strategy didn't take place for a minute. Podesto's aim was victory—just as it had been when he pitched ball in high school or when he competed for business. For him, the Coalition members and their ilk were classic losers—the butcher, baker, and candlestick maker. For OMI and Thames, the battle was about money already on the table, an investment of time and cash that would have to be justified to company directors and stockholders. It was also about avoiding a precedent-setting defeat. Even if the companies lost money for awhile—and they were not ready to concede that possibility—a setback on this benchmark project at the hands of an ad hoc community coalition would slow their privatization agenda nationwide and fuel opposition efforts elsewhere. They were willing to put in whatever money it took to win.

A few days later, the headline in the *Stockton Record* said it all: "Privatization Foes Dealt Setback."[10] The signature-gathering effort was shy by just a few hundred signatures, but that was enough. There would be no referendum. For Podesto, the result was a big relief, and he hoped the city would now move on past the divisiveness.

Round Three: Into the Courts

Mayor Podesto moved quickly to push up another deadline to circumvent his opponents. One of the conditions of the contract was that there be no legal actions under way against either party regarding the deal, but a court date of August 11, 2003, had been set for the Coalition's lawsuit challenging the privatization. So Podesto and OMI/Thames brazenly decided to put the privatization into effect August 1. The decision was not a surprise to McDonald. "A contract is only as good as the paper it's written on," and he predicted that if the companies had a problem, they had enough attorneys "to figure out how to get them out of it."

On July 31, MUD employees turned in their city badges for ones with the OMI/Thames logo. McDonald was not one of them. He had said all along that he would not work for the private company. On the last day of public control of the municipal utility department, his friends at MUD held a going-away barbeque in his honor. They had even collected money to give him a gold watch. In tears, McDonald thanked them. "I'm sad, and I'm angry, but I'm happy I've got all these wonderful people in my life that will always be there." With that, he walked out of the plant's maintenance yard after twenty-six years on the job.

The Coalition's case moved forward before conservative Superior Court Judge Robert McNatt. In October 2003, McNatt shocked observers by throwing out the privatization and giving the city 180 days to unravel the deal. His ruling was dramatic and radical. He said that privatization in and of itself creates a significant change in the environmental status of the water department and requires an environmental impact report. He called the city's self-declared exemption from such a report "an abuse of discretion."[11] However, the city and OMI/Thames announced they would appeal, and, on a technicality, they won a last-minute ruling from Judge McNatt ordering a new trial sometime in the future. After its initial victory in the courts, this turn of events was a major blow to the Coalition.

The Results

Success in court is always a long and uncertain process, and time can turn potential court victories into defeat. Stocking admitted more than two years later, "I never thought we'd be in court this long." Every month that passed left OMI/Thames still in control of the water department, creating facts on the ground by starting construction to expand the sewage plant.

However, the Coalition's forecasts were accurate on other fronts. Water rates that were stable for five years under public control have risen every year since privatization, just as the Coalition predicted. Mayor Podesto had claimed that rates would rise only 7 percent over the twenty-year life of the contract, but a detailed Coalition analysis reported increases of 8.5 percent in just the first three years. In addition, leakage doubled, maintenance backlogs skyrocketed, and staff turnover was constant, even on the management level, where there were two general managers and four operations managers in the first two years.[12]

Some residents of Stockton also notice a difference when they sniff the air. McDonald's mother lives not far from the wastewater-treatment plant, and she and her neighbors complain about the stink. Workers at the plant told McDonald that OMI/Thames cut back on odor-control chemicals as soon as they took over to save approximately $40,000 a month. "I don't want our citizens calling because they can't sit in their front yards because the odors are so bad," said McDonald. "That's a service we should provide our citizens."

Although that is the most odoriferous example of OMI/Thames's management style, it is hardly the most serious. To put a new well on-line and test it with chlorinated water, OMI/Thames hired an out-of-state, nonunion subcontractor whose workers pumped residual chlorine into a waterway, killing fish. That landed the city a $125,000 state fine. Months later, on the Friday before a hot summer weekend, the wastewater-treatment plant spilled eight million gallons of sewage into the San Joaquin River, contaminating a mile-long area where people go swimming. It was the largest spill since the private company took over, but it took ten hours for managers to notice the error and another three days to notify the public about the health danger. The city and the company blamed one another for the delay, a confusion of authority not unusual in public-private partnerships.[13]

As for Mayor Podesto, he was able to make good on his dream of a downtown ballpark, which attracted a minor-league team. However, the team later sued the city for design flaws at the ballpark, and a scathing grand jury report condemned huge cost overruns on the project. Another report, *Pillaging the Public Trust*, by a former city finance commissioner, concluded the city had inappropriately drained $36 million from water and sewer accounts to pay for the ballpark. Those balances, which had been built up over years for future MUD projects, became a development slush fund after privatization.[14]

Forced to retire because of term limits, Podesto ran for the state Senate, hoping to upset the Democratic incumbent. Governor Arnold Schwarzenegger stumped regularly for him, and the Republican Party made his election a top priority. The $10 million battle became the most expensive state legislative race in U.S. history. During the campaign, Podesto's opponent came out against Stockton's water privatization. He reminded voters of Podesto's opposition to a public vote and portrayed the mayor as being in the pocket of developers. In the end, the voters clearly had had enough of Podesto's high-handed style. Not only did he lose the campaign, he failed to win a majority even in his own county. Looking back, Podesto told the *Los Angeles Times*, "A lot of people would say I was short on process. I think our city had plenty of process for a long time but never got anything accomplished. . . . At some point, you have to be a bully."[15]

Three years after OMI/Thames took control of Stockton's water services, the legality of that action was still unclear. In November 2006, the Coalition won yet another important court decision that the privatization required environmental review. The judge went further in finding that 180 days would be a reasonable time for the city to "resume municipal operations and management."[16] The city government and OMI/Thames could still appeal. "There is still some climbing to be done before we reach the peak," said a cautiously optimistic Stocking. "And remember, once you reach the peak, you need to return safe and alive."[17]

Working now in Stockton's Public Works Department, McDonald stays in touch with friends at the sewage plant, who tell him upsetting stories about unreported spills, delayed maintenance, and low morale. "Nothing works," said McDonald. "It really breaks my heart to see what they've done to my plant." Asked about his decision to leave, he paused. "I took a solid stand, and I look back now, and I'm kind of proud of that. This wasn't a fight for personal gain but for principle. It wasn't about the employees. It was about our community."[18]

3

Small-Town Surprise for a Corporate Water Giant

Felton, California

Felton is one of a chain of small hill towns tucked among ancient redwood trees in the San Lorenzo Valley, some nine miles up a narrow, twisty road from the oceanfront college town of Santa Cruz. Most of Felton's forty-five hundred people live up the hill, their houses invisible from the two-block-long main drag. It's easy to think of the place as a haven for turned-on, tuned-in folks who live off the land and keep to themselves, but as California American Water Company discovered to its regret, Felton is populated largely by highly educated professionals who moved here from Silicon Valley, San Francisco, and various other traffic-clogged metropolises because, as one loyal resident put it, "It's heaven here." As always, heaven has its defenders.

The water system in Felton was privately—and locally—owned from 1868, when the town was incorporated, until it was sold to a small regional utility in 1961. Few people paid much attention or noticed that they paid a little more than their neighbors served by public systems. But the purchase of the Felton system in 2001 by a large, U.S.-based water company and its subsequent purchase by an international conglomerate set off alarm bells among people chatting in the local health-food store, which counts as big business in Felton.[1]

Now, locals would be getting their drinking water from California American Water (Cal Am), a subsidiary of the largest U.S.

private water company, American Water, itself a subsidiary of England's largest water company, Thames Water in London, which had recently become a subsidiary of German energy conglomerate Rheinisch-Westfälisches Elektrizitätswerk Aktiengesellschaft (RWE). The *San Jose Mercury News* reported, "Globalization is flying its flag in the Santa Cruz Mountains, and the people of Felton don't much like it."[2]

Doing something about it, however, would not be easy. Felton, like other towns in the San Lorenzo Valley, doesn't have its own government. Instead, the towns are administered by the county and represented by a county supervisor. If a certain self-sufficiency defines Felton residents, it isn't mountain-man isolationism or hippie anarchy. Natural disaster is a regular phenomenon in this earthquake-, flood-, and landslide-prone region. "Groups come together as volunteers when needs arise, then disappear when needs are met," writes Barbara Sprenger in a case study of the town's water services.[3] For Felton, the arrival of Cal Am/RWE posed an existential challenge. To fight for control of their water, Felton would have to become something more than an ad hoc collection of resourceful and occasionally cooperating individuals.

Throughout history, the need for clean water has stimulated the creation of local political institutions. London's first metropolitan government was a board of works created to deal with the "Great Stink" of 1858, when the stench of sewage in the River Thames drove the prime minister out of the Houses of Parliament with a handkerchief over his face. The *Times* of London editorialized that only such a governing body "would have strength enough to double the work of Hercules and to cleanse not only the filthy stables, but the river which runs through them."[4] Felton's Bull and Fall creeks may not compare with the Thames, but the town now faced a similar challenge of self-creation in wresting local control of its water.

The first organized response to RWE/Thames's entrance on the scene came from Felton's political representative, who clearly saw the challenge to the town's future. County supervisor and Felton resident Jeff Almquist believed that RWE/Thames had taken on so much debt to buy Cal Am that he and other ratepayers would suddenly be at the mercy of international finance. "In layman's terms," he said, "this water comes down the creek right behind my house and runs downhill to the collection point. We pay for pumping it back up to our homes, and we buy the water. It was one thing to pay for that service," he continued, "but now we're paying profits to a CEO in Germany for moving this water a little distance, and that's bizarre."[5] In 2002, Almquist spearheaded the founding of a grassroots group called Friends of Locally Owned Water (FLOW) to discuss the fate of the water system. Almquist's call elicited an overwhelming response from the public. The throng that showed up for one meeting at the fire station was so large that the fire trucks had to be moved outside to make room.

Residents were already dissatisfied with Cal Am's service in its first year in Felton, but then Almquist briefed them about Thames's less-than-stellar environmental record in London. The company had been named "Worst Polluter" in the U.K. several years running. London's rowing crews had even formed an alliance, Rowers Against Thames Sewage (RATS), and held a "Thames Turd Race" during which rowers wearing gas masks pulled ten-foot-long inflatable feces behind their boats on their way to deliver petitions against sewage overflows into the river.[6]

The news that really catalyzed residents, though, was Cal Am's application to merge its Felton and nearby Monterey operations and to raise rates by 74 percent over three years. Suddenly, it was a pocketbook issue as well as a debate over local control. Cal Am's spokesman, Kevin Tilden, seemed genuinely surprised by the upsurge. "We'd like to have a chance," he said, promising economies of scale. "We can send out bills cheaper. We can buy chemicals cheaper. We can answer phones cheaper."[7] That promise didn't impress residents upset when their calls to customer service were answered in Alton, Illinois. The big rate increase also didn't help Cal Am's cause when residents learned they were already paying considerably more than their neighbors down the road, who were served by the publicly run San Lorenzo Valley Water District.[8]

Eminent Domain

In November 2002, California's Public Utilities Commission, which regulates private water companies, formally approved the RWE/Thames purchase of American Water and its Cal Am subsidiary. Not discouraged, Almquist pulled together a coalition that included the Felton Business Association, FLOW, and key county and state officials. Almquist's ambitious strategy was aimed at ultimately convincing the San Lorenzo Valley Water District to purchase the Felton water system from Cal Am through eminent domain.

The doctrine of eminent domain is derived from a tiny phrase in the Fifth Amendment to the Constitution: "Private property [shall not] be taken for public use, without just compensation." This idea has been fought over ever since the passage of the Bill of Rights, but many of the nation's greatest and most controversial public-works projects could never have been built without it. Eminent domain made possible the creation of the Tennessee Valley Authority during the New Deal, the construction of the interstate highway system in the 1950s, the destruction of inner city neighborhoods for urban renewal in the 1970s, and much more.

Over the years, Cal Am's parent company, American Water, had become expert in resisting efforts to use eminent domain to buy its local water operations. In the late 1950s, after the company fought eminent domain efforts in Lexington (Kentucky), Peoria (Illinois), and Ashtabula (Ohio), the company feared that it was being nibbled to death, and so it took a stand, declaring in its 1959 annual report, "We consider it our prime responsibility to maintain the integrity of the company's investment in the water works field."[9] Cal Am's community-relations representative in Felton, Evan Jacobs, was only reiterating company policy when he said Cal Am was "willing to spend what it's going to take to defend our property here."[10]

Clearly, a hostile takeover by the community was not going to be easy, and the process itself had many steps, any one of which could stop the effort cold. FLOW would have to convince the county to issue bonds to cover the county's own expenses in the acquisition process. Then, Felton's citizens would have to approve a separate major bond measure for the actual purchase price of the system through eminent domain.

However, the most significant step was not financial or political. To assert control over their water, Almquist and Felton's citizens had to create a community identity and the basic mechanisms for decision making and self-government. Because Felton was unincorporated, the citizens had to establish a legal entity authorized to manifest the will of the people. The proposed solution was the creation of a community services district, which, with the voters' approval, would allow Felton citizens to vote on bond issues and to raise taxes to cover the bond payments. Even to get that far, Felton citizens first had to petition the county board of supervisors.

In October 2003, in the midst of this arduous process, Almquist was nominated for a Superior Court judgeship. It was a position he had long desired, and he accepted instantly. His departure left a void in the campaign for local control. A new county supervisor, Mark Stone, had to pick up where Almquist left off.

It took several months for FLOW to regain its footing after Almquist's departure. But instead of relying on one person at the helm, the community itself came together and took leadership. Committees were formed, headed by an attorney, a web designer, an environmental scientist, a CPA, and several talented organizers. Significant progress was made on a number of fronts, from outreach to fundraising to polling. This new group of volunteers did everything from gathering signatures to organizing events to attending meetings of the board of supervisors. One woman organized a tour of Felton gardens as a fundraiser—with FLOW information tables at every stop. It turned out to be hugely popular. "We were very conscious always that we were building community and raising community consciousness," said tour organizer Michelle Moser. There were water poetry contests for the children, street-theater performances in the center of town, screenings of the film *Thirst* on the wall of the local grocery store, as well as meetings with out-of-town activists like Juliette Beck of Public Citizen's Water Campaign (now called Food & Water Watch). An electrician made sure banners were up everywhere so that everyone stayed up-to-date on the campaign. "Previously, there would be little neighborhoods of people," observed resident Beth Algrin. "Now it's a big neighborhood. People who never knew each other before got together."[11] Every FLOW activity was hands-on, up-close, and personal.

Rate Shock

The key issues of rates, services, and local control were always at the forefront, but the rate issue became even more important when Cal Am asked for yet another increase; the proposed 64 percent hike brought the total to over 100 percent. That increase was too much for Dominga Moldes, the director of Rose Acres Residence, a facility that houses more than twenty people in need. "At first I paid $250, then $500, and now I pay $1,275 a month," she said. "When my water rates increase over 100 percent I can't run this facility for the most helpless, homeless, and mentally ill."[12] Moser agreed: "I learned about the term *rate shock* from this. We are beyond rate shock and into 'rate terror.' People are really wondering how they are going to pay for their service."[13]

Fortunately it's easier to engage in one-on-one dialogue in an area with twenty-five hundred registered voters than in a city of several hundred thousand, because doing so was FLOW's only chance for success. Eighty-five-year-old FLOW member Frank Adamson, a retired psychologist and Congregational minister, walked up and down Felton's steep hills to find and talk to voters whose homes weren't visible from the road. Adamson called himself "a specimen to show what a senior citizen looks like who wants to purchase the water system."[14] He and other volunteers gathered signatures to petition the board of supervisors to allow Felton to vote on acquiring the water company. Adamson's wife, Fran, a former psychiatric nurse, compiled a weekly newsletter and posted it in local hangouts.

While subcommittees convened on their own schedules, FLOW met twice a month to trade information and arrive at group decisions by consensus. A different member started each session with a "reflection" and a "celebration." Sprenger observed that this ritual "became an absolutely vital part of the meeting as times got more difficult."[15]

On August 3, 2004, the county board of supervisors recognized nearly a thousand verified signatures—out of just 1,350 water hookups—and unanimously approved the right of Felton's residents to vote on acquiring their water system and merging it with the neighboring public San Lorenzo Water District. Once it became clear to Cal Am that FLOW would not be deterred by categorical statements that the system was not for sale, the company initiated a pricey campaign of direct mail, radio ads, and phone calls.

FLOW had been growing steadily by the time Jim Graham came on board in December 2004. The forty-four-year-old had his own public relations consulting company in Felton, but he had never done any work with the local community. He moved to town after four years in Washington, D.C., to get away from big-city hubbub, and, he told his wife, "If I get to the crossroad, and I have to wait for four cars, we've got to move. It's getting too big here."[16] It's a fear that many people express when a big water company comes to town because the water industry makes its money not just from raising rates but also from real estate development and the new ratepayers that brings.

Graham had an unusual set of talents to offer. In addition to his paid consulting work, he had volunteered for seven years overseeing a staff of sixty-five as media coordinator for the Burning Man festival, an annual party/be-in/happening in the Nevada desert that attracts tens of thousands of scantily clad people to create community and, on the last night, to celebrate the ritual of burning an enormous wooden sculpture.

Graham had also worked for Lockheed Martin, the big defense contractor over the mountain from Felton in Silicon Valley. As part of that work, he learned how companies case a town for possible future expansion. "At Lockheed, we put community-relations people into a town before the company came in to propose a missile plant or manufacturing facility, and that person would join the right church groups, would get their kids in the right school, would get involved in Boy Scouts, the whole thing. And they'd get a feel for the community and then report back regularly to Lockheed. And now I'm on the other side, and I know how to fight it."

Graham volunteered to help devise communication strategies for FLOW and immersed himself in studying the campaigns by American Water Works subsidiaries against community groups across the country, from faraway Lexington, Kentucky, to nearby Montara, a little town that had successfully bought its water system from Cal Am. Graham put together a plan and, together with FLOW members, came out swinging.

In anticipation of Cal Am's upcoming deluge of mass mailings, Graham designed a post card with a row of mailboxes on the front and a single line, "Get ready for the flood." The back of the card began "Hope you like it. You're paying for it." As a preemptive strike, it was brilliantly effective for two reasons. First, the card seeded a negative reaction to Cal Am's mailings—even before they showed up in mailboxes. Second, it debunked the usual water company claim—repeated in Felton—that local ratepayers weren't footing the bill for company marketing and public relations. If Felton residents weren't paying, then American Water Works customers elsewhere in the country must be. And one could assume that revenue from Felton would soon cover American Water's campaign in the next town.

Graham also handled relations with the local media. "Anything I told a reporter, I could back up with documentation," he asserts. "If I was speculating on something, I'd tell them I was speculating." Not only did that procedure increase FLOW's credibility with the media, it also threw any false claims and misrepresentations by Cal Am into sharp relief.

Cal Am's response took several forms. Seeking a grassroots association to give the impression of organic local support for the water company, it backed an existing organization called the San Lorenzo Valley Property Owners Association, which was led by Patrick Dugan, a self-described libertarian who believed that eminent domain was a government attack on property rights.

The water company hooked up with another local resident, Mary Anderson, who ran a new group called Valley Information Alliance. They claimed a couple of hundred supporters, sent out three mailers, and set up a website. When Anderson surfaced, Graham cannily proposed that she replace Jacobs in public debates because there was now "legitimate citizen opposition." Not wanting any part of a public forum, she declined to make appearances, and FLOW often got to make its case uncontested.[17]

Cal Am constantly underestimated the skills and tenacity of its opposition. The company distributed a flyer favorably comparing its rates with those in neighboring districts, but Sprenger, a warm-spirited but hard-headed businesswoman, discovered that Cal Am had cooked the figures. The company was comparing two months of another district's charges with one month of its own. Another false Cal Am comparison was between Felton and a system whose rates included ancillary charges such as road and community-pool maintenance and recreation fees.[18]

While FLOW—and the local newspaper—didn't hesitate to make residents aware of such maneuvers, the citizens' group itself decided to be forthright about the significant costs to each household of acquiring the company. Homeowners would have to pay an additional annual property tax of $598, but they would enjoy a reduction in water rates, and they would own their water system. With Cal Am continuously asking for bigger and bigger rate hikes, FLOW believed a crossover point would be reached in about seven years.

A Damaging Leak

Broad-based social movements sometimes sweep in unexpected allies, whether it's Daniel Ellsberg leaking the Pentagon Papers or the mysterious source inside Cal Am who leaked the company's confidential communications-strategy document in the spring of 2005. The plan described how "community operatives" had "conducted a reconnaissance" of Felton and prepared "for hostile action." "Our strategy is to make the road a rocky one for proponents [of eminent domain]."[19]

The brain trust behind the plan, which was dated December 1, 2003, was clearly identified as the Moriah Group, a Tennessee-based public relations firm known for its work with conservative candidates, churches, and causes. Moriah had been hired by American Water for a series of campaigns in the Midwest aimed at building community opposition to eminent-domain efforts. The firm boasted on its website that, as a result of its integrated communications strategies, "American Water Works has yet to lose a property that The Moriah Group has had the privilege to assist."[20]

Nevertheless, the leaked document was not optimistic about the state of affairs in Felton, which it called "a grim environment in which the only viable argument appears to be increased taxpayer cost." To turn the situation around, the Moriah plan specifically suggested making life "an unpleasant experience" for County Supervisor Mark Stone, who was new on the job when the document was written. Cal Am was going to employ a "push-pull" phone poll, a technique in which the goal is not to solicit an opinion but to surreptitiously form one. The hot-button issue, the firm concluded, was the tax hike that would be required to cover the purchase price of the company. Callers would ask, "Did you realize that your taxes could go up six or seven hundred dollars a year if you vote for this thing?" The person on the other end of the phone would likely have an adverse reaction, at which point the pollster would say, "I can forward you right now to Mark Stone in the Supervisor's office, and you can tell him personally how you feel about this." The Moriah Group projected that as many as eight hundred calls would be patched through to his office.[21]

The Moriah plan went on to recommend mailings that would accuse "outside organizers" of imposing another tax on Felton residents. FLOW members relished the irony of a German-English multinational hiring a Tennessee company to accuse them of being under the influence of outsiders. The strategy document also referred to "an experienced community relations and political organizer [who] was retained to live and work in the community and serve as both an ambassador and a strategist." This person was part of Moriah's overall strategy to build "large, organized grassroots coalitions to support the company's position."[22]

One allegedly grassroots group that emerged in Felton set up its website at www.notakeoverinfelton.com. FLOW member Graham had anticipated this move from his own experience, and he set out to research the site designer. Lo and behold, the designer's office turned out to be just a few doors away from the Moriah Group's headquarters in Chattanooga. A coincidence? Well, the same firm designed the Moriah Group's own website, where it is duly credited.

The revelations may have been embarrassing for Cal Am, but the company didn't abandon its strategy of "grassroots development" or its spending to defeat FLOW, now estimated in the hundreds of thousands of dollars. When FLOW proposed its language for Measure W to take local control of water, Cal Am ally Dugan of the San Lorenzo Valley Property Owners Association sued to challenge the wording. It was an expensive court procedure for Cal Am, which eventually paid Dugan's bill of $36,800. Dugan did win a change in the wording of FLOW's ballot argument, in which it described Cal Am as a "corporate monopoly with no competitors and guaranteed profits." However, it seemed like a high price to pay for the change. The new wording described Cal Am as a "corporate monopoly with no competitors and the legal right to generate a profit."[23]

If approved, Measure W would authorize the sale of $11 million in bonds to be repaid through added property taxes over the next thirty years. The money would cover the cost of appraisals and legal work as well as the acquisition of the water company. Felton residents would have to make the bond payments, a cost that would amount to about $600 per year per household. It was quite a commitment.

Eyes on the Prize

In spite of all of FLOW's organizing and support, the election was far from a slam dunk. The vote was to be by mail-in ballot, and because the measure called for new taxes, FLOW needed to win a supermajority of two-thirds plus one against a multinational with abundant cash and a willingness to spend whatever it took. "It's a case of deep pockets against a piggy bank," said Sprenger.[24] Leading up to the election, FLOW mapped and divided the district into six areas. A captain was assigned to each and was given a team. Altogether, some sixty-five volunteers had the task of visiting homes and getting out the vote, with each volunteer responsible for about fifty people. With its mountainous and rough terrain, Felton is not what you'd call precinct-walking territory. But walk they did.

The ballots were mailed in June 2005, and citizens were allowed a month to mail them back. FLOW worked the election like an underdog. The group had already done phone polling to identify who planned to vote in favor and who planned to vote against the measure. After the ballots went out, they put that information to use. Twice a week, FLOW representatives went to the election offices to get an update on who had voted. They couldn't find out how they had voted, but they didn't need to—they had a good idea from the phone polling. Supporters who hadn't voted yet received regular phone reminders or visits from volunteers.

On July 26, 2005, Measure W supporters gathered at a local Italian restaurant to await the election results. The battle in this little town was being followed across the country and beyond. A TV crew from Japan had flown in to film the event. When the news came in at 8 P.M., the champagne corks started popping. "I'm almost speechless with joy," said Frank Adamson. "They've got a lot of money, but we've got spirit." FLOW's ballot Measure W passed by a three-to-one margin with nearly 75 percent of the vote. "It's fantastic," said Graham. "The only thing missing was someone dumping buckets of Gatorade over our heads."[25] Although it required extraordinary organization and effort to succeed, the Felton campaign benefited from a savvy electorate as well as Cal Am's surprisingly inept campaign. A neighbor wryly observed, "They thought they had a hippie enclave, and what they had was a yuppie stronghold."

But FLOW's success in Felton was far more meaningful. Sprenger, writing about the Felton battle for her master's thesis in public policy, concluded, "FLOW's success was not predetermined. Indeed, Cal Am appeared to see the town as a fly to be swatted, never believing that the community could succeed against the company's enormous wealth and willingness to spend whatever it took to change minds and set one group against another."[26]

Sprenger was right about Cal Am's willingness to pay a high price for control of water. After the passage of Measure W, Cal Am's Jacobs told the press, "I think this is the end of the beginning, and we move out from the court of public opinion to the legal aspect."[27] The corporation quickly expanded its legal and legislative counterattacks. In 2005, Cal Am helped draft legislation to rewrite the state's eminent-domain laws. A lobbyist convinced a state legislator to carry the bill, assuring him it was just a simple, technical amendment without any significant opposition. Not quite. The bill would allow a public agency to acquire a private utility through eminent domain only if it demonstrated that the private company had "continually failed to comply with governing rules and regulations." FLOW activist Jim Mosher called it "a real sneak attack" to overrule the voters. "If this bill was to pass as currently written, our campaign would be over." FLOW supporters around the state flooded the legislator with calls until the legislator withdrew the bill, admitting that he had not realized what was at stake. It was only a first skirmish. Similar bills are on the drawing board.[28]

In addition to challenging eminent domain and threatening legal action, Cal Am adamantly refused to negotiate a price for Felton to buy the system. The appraisal process alone would take months. FLOW estimated the local system's value at $8.5 million. Cal Am wants the price to be higher, somewhere between $15 and $40 million, but the company says it doesn't want to place a price on a system it doesn't intend to sell. "We are concerned it would create a domino effect and we want to stop that from happening," said Kevin Tilden, Cal Am vice president for external affairs.[29] If there's no agreement on a sale price, then it will be up to the San Lorenzo Valley Water District to use eminent domain to condemn the system, but as we have seen, Cal Am has promised to challenge any such action in court. Felton's fight is far from over, but in the process of fighting the town has forged a new sense of identity as a community.

Scandals in the South

4

The Price of Incompetence
Atlanta, Georgia

A conundrum for opponents of privatization has been the un-
critical enthusiasm for outsourcing water services among many
of the nation's mayors and city-council members. Elected to office
claiming a desire to serve, these officials work assiduously to rid
themselves of the risks and responsibilities they presumably ran for
office to assume.[1]

In many cases, the urge to privatize is based on desperation.
More than twenty-five years of anti-tax crusades and conservative
hegemony in Washington have decimated local government
finances. The possibility of pushing an entire municipal department
and its workers off the books and under an outside company's
purview seems like manna from heaven. In other cases, mayors are
true believers in an almost mystical private-sector mastery that can
rescue their towns from rate hikes and budget crunches while
improving services. Often, this promise of a win-win situation is
politically irresistible. However, in a few cases, a turn to the market
is less about desperation or delusion than about old-fashioned corruption, sometimes criminal but more often of the wink-and-nod
variety that has greased the gears of government for developers, lobbyists, and special interests from time immemorial.

In Atlanta, water privatization was linked to corruption at the
highest level. In 2004, two years after he left office, Bill Campbell,
a former Democratic mayor, was indicted on a series of charges,

including racketeering, taking payoffs and favors from city contractors, accepting illegal campaign contributions, tax evasion, mail fraud, and obstruction of justice. One count of the indictment claimed that Campbell accepted favors and campaign contributions from the city's private water contractor, United Water, a subsidiary of Paris-based water giant Suez. In 2006, a jury acquitted Campbell on bribery charges, but it did convict him of tax evasion and mail fraud. Campbell claimed victory, but, with many of his closest aides, friends, and allies in jail or facing trial for raiding the public treasury, many Atlantans now look back on Campbell's mayoralty as a criminal enterprise.[2]

The corruption at City Hall was a tremendous blow to Atlanta's pride, especially because Campbell himself had once been considered an inspirational figure, the janitor's son who as a first grader was the first black child to integrate the schools in Raleigh, North Carolina. Handsome, energetic, and combative, Campbell eventually graduated from prestigious Vanderbilt and Duke universities, but not without bitter memories. One of Campbell's mentors, former mayor Andrew Young, recalled, "The only thing [Campbell] told me about his time in college was going to a swimming hole and everyone getting out."[3] Many Atlantans, particularly white Atlantans, didn't like Campbell's abrasive style, his closed inner circle of associates, and his frequent gambling trips, but such issues could be overlooked in the midst of the growing optimism and economic expansion of the 1990s. Mayor Campbell led the city successfully through the 1996 Olympic Games, and the nation's economic boom had its counterpart in Atlantans' rising hopes for the city's future.

A Decaying Infrastructure

One major problem threatened Atlanta's potential. The city's public water and sewer systems were in disastrous condition and required massive investment. City leaders feared that the federal government would demand a moratorium on new development if the city failed to prevent regular sewage spills into the Chatta-hoochee River.

Atlanta's decaying infrastructure had been an issue of public concern well before Campbell was elected in 1993. Residents had long been familiar with Dickensian sewage backups and what sani-tation workers called "fecal fountains" spewing through manhole covers. The problem was not just the stench. Every year, heavy rains overwhelmed the sewage system time and again, releasing raw sewage into Atlanta's four main creeks, killing fish, and giving the water a repulsive green tint. One resident told state inspectors, "There is more life on Mars than in our creek."[4]

Even in dry weather, broken pipes leaked untreated sewage, and the overflows, leaks, and chemical pollutants all eventually flowed from the creeks into the Chattahoochee, the source of drinking water for 70 percent of metro Atlanta's 3.5 million residents. Sewer backups were a problem that crossed boundaries of race and class. "It happened to us in January, while we were giving a dinner party," a resident of one of the city's most exclusive neighborhoods told the *Atlanta Journal-Constitution*. "There's nothing worse than sewage in your basement to spoil a dinner party."[5]

Under the federal Clean Water Act, the state and city were required to clean up the river, and Georgia set a deadline of Decem-ber 31, 1993, for the city to fix the sewer overflows. Failure to com-ply would result in fines of $100,000 per day. Atlanta's politicians debated various plans and leaned toward a quick solution of build-ing small sewage-treatment plants at a cost of $90 million. One Environmental Protection Agency expert called the plants "a waste of money" that would not solve the problem, but construction began anyway.[6]

In the meantime, environmental groups demanded comprehen-sive solutions: either create two separate sewer systems, one for rain-water and the other for sewage, or construct two long tunnels to store excess runoff during storms. The deep tunnels would be less expensive than the separated sewers and would also cause less economic disruption to downtown business, but the price was still huge. According to one estimate, it approached $1 billion. The burden of the expense would fall on residents, and the average household water bill could increase by as much as $105 a month, hitting hard in a city with a large low-income population.

The size of the problem and the huge expense to solve it intimidated Atlanta's political and business leaders, who, according to an editorial in the *Atlanta Journal-Constitution*, were always "chasing after one rainbow or another."[7] In early 1994, when Campbell took office, the City Council finally seemed ready to grapple with the problem; it proposed that an eight-mile-long, two hundred-foot-deep tunnel be built underground to carry wastewater from white north Atlanta south to an existing sewage plant in a black neighborhood. Engineers called the plan a solution; the black community, which makes up 60 percent of Atlanta's residents, viewed it as environmental racism.

In cities all over the country, sewage plants, incinerators, landfills, and hazardous-waste dumps are usually sited in minority or poor communities. African American activists in Atlanta said enough was enough. "The community was not involved in this process," said Na'Taki Osborne of the West Atlanta Watershed Alliance. "So the community got together and got its elected officials, its professionals, and average everyday citizens to advocate for policies in favor of environmental justice." An alliance of churches and community groups demanded construction of separate sanitary sewers to stop sewage overflows rather than tunnels to their neighborhood.[8]

The City Council was besieged with protests. The Council's Utilities Committee chair Clair Muller tried to calm emotions, saying the tunnel presented no dangers and was not an example of environmental racism. But, because of the city's failure to involve the community previously, it was too late to build trust now. Elected officials ran for cover. Campbell had voted for the tunnel as a City

Council member three years earlier, but now, as mayor, he promised to veto the plan if it passed. It did not, failing in a vote almost entirely along racial lines.[9]

One after another, more plans were floated and dropped while the city paid thousands of dollars a day in penalties for the delays. Critics were furious. "They just put it off," said Sally Bethea, executive director of the Upper Chattahoochee Riverkeepers. "Well, we'll let the next mayor deal with that, and the next mayor. . . ."[10] The frustration was not confined to metro Atlanta. The polluted river was also a big issue for people living downstream in Georgia, Alabama, and Florida. They too relied on the river for their water.

Bethea spearheaded a grassroots campaign that kept the pressure on state and federal governments to clean up the river, and, in 1995, the Riverkeepers joined with other environmental groups and downstream counties to file a federal lawsuit against Atlanta for years of violations of the Clean Water Act. "We were trying to clean up the river from all this sewage and crap," she said. "It wasn't Bill Campbell who destroyed the sewer system. It went back for decades."[11] The judge ruled that it was "a matter of undisputed fact" that Atlanta was dumping dangerous contaminants and sewage into the creeks and the river, and he ordered the city to work out a solution acceptable to Bethea and the other plaintiffs. In 1998, Mayor Campbell signed a federal consent decree that required the city to pay a $2.5 million settlement and to come up with a plan to effectively treat its sewage.[12]

Privatization and Its Discontents

In January 1997, while the case was still in the courts, the Clinton Administration handed the private water industry a long-sought victory. The Administration threw out an old regulation that prevented cities from entering into long-term contracts with private companies to manage public utilities. The new regulation allowed cities to enter into such contracts for up to twenty years.

Campbell responded immediately. In February 1997, a month after the rule change, he proposed a plan to solve the sewer problem without inflicting major rate hikes on Atlanta's populace. He announced that he had approached three unnamed engineering firms for suggestions on how to privatize Atlanta's water and sewer systems. He wanted to hand off the city's water problems to a private company by the end of the year. The mayor didn't offer much in the way of details, but he did estimate that privatization of water operations could save the city $20 million a year. Campbell said he would apply those operational savings to capital investments for fixing the sewers.

No U.S. city the size of Atlanta's had ever privatized its entire water and sewer operation. The mayor's announcement was a radical turnaround because Campbell had previously opposed privatization. In fact, he had recently asked the water workers' union to help him find alternatives. Yet now Campbell was telling the press, "It is clear that some of the savings will come from reduction in the work force." American Federation of State, County, and Municipal Employees (AFSCME) union spokesman Lewis Peeples heard about Campbell's about-face from a reporter and called City Hall to ask, "What the hell is going on?" Peeples felt betrayed. "I was livid, Meanwhile, all hell broke out with the workforce."[13]

Criticisms also came from another quarter. A leading local expert on municipal outsourcing, Barry Bozeman, now at the University of Georgia but then at Georgia Tech's School of Public Policy, expressed doubts about Campbell's high hopes. "Privatization has been looked to as a panacea," he told the *Journal-Constitution*. "It's a myth that the private sector can manage more efficiently. This should be undertaken with great caution."[14]

But Mayor Campbell was not an indecisive man, and he wasn't interested in waiting around for consensus, especially in a city whose residents were fed up with water backups, odors, and signs warning "Do Not Swim or Fish in This Creek." He was also facing a tough reelection battle against a City Council president who was already calling for privatization. Bozeman saw "a kind of stampeding effect" as the city's powerful business community lined up behind the idea and as many residents saw in it a way to avoid higher water and sewer bills.[15] The city sponsored a one-day workshop for city offi cials on the issue, inviting representatives from other cities that had already contracted out their sewer operations. Private water companies were eager to participate. Seven of them anted up $1,000 each to attend and reconnoiter, including United Water, OMI, and U.S. Filter.

In late 1997, as Campbell campaigned for reelection, the city's water and sewer crisis became a central issue. In debate after debate, Campbell's opponent, City Council President Marvin Arrington, held up a jar of dirty water that he alleged was from city faucets and blamed Campbell for inaction. With both candidates now backing privatization, there wasn't much choice for the majority of Atlantans, who told pollsters they opposed contracting out city services. Campbell narrowly won reelection in a bitter runoff.

By this time Georgia's political establishment was getting nervous about the delays and saw an opportunity to promote its own agenda. "There has been a sentiment for a long time in Georgia," said Bethea, "that privatizing things will mean they'll be run better."[16] With support from Georgia's Newt Gingrich, speaker of the U.S. House of Representatives, Governor Zell Miller threatened state legislation to force the city to privatize immediately.

Campbell responded by putting the pedal to the metal. A Council vote on privatization was scheduled for February 1998. Campbell now upped his estimate of projected annual savings from $20 to $30 million a year, but members of the Council were resisting. They wanted increased oversight of the process by the Council itself and by independent technical experts. Council Utility Committee Chair Muller had convened a task force co-chaired by Bozeman that came back with a series of recommendations for solving the city's problems, including the creation of an independent city authority to run both the water and sewer systems, a solution that would take politics out of the process. The task force also proposed "managed competition"—allowing city water and sewer workers to organize their own bid for the contract.

The Council finally voted to go ahead with the privatization process, but the acrimony continued for months. Muller said, "I have always been in favor of privatization," but she preferred a shorter contract term—five years instead of twenty. "When you look at a 15- to 20-year contract, you're creating another monopoly." She objected to Campbell's repeated vetoes of Council attempts at oversight. The *Journal-Constitution* also weighed in, supporting privatization but blasting the mayor's "usual bombastic tirades. He huffs and puffs and insists it's all a political conspiracy against him."[17] As usual, Campbell gave as good as he got. In a speech excerpted in the newspaper, he acknowledged that privatization "has become one of the most debated issues in the history of our city," and he castigated "the *Atlanta Journal-Constitution*—I think that's the name"— for suggesting that his "cronies" controlled the bidding process. He concluded, "Let's made no mistake about it. This is a bold initiative. I'm not a fan of privatization. But yet, on this issue, I believe that privatization is the answer for Atlanta."[18]

Campbell rejected calls for oversight, independent experts, a shorter contract, and an independent public authority. His critics had little room to maneuver because at that time there was little organized opposition to privatization in the United States. The Clinton era was marked by avid support of "public-private partnerships" among both Democrats and Republicans, with few political leaders breaking ranks. In addition, the citizens' movement against water privatization was barely beginning, and few strong voices were asserting that water should remain a public trust and responsibility. Campbell formed his own task force on privatization, inviting AFSCME's Peeples and other constituency representatives to recommend how to structure the privatization process for the sewer system. Peeples and his union had strongly opposed privatization, but Peeples agreed to participate. "I wanted to make sure our people weren't thrown out on the streets," he explained, but once again Campbell shifted course.[19]

The mayor faced an intractable problem. In spite of the change in federal regulations, Georgia state law permitted twenty-year contracts only for drinking water, not sewer systems. So, in spite of the long battle over the sewers, Campbell dropped the sewer system from his proposal. Instead, the city released a Request for Proposals (RFP) to privatize only the dilapidated drinking-water system, including water purification, delivery, maintenance, billing, and customer service. "Everyone was blind-sided," said Peeples, who also used the word "double-crossed" to describe Campbell's unilateral change of course. Peeples was left to face his members, who blamed him for endangering their jobs. "They wanted to kill me 'cause they thought I was going along with the project."[20]

To deal with the real problem, the sewer overflows, Campbell wanted to rush the RFP process, hoping that quick savings from drinking-water privatization would allow the city to afford a new bond issue for the sewer improvements. It was a juggling act, and the RFP made it clear to bidders that "cost effectiveness" was by far the city's highest priority. Dead last among the priorities was "performance capabilities"—the bidder's history of successful contracts and its ability to manage operations in a city the size of Atlanta.[21]

There were other warnings signs. According to the RFP, bids were due July 2, 1998, the city would make its decision August 12, and the private company would take over operation on September 4. This compressed time line of less than six months was a red flag to knowledgeable observers like Bozeman, who called privatization "the veneer of a solution." Bozeman was also worried about the lack of specific details on how the city would oversee bidding and how it would then monitor the private company's performance.[22]

Suggestions to delay the bidding went nowhere. Warnings that there was no chain of accountability were unheeded. One expert's warning that a company could come in and exploit the situation was ignored. Campbell was in a rush to sign the contract by summer, and that meant moving ahead without community input. "The public was not involved adequately before those decisions were made," said Osborne. "I think, at the grassroots level, the idea was still that water is a public resource and that government should work for us and should deliver."[23] The city's business elite had no such reservations, and it was bolstered by "the political culture of Atlanta, [which] assumes the private sector is always best," said Bozeman. "You can't say anything bad about business in Atlanta. It's God."[24] Discouraging words were dismissed in the revelry over gung-ho economic growth across the country, a stock-market boom, and predictions that private water corporations would take over most U.S. water operations in just a few years.

The flawed RFP process did not discourage the private water companies, which hired fleets of former city officials, Campbell campaign fundraisers, and friends of the mayor to help them win the deal. All told, five companies bid to take over the water system. In late August, the city picked United Water of New Jersey in a joint venture with the French water conglomerate Suez Lyonnaise des Eaux. But it was a joint venture in name only. Suez already owned half of United Water and was poised to acquire the rest of the U.S.-based company within the next year.

United Water had clinched the deal with its low bid of $21.4 million a year over twenty years, half the historical price of running the public system. The figure stunned competitors, and even city officials admitted that the bid was far lower than they had expected. But *Atlanta Journal-Constitution* editorials were enthusiastic, even citing the water contract—with its provisions for firing United Water if it didn't do the job—as a model that should be applied to reforming the public schools.[25]

In mid-October 1998, the City Council approved a $428 million, twenty-year contract with United Water. "I predict every city in America will go to privately run water systems," the mayor told the *Journal-Constitution*. "It's virtually impossible to finance the improvements without going to ratepayers, without privatization."[26] Because Atlanta's was the largest water-privatization contract in U.S. history, United Water's and Suez's reputations got a huge boost, and they had every reason to expect that successful implementation would translate into a flurry of deals with other cities. "Atlanta for us will be a reference worldwide, a kind of showcase," crowed Suez Chair and CEO Gerard Mestrallet.[27]

Securing that showcase may have been the key rationale for United Water's low bid in Atlanta. Some years later, a high-ranking Suez executive, who did not want to have his name used, acknowledged that Suez and other multinational water companies had been eager to grab a significant share of the U.S. market even at the expense of short-term profits. That strategy was consistent with the speculative psychology at the time; dotcom millionaires were similarly supporting the idea of forgoing near-term profit in order to focus on increasing market share. For United Water, the Atlanta bid was a strategic loss leader, designed to secure a large market and position the company as a major player in future deals.

United Water Takes Charge

United Water took over on January 1, 1999, gaining 1.5 million customers and 479 employees. It was also responsible for operating and maintaining two drinking-water treatment plants and 2,400 miles of pipe, some of it more than one hundred years old. Although between 85 and 90 percent of the city water department's employees had accepted jobs with United Water, some 250 workers filed suit to block the takeover, arguing that their benefits and pensions would be worse under the new bosses. A judge dismissed the case.[28]

Atlanta could be forgiven for its flush of optimism after so many years of neglect and half-steps. Desperate hope banished doubt, at least publicly. In private conversations, however, Osborne discerned widespread skepticism. "I tried to keep my finger on the pulse of the community, my neighbors in Southwest Atlanta, and they saw privatization as wasting our money." She also had misgivings about possible corruption and backroom deals.[29]

Atlanta's honeymoon with United Water did not last a single year. In July 1999, a water-main rupture interrupted service to two hundred homes, and the company was forced to deliver cases of bottled water. In another neighborhood, it took two months for the company to fix a broken pipe that spewed aboveground a stream of muddy water that covered more than a block.

Problems continued to mount. From December 1999 to February 2000, it took United Water an average of seventy-nine days to fix a broken water main; in early 2000, it took two months from order to completion to install a meter. Then there was the problem of the floating debris in the drinking water. And, in the affluent neighborhood of Buckhead, the kids' Kool-Aid was made from water that looked like iced tea. "You go run a load of laundry, and it comes out brown. You can't even bathe your kid," a resident told the *Journal-Constitution*, which was flooded with similar stories about problems from neighborhoods across the city.[30]

Where were the maintenance workers? Many had been laid off; others retired and were not replaced. All told, United Water cut staff from 479 to about 300. It also reclassified some employees to count them as supervisors or managers; this change allowed the company to avoid paying them overtime and excluded them from protections under the union contract.[31]

Meanwhile, in August 1999, Suez completed its acquisition of United Water, making the U.S. company a wholly owned subsidiary of the Paris-based multinational. If the local press had assigned its reporters to investigate the story, they might have raised serious questions about the French company's record and methods of doing business. Construction of the Suez Canal in the nineteenth century was part of the company's early history, but by the turn of the twenty-first century, Suez had become a global player in energy markets and one of the world's two largest private water companies. It had contracts in 130 countries, 115 million customers, and revenues well over $40 billion.[32]

On its home turf in France, Suez had a reputation for arrogance, backroom deals, and close financial ties to leading government figures and political parties. Its most infamous deal might have been an object lesson for Atlanta. In 1994, the former mayor of Grenoble in southeast France was sentenced to four years in prison for accepting $3 million in bribes in return for privatizing the city's public water system while in office. Three officials of the local Suez subsidiary were also convicted. The International Consortium of Investigative Journalists reported that the deal and subsequent convictions "revealed how the privatization of water offered the perfect opportunity for personal gain and corporate graft."[33]

The scandal reached into Suez executive suites and the top levels of the French government. The Suez CEO at the time, Jérôme Monod, met with Grenoble's mayor to finalize the deal. Monod was also a close adviser to Jacques Chirac, then mayor of Paris, later elected president of France. Although Monod was accused during the Grenoble trial of having instigated the corruption, he was never charged. Monod left Suez in 2000 to become Chirac's senior adviser at the Presidential Palace.

Grenoble ratepayers were soaked in the deal. A second court action ruled that the city's Suez subsidiary had overcharged customers by using fraudulent accounting. The contract had even permitted the company to raise rates to compensate for revenues lost when consumers conserved water.

As a result of the scandal and protests by citizens' groups and unions, Grenoble's water was eventually returned to public control. Water rates, which had skyrocketed, were slashed, and now Grenoble's water rates are among the lowest in all of France. These events were well documented by the time privatization was put on the agenda in Atlanta, but no one was looking.

Problems Pile Up

Suez corporate culture was soon adopted in Atlanta, where its United Water subsidiary quickly began playing politics. It donated $10,900 to Ralph Campbell, Mayor Campbell's brother, who was running for state auditor in North Carolina, a state in which United Water had no operations. The company also made contributions to Campbell's campaign organization, even though Campbell—now in his second term—could not run for reelection and wasn't a candidate for any other office. Although these contributions were not illegal, they reeked of impropriety and financial payoffs.[34]

Meanwhile, United Water had a series of explanations for the growing cacophony of consumer complaints. Amazingly, the company said that it didn't know about existing conditions when it signed the contract. Executives explained that they could inspect water-treatment plants and other aboveground facilities, but they claimed to have been unable to ascertain the condition of underground pipes. In its eagerness to win the contract, United Water had failed to investigate thoroughly what many Atlantans commonly referred to as the "third-world" conditions of the city's water system. Instead of the twelve hundred water-meter repairs the company expected to do each year, it needed to do more than eleven thousand. Water-main breaks occurred at triple the expected rate. The company's "underground-mystery" excuse did not explain why it failed to ascertain the condition and number of fire hydrants, hardly an underground asset. A top United Water official explained that anyone could have made these mistakes.[35]

What the head of Suez had once called the company's "showcase" had turned into a bottomless pit. Its excuses inspired disbelief. After all, water was the company's business, and Atlanta's problems were not a secret. Every other city in the country considering privatization was now looking at Atlanta and scoffing at United Water's excuses. "This will haunt United Water," said Stockton, California, mayor Gary Podesto as he evaluated privatization proposals in his own city. "Any of these companies are only as good as their last project."[36]

United Water was being inundated by complaints about pools of water on the street during a drought, erratic customer service, and "boil-water" advisories to residents in upscale and working-class areas. By the summer of 2000, *Journal-Constitution* metro columnist Colin Campbell called the water system "out of control."[37] A year later, the same columnist took a walk around the Wildwood neighborhood, a quiet middle-class enclave consisting primarily of ranch houses occupied by increasingly disgruntled residents. "City services have never been great," a resident told the reporter. "But it seems in the last three years there's been a definite decline, and in the last year we've been going to hell in a hand basket."[38] That was not exactly the kind of testimonial United Water was looking to emblazon on a brochure, especially one going to a mayor of another town considering privatization.

There were also hints that the city was not going to realize all the savings promised in the run-up to privatization. The city had hoped that it would take in more revenue as United Water installed meters and improved the collection of unpaid bills. In fact, the company was less than efficient in both areas.

When even the city's business establishment became affected and upset, the tide began to change. "It's my personal opinion," said Osborne of the West Atlanta Watershed Alliance, "that until you get the white business interests and the really affluent people involved, then the wheels don't turn in Atlanta city government because that's who runs the government."[39]

However, United Water had an ace in the hole to compensate for its excessively low bid and ongoing problems. Although privatization deals are usually sold to the public as ironclad contracts, almost any contract can be litigated or changed through negotiations, lobbying, or well-placed campaign contributions. Often, the terms of a contract are altered—sometimes justifiably—through "change orders" negotiated with cities long after the ink is dry on the original deal. Such change orders are a normal part of doing business, and corporate attorneys tend to be much more skilled at such negotiations than overworked city attorneys or water-department employees.

At the end of 2001, in the waning days of Campbell's eight years as mayor, the company suddenly asked for more money—a lot more money—to do its job. It filed a change order with the city seeking to increase its yearly contract fee by $4 million; the amount was backdated to the beginning of the contract and extended over its life. That adjustment alone would have added up to $80 million over twenty years.

United Water claimed that the city, rather than the company, should be responsible for the excess cost of hydrant and line repairs over what had been anticipated in the contract. The company also blamed the city for costly delays in capital projects. City Water Commissioner Remedios del Rosario refused to sign off on the change order. "I don't put my name on documents that are not ethical or legal," she said.[40] At the time, it seemed that the proposed change orders were dead on arrival, but months later United Water sent the city the same change-order documents, which reputedly had been signed by Mayor Campbell just days before he left office.

A Changing of the Guard

The public and the incoming administration of the newly elected mayor, Shirley Franklin, knew nothing about those documents when she took office in January 2002. Franklin herself was not an ideological enemy of privatization. A savvy, well-connected politico who had worked for previous mayors Maynard Jackson and Andrew Young, she had even participated in the 1998 bidding for the contract on behalf of another private water firm, U.S. Filter.[41]

Nevertheless, Franklin quickly made it clear that she wasn't pleased with United Water's performance. By this time, neither was the *Journal-Constitution*. "It was a bad idea to give United Water a 20-year contract in the first place," the paper declared, reversing its earlier editorial positions in support of privatization. The editorial went on to berate Campbell for hastily pursuing a privatization deal in order to help his reelection campaign—and, once he won his second term, for failing to oversee United Water's performance.[42]

That summer a drought forced Atlantans to follow strict water rationing. But when a broken fire hydrant began to gush, it took United Water ten days to fix it despite innumerable calls, and, by then, the pavement was washing away. Atlanta residents in several neighborhoods received still more boil-water alerts after water-line breaks threatened contamination of their drinking water.

Mayor Franklin, spurred by the boil-water alerts and continuing problems with the system, ordered a report on whether United Water was in default of the contract. Released in August 2002, the report confirmed the anecdotal complaints in the daily press. In addition to the murky tap water, staff cutbacks, and delayed maintenance, the report blasted United Water for refusing to give the city access to billing and other information on the water system's computers. "The city views such refusal as a blatant attempt by United Water to keep from the city information pertaining to United Water's wholesale failures in these areas." Franklin responded by giving the company ninety days to improve; otherwise it would face contract termination.[43]

Peter Gleick, president of the Pacific Institute for Studies in Development, Environment and Security, interpreted the report as evidence of a lesson learned too late. "The cities, in particular, are left out in the cold to figure out how to design these contracts and how to protect their interests," he told the *Atlanta Business Chronicle*. "I think this is going to slow down privatization, and force a closer second look."[44]

In response to the criticism, United Water replaced its regional president and attempted to improve service, but its efforts were insufficient to convince Mayor Franklin that the company should stay on the job. In January 2003, the city released an audit showing that the company had failed to collect bills totaling $57 million, twice the amount outstanding when United Water took over three-and-a-half years earlier. The audit also confirmed that United Water had not come close to delivering the promised $20 million in annual savings (a reduction from the $30 million tossed out by Mayor Campbell at various times). The amount saved was closer to $10 million a year, and no one thought those savings made up for the incompetent water service. The feeling was summed up by City Council member Howard Shook: "My inner conservative no longer worships at the altar of privatization as I might once have done," he said. "That is for sure."[45]

Atlanta's much-touted experiment with privatization of its drinking-water system ended with a whimper. Franklin announced that she was terminating the contract, but she allowed the company to save a tiny bit of face. On January 24, 2003, Franklin and United Water Chairman and CEO Michael Chesser put out a joint press release announcing the "amicable dissolution" of the contract. "The joint decision to dissolve the relationship," Mayor Franklin said, "reflects the City's and United Water's conviction that the contract does not accommodate the reasonable customer service and business interests of both parties."[46] When a senior United Water executive was later asked whether upper management held its local honchos responsible for the Atlanta fiasco, he laughed derisively, "They're not with the company anymore, are they?"[47]

Campbell Redux

The saga of Atlanta's privatization was far from over. In a curious development, some of the controversial $80 million worth of change orders submitted by United Water had finally surfaced with Campbell's signature. He denied that he had knowingly signed the documents just before his term expired. The *Journal-Constitution* got into the act, asking handwriting experts to authenticate Campbell's signature, which they did with what they considered reasonable certainty.[48] The U.S. Attorney who had been investigating corruption in Campbell's administration since 1999 now wanted to know whether favors, junkets, and campaign contributions from United

Water could be considered bribes to get Campbell to sign the change orders. There was no direct evidence, but the U.S. Attorney's office hoped to establish a pattern of behavior among Campbell's staff to support charging the former mayor himself.

The scandals had already reached deep into Campbell's administration. The men he appointed as chief and deputy chief operating officers, among other officials, were convicted of taking bribes, and it was an open secret around Atlanta that Campbell was the next target. Finally, in August 2004, Campbell was indicted on seven counts of racketeering, tax violations, and taking corrupt payments from various developers, political supporters, and contractors.[49]

One of the charges against the ex-mayor was that he had received "undisclosed benefits" from United Water, which were subsequently revealed to include an all-expense-paid trip in July 1999 to Suez corporate headquarters in Paris with a mistress in tow. Prosecutors released snapshots of Campbell posing at Napoleon's Tomb and the Arc de Triomphe. The $12,900 trip was supposedly to allow Campbell to hold high-level talks with water-company officials, but the two-and-a-half-hour meeting hardly justified the company's treating Campbell to five days of tourism. The implication in the indictment was that Campbell may have repaid these favors by signing the change orders, but Suez denied any quid pro quo. All told, from all sources, not just the water company, the indictment accused Campbell of accepting $160,000 in payoffs and $137,000 in illegal campaign contributions.[50] Campbell steadfastly maintained his innocence on all counts, regularly appearing on a radio talk show with a friendly host to criticize the prosecution as a tool of a white establishment set on vengeance for his independence.

The trial began in February 2006, and it riveted Atlanta's attention. Everyone, it seemed, had an opinion about Campbell's guilt or innocence. After almost two months of testimony by witnesses and arguments, the jury reached a split decision, convicting Campbell on two counts of tax evasion for not reporting $147,000 of outside income earned while he was mayor. Campbell was also found guilty of mail fraud for using funds raised for campaign debts to pay his personal expenses. Several jurors later said that if the prosecution had stated exactly when a city contractor allegedly put $25,000 in the mayor's golf bag, they would have convicted him of bribery as well, but on that count Campbell dodged the bullet.[51] Three months later, at the sentencing hearing, the judge said there was enough evidence of corruption to sentence Campbell to two and a half years in prison. He was ordered to begin serving his sentence in August 2006.[52]

Unfinished Business

Atlanta was in disastrous shape after eight years of Campbell. The reserve fund had been ransacked, and the city faced a massive budget deficit, not the best circumstances in which to take back control of the water system. Mayor Franklin had so much bad news to deliver that she took to wearing a large flower on her dress "to give people a smile to compensate for all the bad news I had to deliver."[53] Atlanta resumed control of its water on April 29, 2003. Mayor Franklin hired additional workers and raised water rates but faced little opposition from the public. After suffering through the United Water period, citizens were willing to pay for the promise of improved water and service. "You get applause if you talk about sewers and water in Atlanta," said Franklin in an interview on C-Span. "I'm the sewer mayor."[54]

In spite of all the hopes that the savings from privatization would pay for the sewers, the city had accomplished little on that front under Campbell and now faced looming deadlines and huge potential fines. After years of debate, Franklin resisted the broad consensus among community groups for separated sewers, and instead she chose to build the underground tunnels to limit sewage overflows into the Chattahoochee River. Debates over how best to rebuild Atlanta's water and sewer systems continue, but AFSCME's Peeples said privatization is not likely to be an option. "It will be a cold day in hell before they try this kind of thing again."[55]

5

The Hundred-Year War

Lexington, Kentucky

Lucy Winchester Breathitt became interested in Lexington water issues in the late 1990s for unequivocally personal reasons: somebody wanted to dig up her family property in neighboring Woodford County and put in a pipe. Actually, the scope of the job was quite a bit more extensive than that: Kentucky American Water was proposing a pipeline running some sixty miles to bring water from the Ohio River to sell in Lexington. Breathitt was one of a number of people whose land would be churned up by backhoes, but three factors set her apart: (1) she had been the social secretary in the Richard Nixon White House; (2) the pipeline route included her ancestral home in the famed Bluegrass Country—a home that was the historic location of the first thoroughbred horse field in the United States; and (3) she was the wife of a former governor, Edward T. "Ned" Breathitt, a powerful Democrat who could still make things happen with a phone call. Ned Breathitt was well known as a courageous leader and a man of character: he was the first southern governor to sign a civil rights act and the first governor in the nation to sign a strip-mine reclamation law. He had a history of doing the right thing. But he wasn't all that interested in water—not at first.

Breathitt was an extraordinarily genial man who, even if he disagreed with you, would still part company as a friend. So Roy

Mundy, the president of Kentucky American Water, felt no hesitation about sounding out the ex-governor about the pipeline over a friendly round of golf. "Just don't make those women from Woodford County mad," Breathitt advised. Perhaps Mundy didn't take Breathitt seriously, or perhaps the construction project was too lucrative to pass up. Either way, Mundy ended up provoking a group of women, including Lucy Breathitt, into starting an organization called Neighbors Opposing Pipeline Extravagance (NOPE).

"They weren't just dedicated and angry," recalled Chetan Talwalkar, a young Indian American who was asked to join NOPE's efforts early on. "They were also very strategic and operated in a coalition-building mode. They didn't assume they were alone and had to fight the corporate giant by themselves. They made common cause with the Sierra Club in the big population center of Fayette County [Lexington] and other counties to be affected by the pipeline."[1]

Talwalkar was unusually well informed and articulate about Kentucky American, and his reputation preceded him to NOPE. Born in India and raised in Lexington since childhood, Talwalkar earned a degree as an electrical engineer but found his real calling in his thirties. He became a grassroots political organizer working for nonprofit groups and making life difficult for Lexington's powers-that-be, including Kentucky American. "I realized the pipeline was a big boondoggle," Talwalkar relates. "The stated purpose was [to have] a backup water supply in case of a severe drought. If you're trying to solve the problem in the optimal, least-cost manner, you study all other alternatives. They didn't do that. It was a straw man; they had already decided to build the pipeline. The rationale was devised later on."

As Kentucky American made additional information available to the state's Public Service Commission, it became clear that the company's goal was to get the existing ratepayers to pay for a huge expansion of its service territory into the farmland surrounding Lexington. The project was a developer's dream but a horse breeder's nightmare. Some of the commissioners, along with the state's attorney general, echoed Talwalkar's suspicions, and the Commission eventually denied a rate increase intended to pay for the pipeline. It was an early victory for the Breathitts and Talwalkar. The pipeline was halted, the Commission began to study whether it was actually needed, and Kentucky American shelved the project, at least for the time being.

Lexington is a mid-sized city of 270,000 and is known primarily as the world's horse capital, the place where Kentucky Derby winners command stud fees of $150,000 for a romantic interlude. The horse industry is valued at $4 billion and provides one hundred thousand jobs, but that amount may not be enough to save large swathes of the region's spectacular bluegrass from suburban development. Local writer Bobbie Ann Mason writes, "Developers are hot to fill the green fields around Lexington with grand illusions of country life—each with its patch of grass and barbecue grill and double garage." But tradition dies hard there, and the horse-breeding establishment, the "equine elite," is close-knit and influential. Its members resist the development onslaught, but these old-line breeders are dying out.[2]

There are and have been other economies here, now often denied or forgotten. The coal mines that destroy the land and pollute the water still demand blood and sweat for electricity, a price most people ignore. And then there's the largely forgotten old economy of Cheapside, the square in Lexington that before the Civil War was Kentucky's largest slave market. Abraham Lincoln was said to have seen African slaves beaten and sold there on visits to his wife's hometown.

Battles for control of Lexington's water go back almost as far. In Lexington, drinking-water services have been privately owned for over a century, and, for almost as long, the city has been exploring various ways of purchasing the water company to bring it under public control. In 1883, after receiving a charter from the state legislature to establish a water operation, Lexington Hydraulic & Manufacturing contracted with the city to build and operate the first waterworks. As early as 1899, the city tried to buy it, only to be beaten out by a group of local businessmen. In 1904, a local newspaper story suggested that the profit motive, rather than public service, was at work: "There are strong and persistent rumors to the effect that one of the main reasons for the purchase of the Lexington water works plant by the Stoll family and other Lexington businessmen was for the purpose of considerably inflating its stock and capitalization and then disposing of it to the city at a greatly increased figure over what they paid for it."[3]

The owners eventually did sell Lexington Water (as it was rechristened along the way) to a Chicago holding company during an era of robber barons, speculators, and vast utility empires that soaked consumers and defied regulation. In 1927 the Chicago holding company peddled the Lexington property to a New York holding company, which, in turn, was taken over by American Water Works & Electric in 1936; that company was then gobbled up in 1947 by Northeast Water, which—no longer being only in the Northeast—eventually adopted the more expansive name of its subsidiary. The city of Lexington considered buying American Water's local subsidiary at various times during this period; in 1937 a ballot measure to do so was presented to—and rejected by—the voters.

By 1959, Lexington's leaders began to float a new plan—to acquire the water company via eminent domain. American Water Works responded swiftly and aggressively, stating in its 1960 annual report, "Because we were convinced that the best interests of the company would not be served by the sale of this subsidiary, and that it would not benefit the public served, we advised the City that we would be unwilling sellers, and we were prepared to conduct a vigorous campaign to gain support of Lexington citizens in opposition to the acquisition." That has been policy ever since, and top company officials came to be judged by the eminent-domain efforts they won or lost.[4]

In September 2001, just days after the attacks on the World Trade Center and Pentagon, American Water's chair, Marilyn Ware, announced the sale not of a local subsidiary but of the whole company, lock, stock, and barrel, for $7.6 billion to German conglomerate RWE, at the time the world's fifty-third largest corporation. The price was far higher than any previous valuation of the company's worth, but those were heady times in the water business, with exuberant predictions that water would be the oil of the twenty-first century, that wars would be fought over a dwindling resource, and that water was a hot speculative "buy." As with the go-go Internet boom of the late 1990s, the water hype was often believed most earnestly by its own practitioners. RWE's leaders thought that it made perfect sense to own both energy and water utilities, and they were willing to pay almost any price to realize these "synergies" and fulfill their company's destiny.

And pay they did. The high price for American Water Works forced RWE to assume $3 billion in debt in order to close the deal. It was a price that would come back to haunt not just RWE but American Water and the people served by its subsidiaries. Highly leveraged takeovers follow a consistent pattern: the new owner must quickly slash costs and raise prices to maximize cash flow and pay down the debt.

Ned Breathitt was well aware of the consequences of RWE's bottom-line strategy. In an op-ed piece in the *Lexington Herald-Leader* in February 2002, he cited the example of a municipal power company elsewhere that had slashed staff and transferred its administrative personnel out of state after it was acquired by a foreign company. He asked why Lexington and Kentucky should become "colonies of companies out of state, and even out of the country." Breathitt's conclusion was dramatic and attention grabbing: he called for the city to buy Kentucky American.[5]

Bluegrass FLOW and the
Case Against Kentucky American

To that end, the Breathitts joined other prominent citizens in founding Bluegrass FLOW (For Local Ownership of Water) in the spring of 2002. The core group included attorney Foster Pettit, who had been mayor of Lexington in the mid-1970s, and Talwalkar, who had helped expose and defeat Kentucky American's pipeline proposal several years earlier.

From the beginning, FLOW cast a wide net. "Lucy is the die-hard Republican, Ned is the die-hard Democrat, so they didn't always see eye to eye politically," recalled Talwalkar, who became FLOW's coordinator. "But this was an issue that expands those boundaries. That's held true if you look at who our supporters are. It's old Lexington, it's the progressive crowd, it's the environmental community, it's even some of the die-hard nationalists because we fought the damned Germans in World War II. Rural preservationists, neighborhood activists, parts of the farming community. People of every political stripe." But fundamentally FLOW's leadership consisted of Lexington's elite. "These are the landed gentry," added Talwalkar, "but they had a vested interest in caring about the community."

As coordinator, Talwalkar first turned his attention to researching RWE. "We looked into it," he remembers, "and it was clear they were not the kind of company we wanted in control of our water supply here—from mismanagement of nuclear waste to price-fixing to bid-rigging to buying politicians. RWE's record in Germany provided the spark that got people moving on the issue."

One of those moved was community leader William T. Young Sr., a venerated local businessman, philanthropist, and prominent thoroughbred breeder who sent many of his horses to the equine hall of fame. A peanut butter mogul, Young had made a fortune selling his Big Top brand to Procter & Gamble. He also served on numerous company boards of directors, including the boards of

Royal Crown Cola, Kentucky Fried Chicken, and Kentucky American itself. Young did his own financial analysis of the water company. He concluded that it was a profitable business and that the Lexington city government should indeed take it over. Young's findings shouldn't have surprised anyone. A study had found that Lexington water bills were higher than those in ten other cities in Ohio, Kentucky, and Indiana, and they were more than three times higher than water bills in the publicly-run Toledo system. Clearly, Lexington's citizens were paying a price for having a privately owned water system.[6]

Young identified other economic factors that favored city operation of the water company over acquisition by RWE. "Lexington, free of income tax and with access to low-interest, tax-exempt bonds, and free of several layers of overhead, can recover its costs much more quickly and earn substantially more than RWE over the long term," Young wrote in the *Herald-Leader* in October 2002. "Income remaining after payments on the bonds issued to pay for the utility will be available to help finance local services in amounts growing over time as Lexington grows. When the bonds are paid off, the water company will produce tens of millions of dollars annually for city services." Young concluded with an unequivocal recommendation. "I urge the city to leave no stone unturned in pursuing the purchase of Kentucky American at a fair and affordable price."[7] Coming from a man of his standing, the recommendation forced members of the business community to take the idea seriously, but to no one's surprise RWE and American Water Works declined to sell.

A month after Young's op-ed piece was published, Teresa Isaac was elected mayor of Lexington on a platform that included buying the water company through eminent domain. "It's a smart business decision for the community," she explained. "If you want to control your community's destiny you need to have local control of your most precious resource." Behind that pragmatic reasoning lay a personal history. "I grew up in eastern Kentucky, and I saw what happened with the coal mines. I saw companies come in and suck the life out of those communities and just bleed them dry economically."

Mayor Isaac was no newcomer to rough-and-tumble local politics. Her family had been in real estate development, and she had been a prosecutor in the county attorney's office before serving for nine years on the Urban County Council. A Democrat, she was bipartisan in her choice of role models—the Republican New York City mayor Rudolph Giuliani and Congresswoman Barbara Jordan of Texas, a Democrat. When Isaac ran for mayor, she already knew about the power of Kentucky American in the community, but when she moved into her new quarters in City Hall, she saw the evidence. There in the office the company had its own dedicated direct phone line. One of her first acts was to have it removed.

Isaac was ready for the fight, and the battle was joined. In early 2003, she urged the Urban County Council to begin the lengthy legal process of using the eminent-domain powers of government to condemn and acquire the assets of the water company. In July, the Council voted nine to six to move ahead with the process. Among other steps, the eminent-domain process entailed appraising Kentucky American to determine the fair-market purchase price, a process fraught with risk for both sides. A high appraisal could discourage citizen support for a buy-out and aid the company's campaign to convince people that a buy-out would raise rates and taxes. A low appraisal would mean that RWE would be surrendering one of its major assets for a lot less than the company had paid for it. As a result, the appraisal process would be political from the get-go. American Water would push for the much higher "replacement cost" as the basis for evaluation. The city would push for the much lower "original cost."

Young, Ned Breathitt, and ten other well-off, well-connected allies did more than publicly express their opinions. They put their private money behind their public convictions. Grassroots coalitions opposing privatization almost always struggle to raise funds, but in Lexington high-net-worth power brokers were central to the campaign for local control. These allies took the highly unusual step of proposing to guarantee a $750,000 bank loan to the city to cover expenses for the eminent-domain condemnation. The generous dozen would be obliged to repay the note if a judge blocked the effort to acquire Kentucky American. The legal costs of a buy-out campaign are significant for both sides. By mid-2003, the city had already spent close to $300,000 just in preparing initial appraisals and in legal fees. American Water had expended more than a million.

Although advocates of local control hadn't looked warmly at the New Jersey-based American Water Works over the years, the entrance of RWE generated overt opposition. "What we don't need here is an international corporate giant that siphons profits off our water and invests that money into a new overseas venture instead of our city," Breathitt said.[8]

The case against the foreign company's control of local water was visceral and persuasive, but sometimes it had a xenophobic undercurrent. Some Lexington veterans of World War II took the opportunity to lambaste RWE because it was a German company. Supporters of the company said the campaign for local control was based on jingoism, to which Pettit, the courtly chairman of Bluegrass FLOW, responded, "I don't think people are worried about the Germans as *Germans* owning our water system. It's the fact that they are far away and don't give a damn about us."

If the water business was as lucrative as the local-control folks figured, it stood to reason that RWE and Kentucky American would do anything to hang onto it. In the high-stakes battle for public opinion, Kentucky American argued that the city would have to substantially hike water rates to cover the purchase cost. Its merit and accuracy aside, this argument was neatly double-barreled in a politically conservative city: it evoked the vague but widely held perception that (1) government was exceedingly adept at raising taxes but at nothing else, while (2) corporations and the private sector were inherently more efficient than the public sector. As veteran *Herald-Leader* reporter Andy Mead said, "The thing they've hit on again and again and again is, 'We're a well-run company and there's no reason for the government to take us over.' Antigovernment messages play better in the country these days than they did a decade ago, and they're playing very well in Lexington."

The argument that City Hall was bad for the private sector received a symbolic setback in early 2004, when *Forbes* published its annual rankings of the best cities in the United States for business. Lexington was listed in ninth place. The *Forbes* listing is an arbitrary and dubious measure, but it did provide a rebuttal of sorts to the underlying Kentucky American message that City Hall was an obstacle to Lexington's progress, especially because the city had placed fourteenth on the *Forbes* list a year earlier.

The company was taking a pounding more serious than that given by the *Forbes* article on another front. Way back in 1960, American Water's leaders learned an important lesson from their success in beating back Lexington's takeover attempt that year. "Part of the success of Lexington," said then company president Jack Barr, "has to be assigned to the manager's local position." The company's aptly named corporate history, *A Dynasty of Water*, observes that to avoid being perceived "as a faceless entity, a puppet whose strings are pulled and whose profits are siphoned off by some remote, impersonal corporation," the local company manager must be accepted as "Mr. Water Company, a real human being, a neighbor and a friend."[9] However, a Kentucky American filing for a rate increase revealed that the person now in charge of local company operations wasn't local at all but was based in West Virginia, where he oversaw five states. This revelation was a vindication for Bluegrass FLOW leaders, who had claimed that Kentucky American had been run from afar even before the merger with RWE/Thames.

Kentucky American's supposedly local man in charge, Mundy, tried to counter that perception. He told the *Herald-Leader* that he was still "effectively the head of all aspects of the company" but that his primary focus currently was fighting the takeover, so he had asked the West Virginia executive to step in to help.[10] The statement was not unreasonable given American Water's record of sending in its top executives to take up residence in battleground cities while others in headquarters handled day-to-day responsibilities. However, the damage was done, and less than two months later Mundy walked away from Kentucky American after thirty-one years with the company. His next stop? The post of state vehicle regulation commissioner, courtesy of the Republican governor, Ernie Fletcher.

About the same time, in mid-2004, another revelation blew the lid again on the company's image as the responsive local water guy. As part of its cost-cutting campaign, RWE centralized its subsidiaries' customer-service call centers. The call center in Lexington was relocated to Alton, Illinois—a move the company didn't announce and clearly hoped to finesse—but customer Bill Varallis's letter to the editor at the *Herald-Leader* brought hoots of derision from company critics:

> Believe me, when I got a water bill in April for $40,768.51, I wanted to talk to someone fast. The water bill for my business usually runs about $53 a month. . . . I started calling the customer service number printed on my bill. . . . It took 45 minutes of continuous dialing before a real person answered. I remember thinking that it was a good thing my water bill wasn't paid by automatic withdrawal. What I really wanted to do that day, however, was to talk to someone in Lexington. I used to be able to do that when the people who ran the water company actually lived here. No can do, said the operator, . . . who I now know was in Alton, Illinois. Ten days after my first call to Alton, someone from the water company showed up to tell me that I didn't have a leak. . . . The good news is that the bill was adjusted. . . . I even received a letter from someone telling me that my meter had been misread. . . . The bad news is that the letter says that if I have any problems, I can call customer service anytime.[11]

The Corporate Campaign

In spite of such largely symbolic setbacks, Kentucky American, and its parent, American Water Works, were prepared to fight back in the public arena using the enormous resources at their command to shape public opinion and public policy. Kentucky American employed four public relations and political-consulting firms to design strategy and implement tactics against the local-control movement.[12]

A stinging editorial commentary in the *Herald-Leader* highlighted one corporate strategy in particular: it accused Kentucky American of creating a fake grassroots coalition to advocate on its behalf. Calling the coalition "Manicured Astroturf," the unsigned editorial concluded, "That's just the kind of civic engagement we've come to expect from Kentucky American and its bought and paid for allies."[13] The best-known ally recruited by Kentucky American was Public Opinion Strategies, one of the largest Republican polling firms in the country, with headquarters in Alexandria, Virginia. Its strategic information gathering has been deployed in the successful Republican campaigns of Governor Jeb Bush of Florida, Senator Saxby Chambliss of Georgia, and Senator John Sununu of New Hampshire, among others.

However, arguably the most important of Kentucky American's hires was a less-well-known firm, the Moriah Group, a Chattanooga company that devised or assisted in devising strategy for a number of besieged American Water properties in California and Illinois. The firm's list of services includes strategic planning, media relations, advertising, and "grassroots and coalition development." Moriah's website declared, "While the community campaigns varied in nature—some ended in successful referendums while some ended or were based on changing the direction of the local governing body—all involved intensely integrated communications strategies," which included working with media outlets hostile to the company's position to get "balanced news coverage." On that front, Moriah clearly had its work cut out for it with the *Herald-Leader,* whose publisher, editorial writers, and caustic political cartoonist were unwaveringly in favor of local control and distrustful of Kentucky American.

The Moriah Group's machinations on behalf of the water company were augmented by yet another company, Tactical Edge, a lobbying, political-campaign, and land-use consulting firm based in Columbus, Ohio. Its success stories include implementing rezoning to support big-box stores, defeating antigrowth initiatives, and other business-friendly campaigns. Its website diplomatically stated, "We also engage our clients in proactive efforts to lay groundwork in communities in an attempt to avoid an adverse environment." Although Tactical Edge lists Kentucky American as a client, its description of its product—"grassroots coalition opposing a government takeover of the local water utility"—suggests that its actual work was connected with the formation of the Coalition Against a Government Takeover in July 2002.

The Coalition was led from its inception by Warren Rogers, the burly, well-spoken president of W. Rogers Company, a Lexington-based municipal-utilities contracting firm founded by his father. Rogers denied receiving any financial benefit from his role and said it was a matter of personal conviction. "I have a deep concern that government will use eminent domain to condemn and take a well-run private water system. American Water has a stellar reputation."

The construction and real estate industries signed on as members of the Coalition early on, a fact that did not surprise the *Herald-Leader*'s Mead. "The interesting thing," he said, "is that when it comes to approving a new subdivision or new development, the question is never, 'Is there enough water? Will it strain our water supply?' But I think the idea is that, put in the hands of the Council, it might someday come down to that. 'No, developer, you can't have this big area rezoned for housing because there's not enough water.' But a private company running the water company, they're not going to say, 'No, we don't want to sell more water.'"

Several labor groups also backed the Coalition, including the Fraternal Order of Police (also a Moriah Group client), Lexington Firefighters Local 526, and Service Employees International Union (SEIU) Local 320, which represented Kentucky American workers. The police and firefighters believed that the money spent by the city to buy Kentucky American would mean that their members would not get raises. The SEIU support was a different matter; it pointed to FLOW's failure to reach out to the company's workers and their union, perhaps a result of FLOW's having been established by members of the city's elite. Union Business Manager Bob Gunter said his members "don't see Lexington as real labor friendly." Lexington city workers do not have union contracts, and the water workers feared losing their contract and benefit package if eminent domain were successful.

Although the Coalition consistently presented itself as a grassroots organization with broad local support, independent of Kentucky American, Rogers was the Coalition's face, voice, and only member who ever seemed to be quoted in the paper. The Coalition was organized as an "unincorporated public issues association," rather than a nonprofit, so it did not have to reveal the sources of its funding, which FLOW suspected came from Kentucky American. The Coalition's veneer of independence was also undermined when it retained Kentucky American's fourth public relations firm, a Lexington outfit by the name of Preston-Osborne, which also claims on its website to have been instrumental in forming and even managing the Coalition. Preston-Osborne's employees sat in on Rogers's interviews, accompanied him to public events, and regularly took the trouble to tape-record and video public meetings on the water issue, even though surveillance work is not listed on its website.

As the Coalition squared off against Bluegrass FLOW in the arena of public opinion, it was hard to discern precisely where the citizenry stood. A University of Kentucky poll in October 2003 had found that Lexingtonians favored FLOW's position when the question was posed as "local control" but opposed it when the issue was posed as "costly condemnation."[14]

Playing Politics

During the election year of 2004 the opponents of local control quietly plotted a strategy that didn't become fully apparent until late in the game. According to Kentucky American's business plan, which hit the press two months before the election, "We need to work harder to get people elected to the Lexington Council who have a pro-free enterprise philosophy." The aim was to change the balance of power on the Urban County Council and reverse the Council vote for eminent domain. The company plan allocated $2.7 million dollars to an outreach and organizing program.[15]

No smoking gun proves that Kentucky American, its public relations firms, and its political consultants coordinated all aspects of their candidates' campaigns, but plenty of dots beg to be connected. Candidates who supported the company seemed to benefit from the expertise of its public relations and polling firms. They adopted a unified campaign theme, "Are we moving in the right direction?", a message which had galvanized conservative votes in other elections. And other signs indicated that the company's consultants were in control. "If you look at many of their mailings," said reporter Mead, "many of them were exactly the same except you switch out the person's photo." Mead concluded that "there was a clear line of communication" between the candidates and the company.

Campaign donations also flowed freely. Although Kentucky American itself could not make contributions, its individual managers and political consultants could and did—generously. Mundy kicked in contributions totaling $3,500 to four candidates. Kentucky American's lobbyist divvied up $2,550 among three candidates. Rogers spread $3,750 among three would-be Council members.[16]

These were unusually large amounts for Lexington campaigns but were still small potatoes compared with Vice Mayor Mike Scanlon's generosity. Although it was unusual for a vice mayor to give money to candidates, the outspoken Kentucky American supporter joined with his wife and one of his business partners and his wife to pour a total of $32,000 into five council races.[17] "My feeling," Mayor

Isaac eventually concluded, "was that money that flowed into those council races was controlled by the water company." It shouldn't have been a surprise. The company clearly felt it was fighting for its life—or at least its future profits—in Lexington.

Jay McChord, who raised $43,100 and eventually outspent his opponent by a margin of two to one, was one of the beneficiaries of the largesse from company supporters. A clean-cut, garrulous man in his mid-thirties, well dressed and articulate, he was typical of the anti-local-control candidates who'd been quietly recruited to run in certain districts. McChord had been a three-year letterman at the University of Kentucky; after graduation, he excelled as a New York Life insurance agent before becoming marketing director of a financial-services company. Now he headed his own motivational-speaking and consulting firm. "I see myself offering Idea Drain-O to unclog the sink of the status quo," he says on his company website. With his salesman's effusiveness and Dudley Do-Right smile, he cut a confident figure during the campaign.[18]

In September, with the campaign in full swing, the charges of "dirty tricks" by Kentucky American hit the press. A candidate who had been defeated in the primary claimed that two water-company officials had offered to run his reelection campaign and guarantee him a win if he would vote to oppose local control of the utility. FLOW also filed a complaint with the state attorney general asking for an investigation of the company's activities. Kentucky American denied the charges, and the complaints were later dismissed for lack of evidence.[19]

Supporters of FLOW, however, were unable to use the dirty-tricks issue in the campaign because of a bizarre incident involving FLOW coordinator Talwalkar. A month before the vote, Talwalkar was arrested for removing some of candidate McChord's yard signs, which he believed were illegally placed on public and corporate property. He had even taken the precaution of phoning the city to get a clarification of the law before he took action, but he was snared by a technicality. It turned out that the property was owned not by a corporation but by a limited-liability company, which did have the right under Kentucky's campaign-finance laws to support a candidate. Talwalkar accepted his error and resigned immediately as Bluegrass FLOW's coordinator, but McChord used the incident to depict the local-control folks as fanatics and hysterics. "I think this is a real good opportunity for the Bluegrass FLOW group to re-examine their campaign and try to move forward based on facts and not emotion," he told the *Herald-Leader*.[20]

The candidates in favor of local control were mostly fresh faces with little political experience, and Pettit later admitted, "We were not proactive enough in seeking the right candidates to run." The inexperience of the local-control candidates was magnified by the sudden, tragic death of Ned Breathitt in late 2003 and the passing of Young in early 2004, losses that deprived the FLOW side of con-siderable political savvy and business acumen.

Even Mayor Isaac didn't help her own cause. She refused to endorse any candidates out of her belief that the executive branch shouldn't in any way manipulate the legislative branch. For her, that would have been a violation of her "take-the-high-road," hands-off philosophy, an attitude that has undone many community-based campaigns that enter the hardball arena of politics, endorsements, and campaign finance.

But voters can be forgiving if they are paying attention, and by all accounts the water battle was the central issue in the campaign. "Every debate we had, and we did about four a week, that question came up," recalls Mayor Isaac. "And it was probably the only ques-tion that came up in every debate."

As election day approached, hopes ran high, as they always do, but in hindsight the results were not a surprise. The Kentucky Amer-ican–backed slate seized four seats, shifting the balance of power on the Council. Mayor Isaac claimed that Vice-Mayor Scanlon had told her he was buying himself a new Urban County Council for his birthday present, according to an article in the *Herald-Leader*. The vice mayor denied Isaac's version and accused her of being a "sore loser."[21] The post-election analysis was straightforward. Not only were the pro-local-control candidates unprepared, but, Talwalkar concluded, "Most of FLOW's resources got directed toward legal fees instead of effective PR and media. This campaign called for more organizing and education."

Although the new Council members had denied that they were one-issue candidates, their first steps after taking their oaths in January 2005 were aimed at stopping the local-control proceedings cold. By a nine-to-six vote, they reversed the previous Council's plan to create a municipal water authority that would own Kentucky American's assets after acquisition. One week later, a majority voted to end the eminent-domain case against Kentucky American. The mayor stood firm, vetoing the Council resolution and temporarily keeping the buy-out plan alive. Among several factors, she cited the $5–6 million that Kentucky American sent to RWE annually, which would remain in Lexington if the city owned the water company.

Taking It to the Voters

Bluegrass FLOW and its allies, well aware of RWE's priorities and the new Council's agenda, met to brainstorm about how to continue the fight for local control. They decided to take the issue directly to the voters with a ballot initiative directing the city to purchase Kentucky American. A new group called Let Us Vote was formed to carry out the campaign, and hundreds of people volunteered to gather the 18,300 signatures needed to put the initiative on the November 2005 ballot.

The national and international movement against water privatization had come a long way since the debacle in Atlanta, and it now had resources to contribute to local campaigns. The Lexington movement took advantage of research provided by organizers from Food & Water Watch as well as volunteer support from the Boston-based Green Corps, a leadership-training group for envi-

ronmental activists. The Green Corps trio of young women organizers generated new energy and brought in student activists from
local campuses. Maude Barlow, chair of the Council of Canadians,
and African water-rights campaigner Rudolf Amenga Etego from
Ghana arrived in Lexington to speak in support of the campaign.

Meanwhile, some of Kentucky American's allies on the Council
began talks with the company aimed at negotiating a face-saving way
for the city to end its bid to take over its water service. The Council group even went so far as to hire a lawyer without bothering to
get the Council's approval. "They began to have meetings which vio-
late our open meetings law," Mayor Isaac said. "And they began to
try to negotiate [with Kentucky American] without any authority,
and of course our law department then had to tell them they had no
authority to do that." That was a small speed bump, however, and in
short order the Council formally gave three of its members the go-
ahead to work out a deal with Kentucky American.

Vice-Mayor Scanlon was exerting pressure behind the scenes
to overturn Isaac's veto, and in April 2005 he finally amassed a
veto-proof majority to do it. At the same meeting, the Council
approved a negotiated settlement with Kentucky American. In
exchange for the city's dropping its eminent-domain case, Kentucky American agreed that in 2011 it would deed the city some
land already used for a public park and golf course. Kentucky
American also threw in $25,000 a year worth of water for public
swimming pools and, as a sop to disgruntled callers, agreed to create a citizens' advisory group dubbed the Customer Service Council, with a local resident named as ombudsman, to take complaints
about the customer-service operation.

Scanlon, Rogers, and their allies declared victory and asserted
that local control was dead once and for all. To the contrary, we've
just moved on to the next phase, said Let Us Vote attorney Foster
Ockerman Jr. In fact, the signature-gathering effort got an instant
boost the day after the Council pulled the plug on eminent domain,
when Kentucky American asked a court to overrule state regulators

and impose a substantial rate increase. "If this is a sign of gratitude from RWE for ending condemnation," said FLOW's Pettit, "I shudder to think how much more corporate monopoly ownership of the water system is going to cost us in the years ahead."

The rate increase request and its timing gave impetus to the signature-gathering campaign. Eight hundred Let Us Vote volunteer signature gatherers collected a remarkable twenty-six thousand signatures in a little over two months. "I've never seen such enthusiasm from volunteers," said Pettit. The Fayette County clerk ultimately validated twenty-three thousand signatures, well beyond the required number, and put a measure to resume takeover proceedings against Kentucky American on the November 2005 ballot. Let Us Vote had done its job, and it was succeeded by yet another new entity, Vote Yes.

But Kentucky American wasn't giving up either; it filed a lawsuit that claimed that the citizens of Lexington had no right to vote in referendums at all and that, even if they did, they didn't have it that November! It was not a legal posture likely to endear the company to the large spectrum of citizens who generally associate voting rights with democracy. But Kentucky American had an answer to head off that critique. In a public relations assault of its own, the overriding theme was that government was not to be trusted. A mass-mailed post card accused the city of irresponsibly squandering taxpayer money to pursue the takeover.

It was a long, wet summer in Lexington as the two sides battled away on legal and political fronts. Hurricane after hurricane battered the South, culminating in the devastation of New Orleans and the Mississippi Gulf Coast and the Bush administration's shamefully negligent response. In late August 2005, a circuit court judge, ruling that the election could proceed, dispensed with Kentucky American's arguments that recent changes in Kentucky law banned voter referendums and that the absence of a regular election in 2005 mandated that the measure be postponed until 2006.

Two weeks later, the Kentucky Court of Appeals upheld the ruling. The water company's next stop: the Kentucky Supreme Court.

While the high court considered the case, Kentucky American was spending hundreds of thousands of dollars to fight the referen-dum if the company lost in court. The wait for the decision was ago-nizing, and the Supreme Court ruling didn't come until three weeks before election day. To the dismay of local-control advocates, the Supreme Court overruled the lower courts, deciding that the refer-endum was not a regular election and, therefore, could not be held in an off year. There would be no vote in November 2005.

The individuals who had worked so hard for local control of the water company were angered but apparently not demoralized by the court ruling. Hundreds of FLOW supporters turned out for a rally downtown on the Election-Day-that-wasn't. They came out not only to support local control of their water but even more to oppose the abrogation of their right to vote on the issue. Janet Tucker, chair of Kentuckians for the Commonwealth, told the crowd, "If we can't vote at the ballot box, at least we can show up today . . . and show that this is not over by any means."[22]

The Bombshell

In early November 2005, RWE dropped a bombshell. It had had enough of water politics and not enough of water profits. It was sell-ing out, looking for companies to buy American Water Works and Thames Water. "The concept of a global water player has not really worked," said RWE CEO Harry Roels. "Scale and synergy effects in the water business are regional, not global."[23]

RWE's decision threatened to spark the dismemberment of American Water, as mayors in several other cities announced they were fed up with having so little control of the fate of such a basic resource. That potential threat forced RWE to announce that it would not sell American Water in pieces. It wanted to find a buyer for the whole company, although it was unclear whether a buyer could be found that would want to take over a series of potential eminent-domain battles as soon as it walked in the door.

RWE may not have bargained for a major battle over the sale of its water properties, but company brass were eager to sell American Water to reduce the enormous debt load. Debt reduction was one objective for RWE; raising its lagging stock price was another. Embattled water subsidiaries like Kentucky American seemed to be a drag on RWE's stock-market performance. The announcement of a potential sale of its English subsidiary, Thames Water, for example, produced a record rise in the RWE share price on the German stock market. Among the companies considering bids for Thames was the U.S.-leveraged buy-out firm Kohlberg, Kravis and Roberts, a company with a long and predatory history of buying companies, slashing costs, laying off employees, and then putting the companies back up for sale. Other bidders included a consortium led by Qatar's state-owned investment fund, the English private equity group Terra Firma, and the ultimate winner of the bidding, a consortium led by Australia's Macquarie Bank. The stability of Thames Water services, management, staffing, and supplies was not likely to be solid for some time to come, and the question for citizens of Lexington was, were they next?

RWE's announcement essentially silenced political opponents of Mayor Isaac's quest for public control of the city's water services. Vice Mayor Scanlon seemed ready to capitulate, agreeing with Isaac's proposal for a committee to investigate buying Kentucky American directly from RWE. Scanlon also decided not to challenge the mayor in the next election or even to run for reelection for the Council.

Then, in May 2006, Kentucky American announced, to everyone's surprise, that it had reversed its position and would no longer try to prevent a city referendum on local control. Kentucky American's new president, Nick Rowe, said in a statement, "The best thing for all of us is to let our customers vote."[24] That announcement set the stage for a major new election battle in the fall when Isaac herself would be on the ballot against an anti-local-control candidate.

However, RWE's decision to sell American Water gave the debate new legs. It not only changed public perceptions in Lexington but also had ripple effects in other cities across the United States. The mayors of Charleston, West Virginia; Urbana, Peoria, and Pekin, Illinois; and even Moriah's hometown of Chattanooga announced that they wanted to take control of their local water systems away from RWE.[25] City governments, consumers, and grassroots organizations all joined the battle against skyrocketing rates, inadequate service, and for-profit ownership. Enough had apparently been enough. American Water was now facing the possibility that its largest subsidiaries would be nipped off one by one. Sensing the threat, RWE opted not to put American Water up for sale to a single buyer but instead to spin it off in an initial public offering of stock. Water company stocks had risen sharply in the United States, and RWE stood to do quite well with an IPO, while leaving the eminent domain battles for others to fight.[26]

In the fall of 2006, Bluegrass FLOW now mobilized once again to end more than a century of private control of water in Lexington, calling on its supporters to go door-to-door and fighting the fatigue that endangers all community groups in long campaigns. For its part, Kentucky American took the battle into every arena with every resource a major corporation can command.

Kentucky American's strategy was to flood the city with TV ads, mailers, and op-eds emphasizing counterintuitively the grassroots, local nature of the corporation. Company president Nick Rowe constantly stated that "supporters of eminent domain talk only about 'local control,' as if 2300 Richmond Road [the multinational's local office] doesn't exist."[27]

The tie-in with the growing national controversy over eminent domain was also a key theme. "Their ads made 'eminent domain' dirty words as if to say 'What next? Your house?'" said *Herald-Leader* reporter Andy Mead.[28] Ballot initiatives against eminent domain were on the ballot in eleven states that November. Some of the initiatives defined whole areas of government action, including environmental regulations, as takings of private property that must be compensated at market prices. If successful, these measures would make community drives for local control of water much more difficult.[29]

Two days before the vote, the *Herald-Leader* ran its final editorial in favor of local control. Titled "A Wealth of Wisdom Behind Voting Yes," it exposed a weakness in the overall campaign. The editorial praised FLOW's well-known founders, Ned Breathitt, W. T. Young, and historian Thomas D. Clark, all of them now dead.[30] Bluegrass FLOW's web page also featured pictures and sound recordings of Breathitt and Clark. It was as if the campaign focus was on the issue's pedigree rather than its potential to excite a new generation of voters to challenge corporate power and globalization.[31]

FLOW was also saddled by its association with Mayor Isaac, whose popularity had sunk after City Council infighting. Kentucky American tarred FLOW as divisive—the same charge leveled by Isaac's opponent against her. The association could hardly be missed by the voters. Even the pro-eminent-domain *Herald-Leader* endorsed Isaac's opponent.[32]

In the end, it wasn't close. FLOW's ballot measure to finally take public control of the city's water future was defeated, 61 to 39 percent.

Kentucky American's patient war of attrition had succeeded; it had stretched FLOW's resources, delayed a resolution of the issue, and exhausted the public. Company leaders were ecstatic.[33] The victory was a clear warning to other communities considering local control efforts.[34]

However, water wars rarely end, and there are new conflicts already on the horizon. Kentucky American has sparked controversy once again over new plans to build a grid of pipelines, the same issue that once raised Lucy and Ned Breathitt's hackles years earlier.[35] Lexington's hundred-year war may be entering its second century.

New England Skirmishes

6

Keeping the Companies at Bay

Lee, Massachusetts

From her apartment overlooking Main Street, Deidre Consolati can see Lee's Memorial Hall, containing the offices of the mayor, city administrator, and police. The old brick building also holds the tiny courtroom where justice was meted out in the late 1960s to eighteen-year-old songwriter Arlo Guthrie, the son of legendary folk singer Woody Guthrie. In the counterculture classic "Alice's Restaurant," Arlo recounted at great length and with considerable bemusement the shaggy-dog story of his arrest on a garbage-dumping charge on Thanksgiving Day.

A five-minute walk takes Deidre to the high school, where her father coached football for forty years. Her mother came to Lee with her family from New York City in 1920 and wrote a colorful and comprehensive history of the charming town a half century later. Deidre, a slim woman with long hair, is a proud resident of the town. "I did go away and discovered this place is no less lovely than any other place," she says. "So why not make my life here?"[1]

Lee is a small, well-kept town of some six thousand people, but it's not a sleepy hamlet. Founded in 1777, it's located in the southern Berkshires near Tanglewood, the summer home of the Boston Symphony, twenty minutes from the New York border and a couple of hours from Boston. The area is known as one of the country's premier cultural centers; its attractions include the famed Massachusetts Museum of Contemporary Art and the Berkshire International

Film Festival. The summer vacationers and the hordes of leaf peepers who arrive in the fall use Main Street as a thoroughfare, and traffic is continuous. Yet Lee is not a middle-class resort but a town whose working-class history still defines personal loyalties and political outlooks.

Lee was one of many towns in the area that thrived on industry in the nineteenth century, drawing water from the Housatonic River and a reservoir on nearby Washington Mountain. The manufacture of papermaking machinery was a successful enterprise in a region of abundant local paper mills. During the Civil War, Lee produced more paper than anyplace else in the country.

The city was also known for the quarried stone it shipped all over the United States. In 1852, a local businessman secured an eleven-year contract to provide white marble for the expansion of the Capitol in Washington, D.C. The quarry's labor force consisted of about a hundred Italian immigrants, who had been stoneworkers in their native land.

Consolati is an activist by nature, and the battle over water in Lee was hardly the first she had taken up. She co-founded the Lee Land Trust to preserve open space in the town. She organized a group called Concerned Citizens of Lee to prevent the expansion of a sixty-two-store outlet mall erected on the edge of town. She also joined the substantial opposition to a proposed 240-unit time-share resort, winning a reduction to 78 units. In every case, Consolati's campaigns were fueled by the urge to preserve the character of her hometown. Like many Lee residents, she felt a sense of ownership.

Christopher Hodgkins, another longtime resident, also felt a sense of ownership. He had worked as a teacher and a policeman after graduating from the University of Massachusetts at Amherst. In 1983, at the age of twenty-five, he was elected to the state legislature from the Lee area on a liberal platform that emphasized the reform of State House rules. Early on, he helped introduce the live telecast of House sessions over the objections of the House leadership.

Energetic, socially liberal, and savvy about the media, Hodgkins seemed destined for political stardom on a wider stage with his campaign slogan "Slightly outrageous. Very effective." But Hodgkins's career hit an unexpected snag in 1996, when he was on the losing side of a House leadership fight. His influence evaporated in the resulting purge, and he was exiled to a tiny office in the State House basement.

Meanwhile, Hodgkins took on outside work, not unusual for low-paid state legislators. He became a consultant to a Massachusetts water-technology company and to the developer of the controversial 240-unit time-share. For perhaps the first time, but not the last, some of his Lee constituents found him to be on the wrong side of an issue.

Veolia Comes to Town

In 2000, the Massachusetts Department of Environmental Protection approved a consent decree requiring Lee to upgrade its wastewater-treatment facility. The city was given four years to comply. Soon after, town representatives voted for special state legislation to allow cities like Lee to pursue private bids for public-works projects and to suspend competitive bidding; this law opened the door to one-bidder contracts.[2]

Petitioning for "special legislation" is not uncommon in Massachusetts, which gives cities and towns broad local control under the "home rule" doctrine. But this particular form of special legislation was used throughout Massachusetts to push through one-bidder water privatization deals.

In Lee, the single bidder turned out to be the North American subsidiary of France's Veolia, the largest private water company in the world, with operations in fifty countries and water-related revenues of over $11 billion a year. Veolia's favored position was a disturbing coincidence for some because Hodgkins had just recently left his legislative post after twenty years to take a job as a vice president of Veolia Water North America. "It stinks to high heaven," said Consolati, who was one of fifty-four residents elected to vote as representatives at town meetings. There were murmurs of discontent, a powerful force in any small town's politics, but the grumbling didn't slow the process toward privatization as various local boards approved negotiating a deal.

Although Hodgkins was no longer a legislator, he continued to serve as Lee's town moderator, a position that allowed him to lead discussions at town meetings and to appoint the town's Finance Committee. He relinquished the chair whenever a vote was taken concerning Veolia, but it was becoming difficult for residents to see Hodgkins as their hometown guy and neighbor when he was also a key player behind a French multinational's bid to take over the water department. Hodgkins understood his complicated role. "It's always nice to dislike the corporate entity you don't know, but it got harder once my face was connected to it."[3]

Private water companies prefer to go after contracts in places where they have politically powerful "champions," like Hodgkins, who can draw on their local reputations and popularity. Hodgkins was not the only one. Massachusetts has an astonishing pattern of revolving doors between local political offices and water-company executive suites. The mayor of Taunton, who signed a contract with Veolia, subsequently went to work at the company. The mayor of Lynn, another contract signer with Veolia, also went to work at the company after leaving office. Critics of the Lee proposal were asking whether these revolving doors didn't represent the true meaning of "public-private partnerships."[4]

This pattern had been well established in France, home to Vivendi Universal, Veolia's parent company, until the water division was spun off in 2002 to help Vivendi avoid bankruptcy. But the spin-off and subsequent name change from Vivendi to Veolia did little to change the corporate culture of influence peddling and speculative excess. In *The Man Who Tried to Buy the World*, the 2003 biography of former Vivendi CEO Jean Marie Messier, journalists Jo Johnson and Martine Orange write that Vivendi and its giant rival Suez had long been key funders of French politicians and par- ties. "Both companies had 'their' mayors and 'their' deputies and made the influencing of local officials their core competence."[5]

Messier himself is an object lesson in the dangers of privatiza- tion. Many global water companies have used their water-division profits to finance other, more speculative investments, but Messier went all out. Bored with low-profile businesses like water and sewage, he bought a movie studio and a music company. He also overpaid significantly to buy the U.S. water company U.S. Filter. In a *New York Magazine* profile, Michael Wolff wrote that Messier "seemed to see himself as some combination of religious figure and maestro—his idea, I suppose of an American mogul. (Not some- thing, of course, you could see yourself as, if what you are is a CEO of a water and sewer company.)"[6]

The pyramid of investments finally collapsed, threatening Enron- style bankruptcy for one of the world's largest corporations. A key solution was the spin-off of the water division, Vivendi Environ- nement. Germany's giant electric utility, RWE, was interested in buy- ing it (RWE later purchased England's Thames Water and U.S. American Water Works instead), but Johnson and Orange write that French politicians adamantly opposed a foreign sale because they "worried about all the secrets buried in its vaults. For decades the [company] had played a role in the funding of political parties: it was imperative that Vivendi Environnement stay in friendly French hands."[7] (The pattern was repeated in 2006 with France's other water giant, Suez, when the government intervened to prevent its sale to an Italian company.) As for Messier, he was sacked in the crash. Given this history, many residents of Lee were not happy with the idea of having their water and wastewater operations in foreign hands, even if the local representative was their own Chris Hodgkins.

The Opposition Grows

The Veolia negotiations involved two projects: (1) building and operating a new sewage plant and (2) taking over management of Lee's five-year-old drinking-water filtration plant. Veolia said it could save Lee $6 million over twenty years. Concerned Citizens of Lee was more than skeptical. For a little town like Lee, the sheer size of the deal was daunting, but, for a giant like Veolia, it was peanuts. Why, some residents asked, was the multinational so interested? Hugh Jackson, a researcher for Public Citizen's Water for All campaign (now an independent organization called Food & Water Watch), wrote that big companies like Veolia started to avoid big-city contracts after the debacle in Atlanta and the costly battles in Stockton. "They seem to have made a conscious effort to go after smaller towns."[8] However, Consolati suggested that more was at stake than just Lee. "Hodgkins thought there would be a domino effect to more than thirty other towns in the county," she said.

Hodgkins was stunned by such distrust of himself and the company. "I think people in Lee were angry that someone with my background and my relationship with the town was leading the charge against them," he acknowledged. Nonetheless, he denied spearheading the negotiations or using personal connections to push the deal through. "I'm going to sell a project based on engineering ability, operational excellence, and cost savings. . . . I never picked up the phone once and said, 'I need you to vote for this because I know you trust me.'"[9]

With Hodgkins taking a back seat in public and recusing himself from votes on the issue in town meetings, it fell to other Veolia officials to counter the growing unrest. "Look, I understand the immense fiscal pressures a community is under," Veolia project vice president Richard Johnson told the local paper, the *Berkshire Eagle*. "So if you can do anything at all to shift a part of that responsibility to a private company, and let them deal with infrastructure issues and regulatory issues, you do it."[10]

For opponents of the Veolia deal, the political challenge of defeating it seemed enormous. In meeting after meeting through the spring and summer of 2004, Consolati and other citizens demanded additional time to review the proposed contract. They suspected that Veolia figured the task of analyzing a several-hundred-page contract would swamp the town's minuscule staff of one lawyer and one financial manager. And if it came to a fight, Veolia's legal and financial resources would easily overwhelm Lee's meager resources.

Some Lee residents felt they needed to do the due diligence themselves. Part of their research took them to other towns in Massachusetts that had struck deals with Veolia and other private water companies. The reviews were mixed, with some declaring satisfaction and others reporting the experience as a harsh lesson learned, especially when it came to layoffs, which were often carried out in spite of promises made before a takeover.

One of the worst cases was in Lynn, where Veolia started with forty-nine employees at the sewage plant and was soon down to thirty-four. After a state investigator called the deal "a disaster" that had cost the city millions, the City Council finally threw the company out. A participant in the Lynn fiasco warned his Lee counterparts, "All communication should be in writing," and, he added, "you need a full-time chief administrator to review the contract on a daily basis, a town employee stationed at the plants. If you don't do this you are looking for problems. The fox will be in charge of the chicken coop."[11]

Monitoring is an issue that many communities fail to consider adequately when they bring in a private water company. Aside from the pros and cons of privatization itself, close city supervision of a contract requires time, money, and manpower, costs that cities often overlook in their analysis and decision making.

Monitoring for contract compliance was one thing. Monitoring for criminality was another. News reached Lee that Rockland, Massachusetts, had terminated its contract after the company's regional manager and the local sewer superintendent were indicted on charges of embezzling over $300,000 from the sewer department. In addition, an audit suggested that the original bidding process had been rigged.[12]

With such information in hand, the Concerned Citizens of Lee saw the Veolia proposal as a dangerous corporate takeover. The group's members hit the streets, talking one-on-one to fellow citizens and explaining what the city would be giving up by signing the contract. The pros and cons were debated in letters to the *Eagle*, with opponents far outnumbering supporters.

But divisions ran deep. "I hate the word *privatization*," Selectman Frank Consolati, Deidre's cousin, declared. "We're merely hiring a manager. They are running it for us for a fee. If anything goes wrong, it's on their dime. The same people were going to manage the place. What was the difference?"[13]

"The same people" referred to the seven Department of Public Works (DPW) employees whose jobs Veolia guaranteed for the twenty-year life of the contract. The corporation also asserted that it would not transfer workers out of town and argued that it would improve on the worker's current contract. "We recognized the union," said Hodgkins. "We gave them better benefits."

But the DPW employees weren't convinced. "They were supposed to make all the pay and benefits apples to apples," explained longtime worker and Teamsters union steward Paul Porrini. "It wasn't even close. They'd fly in guys from [Veolia's U.S. corporate headquarters in] Texas and say, 'Listen, we're going to change your retirement to a 401K blah blah.' But they'd never put in the money that you were going to lose from your retirement by moving it to a 401K. That sunk the deal for them."[14]

Employee opposition to the deal tapped into Lee's pride in its working-class traditions. "I'd say this town is a mill town," said Porrini. "It's practically all blue-collar people, and they can see when somebody is trying to pull the wool over their eyes." Even though only seven jobs were at stake, in a small town like Lee it seemed that everybody was related to or had gone to school with one of the seven or knew someone who had. "The workers that I knew so long were going to be screwed," Deidre Consolati declared. "You can't sue a multinational and expect to get results if a worker has a grievance." Consolati drew inspiration from the DPW crew's steadfast opposition to the company's pay and benefits offer. "They were under enormous pressure," she confides, "and none of them would sign on the dotted line."

Her cousin, Selectman Consolati, had a different take. "The employees did not believe in the state laws of Massachusetts—if they became employees of a private contractor, they could not be harmed in any way."[15] If Porrini didn't put stock in Massachusetts laws, it's because his gut warned him not to trust the private contractor. He told the Veolia reps, "You guys come in the wrong way. You come in the back door. You wine and dine all the politicians, you try to go the political route instead of working with the workers who, if you can sell it to them, you've basically got it sold."

Hodgkins was in a bind. A liberal with an excellent pro-union voting record in the state legislature, he was saddled with allies in the company who were a lot less sensitive to labor issues than he was. "Our human relations [HR] folks did an abysmal job," he said. At a meeting between Veolia and employees, the head of the union threatened a strike if Veolia took over. As Hodgkins remembers it, the head of Veolia's HR department countered by threatening a lockout. Hodgkins stopped the meeting at that point because the hardball language had alienated the workers. "The HR guy was a moron," he said. But the damage was done.

The Showdown

The workers and the Concerned Citizens were joined at meetings, events, and protests by other activist groups such as the Quakers, Berkshire Greens, Shays 2 (also known as the Western Massachusetts Committee on Corporations and Democracy), and Boston-based Massachusetts Global Action, which was developing a statewide campaign addressing water-privatization issues, corporate globalization, and democracy. The Lee case was also gaining attention nationwide through the advocacy of groups like Public Citizen and the Alliance for Democracy, which provided important solidarity and informational support.

However, the core resistance to Veolia was local. A couple with a house on Main Street put up signs on their roof and front lawn that read "Do Not Privatize Water" and "Thirsty Not Hungry." Volunteers passed out handmade door hangers emblazoned with the message "Water is not for sale." Consolati organized informational screenings of the film *Thirst* in Memorial Hall. To raise money for an ad in the paper, she passed the hat—a cowboy hat in homage to the "Cowboy Up" slogan adopted by the underdog Boston Red Sox on their way to their first World Series title in eighty-six years. Folk singer Tom Neilson came to town and caused a stir with a song he wrote about the battle of Lee in which he rhymed Veolia with "pay-oh-lee-a."[16]

In the dog days of August 2004, the city and Veolia arrived at a contract agreement that surpassed a thousand pages. Incredibly, only a week was allotted for the town representatives to study the massive document before they were supposed to vote on it. But town officials quickly agreed to expand that window when they were confronted by an angry group of residents at a meeting in which Consolati warned them not to "trade dollars for democracy."[17]

With the contract language finalized, the opposition campaign swung into high gear. The second *Thirst* screening at the high school was jammed. Hodgkins was there and told the crowd the contract was a good deal for the town, but the momentum of the opposition seemed to be growing. Citizens perused the contract and discovered that Veolia would be allowed to take almost all the profits from sewage trucked in from other towns for processing at the plant. They also thought Veolia's proposed plant was too small for future needs, and they objected to terms of the deal that limited the public's access to information about system operations.

The *Eagle's* letters' page teemed with arguments against the contract. Letter writer David Norton attacked one of Veolia's main arguments, writing "while the town of Lee would set the water rates, not Veolia, I do believe the town of Lee will use Veolia's operating costs as a major factor in setting the water rates. Thus, Veolia has a large say in the matter since it is a large corporation which operates for its own profit, not for Lee and its best interests."[18]

Veolia was hardly silent, sending out flyers and taking out newspaper ads showing two boys under the headline "We love that our Dad works for Veolia Water." The ad copy was just as cloying. "Our Dad works for Veolia Water, the company that would like to partner with the Town of Lee for water and wastewater services. He says that his company will bring savings and high-quality water services to you in Lee, and you stay in complete control of your water. He also tells us that working for Veolia Water is great. So does that mean we get a raise in our allowance?"[19]

Consolati was not the only one who found the Veolia campaign condescending and arrogant. "Little by little," she said, "we felt that there were more town representatives coming on board." She spent many hours studying the contract and devising ways for the city to keep control of the utility.

The vote on privatization by Lee's fifty-four representatives was scheduled for a town meeting on September 23, 2004, and Main Street was abuzz as the evening showdown approached. Consolati was predicting a slim victory, but it was far from guaranteed. The pressure was intense. "Who knew how many representatives might cave," she fretted.

A large crowd turned out for the meeting that night.[20] Opponents of privatization handed out big price tags that said "Lee can do it," to which people responded, "Yes we can!" The Concerned Citizens also handed out small flags of red cloth, which opponents waved when Veolia or its allies made optimistic assertions about projected cost savings or the employee wage and benefits plan.

"Veolia went through their spiel for the twentieth time," said Consolati. "The number of consultants, people with cell phones and black suits and briefcases, at that meeting! They were like crows ready to pick us apart." Discussion was heated. Hodgkins was also at the meeting, but in keeping with his promise not to intervene he did not speak.

The Board of Selectmen and the Finance Committee both recommended that the fifty-four town representatives approve the private contract. Then came the moment that Consolati had been waiting for with trepidation. She took the floor and asked for permission to present an alternative proposal. The representatives voted to allow her time to make a presentation. "This was the biggest moment of my life," she confided, recalling the culmination of this four-year battle. "I've given birth to two children, but let me tell you, this was a moment!" She had done her homework. Point by point, Consolati argued that Lee could successfully build and operate the plant for little additional cost over Veolia's proposal, and the plant's revenues would remain in Lee rather than being siphoned off to an overseas corporate headquarters.

For another hour, town representatives debated the cost issues, many of them expressing dismay about feeling railroaded. This time, almost all the speakers seemed to be against the contract.

It was finally time to vote, which was taken in New England town-meeting style—not by raising hands but by standing up. Pandemonium broke out as the town representatives surged to their feet to defeat the contract. Veolia and its supporters were in shock. Standing—literally—against privatization were forty-one town representatives; only ten representatives supported Veolia. It was a landslide, and the room filled with cheers. "It was one of the happiest days of my life," Porrini says. "It was like we all hit the lottery. It was democracy at work. People were clapping. It was quite a thing to see that, to see a bunch of regular people defeat a mammoth giant like Veolia."[21] Afterward, Consolati wrote in the *Berkshire Eagle*, "The landmark vote has spawned a movement to run alternative candidates to challenge pro-privatization incumbents. Democracy, in this moment, is at its best in Lee."[22]

Both sides acknowledged the incredibly strong emotions that surfaced during the summer and that all but boiled over during that final town meeting. The Concerned Citizens were convinced that they won on the merits of their arguments; the pro-Veolia proponents viewed the vote as a triumph of emotion over reason and, in particular, as a sign of anger at Hodgkins. Richard Johnson, the project vice president for Veolia, told the *Eagle*, "You're asking me if I've ever seen an issue get this personal in a town. No way."[23] Frank Consolati agreed, although he said he couldn't fathom the source of the animosity toward Hodgkins. "I have not a clue, but you could feel the hatred in that room for that man," he said.[24]

Deirdre Consolati was unforgiving. "Somewhere between being the idealistic, naïve state representative he was 20 years ago, and being a spokesman for corporate America, Chris Hodgkins took a right-hand turn," she said. "I have often pondered this, but I think many citizens' perceptions of him changed over the past few years."[25] Hodgkins denies that he was the flashpoint. "I think the opposition was led at the time with misrepresentations." He predicts the ratepayers will be paying a lot more now that the town is going to do the work.

In the days following the vote, dozens of people came up to Consolati and said, "Thank you for saving our town." She also received thanks from residents in many other nearby towns who had feared a domino effect if Veolia won. She admits that the water war in Lee "changed my life. Fighting this opened my eyes to see what corporate battles really are." Within weeks of the vote, Lee became a model of decisive citizen action for the local-control movement nationwide.

Hodgkins still lives in Lee and continues to consult for the private sector. "I believe in everything 'public-private partnership' stands for, and that's what I'm doing," he said. He threw his hat in the ring in a race for state senator on a liberal agenda that included abortion rights and support for gay marriage; he declared, "I was a tireless advocate for consumer rights, for the elderly, for our communities and for the environment."[26] In a sense, Hodgkins, with all his contradictions, embodies the New Democratic politician of the Clinton era—progressive on social issues, but supporting the corporate agenda of privatizing public resources and services.

Veolia may have been dismayed by the results of the water war in Lee, but the company still had plenty of other potential partners. At the U.S. Conference of Mayors annual meeting, Veolia representatives invited mayors to tape a promotional videoclip giving their response to the question "How have public-private partnerships and public-private initiatives improved services and the quality of life in your city?"[27]

7

Cooking the Numbers

Holyoke, Massachusetts

Holyoke lies in the Pioneer Valley of western Massachusetts on a hillside sloping down to the Connecticut River, a lovely hour's drive east of Lee. It lays claim to being the first planned industrial city in the United States. In the 1800s, pulp and paper mills lined the river, and corporate leaders built a pleasure park on a nearby mountaintop. But after more than a century and a quarter the old brick mills slouch at the riverside, perhaps waiting for yuppies, art spaces, and condo conversion—upscale dreams that probably aren't in Holyoke's future. For despite its bucolic setting, this is a depressed, working-class city—part of the Northeast's Rust Belt.

Unemployment is well above the national average, and Holyoke consistently ranks as one of the poorest cities in Massachusetts, with 26 percent of residents living below the poverty line. From a 1920s peak of sixty thousand, the population has gradually shrunk to thirty-nine thousand today. Most of the buildings are made of dark brick—charming on a sunny summer's day but gloomy in winter. Few people can be seen on the streets after dark, and the first question a visitor is asked at a gas station is, "Do you need to know how to get out of town?"

The city has been overshadowed for years by bustling Springfield, just to the south, but that city is also beset with problems and teeters on the edge of bankruptcy. The region's cultural and intellectual center lies twelve miles up I-91 from Holyoke in Northampton, the home of Smith College and a bastion of upscale shops and ethnic restaurants. Tourists on their way to the Berkshires tend to bypass Holyoke, notwithstanding the Volleyball Hall of Fame commemorating the sport's origins here as well as its heroes. Indeed, the scarcity of interesting restaurants and nightlife in Holyoke causes residents regularly to drive to Springfield or Northampton to dine out.

On the bright side, Holyoke is more affordable than its neighbors. Since the mid-1990s, the reasonably priced housing and entry-level jobs in nearby paper-products factories and at the sprawling Holyoke Mall have attracted a substantial number of Latino families, most of them Puerto Rican. They now constitute 40 per cent of the town's population. Holyoke is the only city in Massachusetts that recognizes Three Kings, the popular Latino holiday, but despite some acceptance and accommodation, tension exists between the old-line Irish Holyokers and the relative newcomers.

Thirty-six-year-old Mark Lubold is an easygoing, fourth-generation Holyoker—his two young sons are the fifth generation—and he has an unshakable affinity for his hometown. Residents describe the Lubold family as Holyoke's Kennedys. Lubold is a hands-on guy who enjoys disassembling and cleaning machines and putting them back together, and after high school he went to machine school before getting his bachelor's degree in mechanical engineering. More than thirty years ago, his father started a business making packaging machines for companies such as candy makers Russell Stover and Hershey Canada. General Machine is still a family operation: Lubold's two brothers are the machinists, and he runs the company. In preparation for the job, he went back to graduate school and got his MBA.

His ability to analyze a business proposal and his passionate loyalty to his hometown are among the qualities that Lubold brought to Holyoke's City Council. First elected for a two-year term in 1999, he was reelected twice—the last time without a challenger. Although sociable and talkative, he is not drawn to the spotlight and somewhat unwillingly found himself the leader of the opposition to a wastewater privatization proposal put forward by the mayor. All Lubold did was read the contract and ask some questions, like any good businessperson. When he didn't get any answers, he grew increasingly skeptical.

Questions Emerge

The story begins when the Environmental Protection Agency (EPA) ordered Holyoke, which had had a public water system since 1871, to stop polluting the Connecticut River. EPA enforcement of the Clean Water Act has often been the trigger for municipal government soul-searching about privatization, and the EPA itself has recommended that cities "consider the use of public-private partnerships that utilize private sector resources to finance wastewater treatment needs."[1] To comply with EPA regulations, cities like Holyoke have had to decide how to increase spending on their water and sewage systems. That moment of vulnerability has been an entry point for private water companies that promise to meet EPA requirements cheaper and faster than the cities can by themselves.

In Holyoke, the EPA wanted to know how the city planned to reduce the sewage overflows that were endangering local drinking-water supplies, recreational fishing, and swimming in the river. It's a common problem in more than seven hundred cities around the country, including Atlanta, Chicago, Milwaukee, New York, and Seattle. The problem is caused by a fairly predictable meteorological phenomenon: rain. Rather than have separate sewers for rainwater and sewage, many towns and cities combine the two streams in one set of sewer pipes. That's a fine system until a heavy downpour sends massive amounts of rainwater mixed with sewage through those pipes into the local sewage-treatment plant. The overwhelmed plant can't handle the flow and dumps the noxious mixture into the nearest river, lake, or ocean; the technical term is Combined Sewer Overflow (CSO). In Holyoke's case, the dumping site is the Connecticut River. In Atlanta, it's the Chattahoochee;

in Milwaukee, Lake Michigan; in San Francisco, the Pacific Ocean. Fixing the problem is expensive; it requires building holding tunnels to retain the rainwater and sewage until the mixture can be treated or installing a separate set of pipes for sewage only.[2]

Faced with the high cost, Holyoke city officials delayed making a decision for years, but in mid-2003 Mayor Michael Sullivan finally asked the City Council for authority to deal with the problem. "The EPA is getting antsy," said Sullivan, who was elected mayor in 1999 after ten years on the Council. "At the end of the day, all I'm looking for is the simplest, most economic, most efficient way to abate the risk."[3] A husky Irish-American, Sullivan flashes a dimpled smile as if to ask "How am I doing?" without really expecting an answer. The former owner of Nick O'Neil's, a popular tavern in town, he puts people at ease and seems happy to engage in lengthy one-on-one conversations about city issues. But Sullivan can also be impatient and stubborn, with an edge that local activist Jeremy Smith called his "darker side." "He's totally willing to engage in a discussion," said Smith, "but it seemed like there was no other way to think about an issue than the way he thought about it."[4]

Sullivan told the City Council he wanted to get multiple bids for the sewer project not only from the city's own Department of Public Works but also from private companies, which claimed to be able to do the work for 30 percent less than the city could. The Council approved the mayor's plan to spend more than a million dollars to hire consultants to come up with options for later Council review. At least that's what Lubold and some of his fellow Council representatives thought they had approved, but from that point on the stories told by each side diverge dramatically.

"About a year went by," recalls Lubold, "and they came in front of the City Council to present what I thought were going to be options. As it turned out, it was just one option, and it was the privatization option. And then it turned out there was only one bid, and if you believed the consultant's numbers, it was a very small savings."[5] In June 2004, the sole bidder was Aquarion Water Services, the largest private water utility in New England and a subsidiary of the Kelda Group, a multinational water company based in Great Britain.[6] Aquarion's bid didn't bear out earlier optimism about savings. It now seemed that contracting out was going to cost the city just 5 percent less than doing the work itself under continued public control. But the Board of Public Works, under the mayor's control, failed or refused to come forward with a proposal of its own.

With millions of dollars at stake, Lubold's colleague on the City Council, Elaine Pluta, was beginning to get suspicious too. She believed the city was perfectly capable of running the system and making the needed improvements. "It's the one department in the city that's in the black, that makes money every year," she said. "Why are we giving that away?"[7]

In spite of Sullivan's claim that he had no stake in privatization unless it saved money for city ratepayers, it was now dawning on the entire Council that the mayor was ideologically in favor of such deals. "It seems, looking back over the evidence," said Lubold, "that it was on the fast track from the beginning to privatize."

The City Council had been caught flat-footed, but the mayor's commitment to privatization should not have come as a surprise. As far back as 2000, the Holyoke Taxpayers' Association had praised Sullivan for advocating "some form of privatization" of the sewer system. In 2003, Sullivan testified before Congress, praising "public-private partnerships" on behalf of the Urban Water Council, the industry-financed task force of the U.S. Conference of Mayors. Mayors who attend task-force meetings are surrounded by water-company brass and regaled with stories of private sector efficiency.[8]

The Urban Water Council isn't the only group with a less than altruistic interest in privatization. Major consulting firms that advise cities on such deals make money only because cities are making such deals. Nevertheless, Sullivan told the *Springfield Republican* newspaper, "We had independent experts. These are people of great integrity and they're all out there staking their professional reputations on this."[9]

For Lubold, "the numbers just didn't seem to add up. I felt, after interviewing other communities, like Lynn, that [the consultants] underestimated the true cost of privatization and overestimated the future costs of the city going forward to make [privatization] look attractive." Several years earlier, Lynn, Massachusetts, had signed a one-bidder contract with Veolia based on consultants' statements that the deal would save Lynn millions. The state inspector general ultimately concluded that Lynn "paid more than $3 million to privatization consultants to assist with these procurements; unfortunately, this expensive investment in expertise has not protected the ratepayers from a bad deal." Lynn eventually threw out the contractor, US Filter.[10] Mayor Sullivan had brought in some of these same consultants, including one who described himself as "the quarterback of privatization in Massachusetts."[11]

In spite of the Council's reservations, Sullivan said the city had avoided Lynn's mistakes, and he wanted to move forward with the Aquarion contract without further delay. It would not be the first time he defied the Council and public opinion to get his way. When the Council voted against the reappointment of the city solicitor, Sullivan ignored the vote and gave her repeated "acting" appointments. When a majority of citizens voted to support the idea of a police commission, he ignored them, sparking an editorial in the local bilingual newspaper, El Dialogo, which condemned the administration's "greed" and "false statements."[12]

Of all these conflicts, perhaps most galling to Sullivan's critics on the Council was how he outmaneuvered them early on about water privatization. Back in 2002, a year before the Council had approved funds to study water-system improvements, the city solicitor—who acts as the city's lawyer—asked the state legislature for "special legislation" to allow private companies to bid on the sewage-treatment system. As in Lee and other cities, the proposed special legislation exempted the city from having to obtain more than one bid. "It was not unprecedented," recalled Sullivan. "'Local allowances,' 'home-rule initiatives,' they call it."[13]

At that time, the consultant who was drafting the legislation for the city had assured members of the City Council that they would continue to have ultimate authority over the privatization contract. As a result, council members voted to support the legislation, believing it would increase the city's flexibility in the bidding process. They didn't realize until much later that the legislation increased the mayor's flexibility, not theirs. The Council had made a fatal error by failing to review the final wording of the law, which never mentions the Council at all but says the contract "shall be subject to the approval of the mayor." Lubold said he and other council members had been misled by the consultant, who later admitted writing the legislation so that the mayor "was free to do whatever he wanted."[14]

By the spring of 2004, it was clear that the mayor was going all-out for the twenty-year, $176 million deal with Aquarion—the largest public-works contract in the city's history. Sullivan appeared willing and able to do whatever was necessary to complete the deal even as he continued to maintain in public that he had no stake in privatization unless it saved money for the ratepayers.

"The deck had been rigged," Lubold recollected, "but I still wanted to keep an open mind and look at all the information." The consultants gave council members a huge stack of paper to read, as well as books and studies of draft contracts. "We were told, 'Have all your comments in to us by Monday because we want to make a decision.' Right away, that was another sign of 'Whoa! What's going on here?' So I started to dive into the figures pretty quickly and generated a lot of questions." Lubold and some of the other council members persuaded the Department of Public Works to extend the time for comments. Lubold then had time to review past studies, read the seven-hundred-page contract, and study the economic analysis.

Lubold shared his research and insights about Lynn and about Aquarion's plan for Holyoke with his colleagues. "Wait a minute," he told them. "There are a lot of unknowns here. The financial analysis doesn't seem to add up; we're not getting questions answered. What's really going on here?" Most of the council members who took the time to review the deal arrived at the same conclusion. But a slight majority was unmoved and unresponsive. "We asked at one of the public meetings, 'Can one of you please tell us why you're in favor of it?' and not one person said anything," Lubold recalled. "Not one person. So I can't tell you why [they supported the proposal] because they can't articulate it themselves."

The mayor dismissed such complaints, saying he was open to hearing citizens' concerns, "but if it's just 'profits are bad' and 'we don't like corporations,' that's not going to carry as much water."[15] In November 2004, the city was moving quickly toward approving the contract. The Department of Public Works recommended an 82 percent sewer-rate increase to fund initial construction work. Few people in Holyoke were paying any attention, but their indifference was about to end.

Holyoke Citizens for Open Government

That November, Carolyn Toll Oppenheim saw a small notice in the *Springfield Republican* officially informing the public of the end of the comment period on the contract. "I called the city to see if I could rush down with some comment," she recalled. "They said it was too late. They closed comment at noon. Then I asked where I could see the contract, and they told me the contract was not finished or available for viewing. I asked how they could close public comment, and they were rude."[16]

Oppenheim was not one to be intimidated. She and her partner Ward Morehouse were leaders of a group called Shays-2, named after Revolutionary War veteran and local farmer Daniel Shays, who led an uprising against rapacious business practices in the 1780s. She had been a journalist and investigative reporter for the *Chicago Tribune* and the *Chicago Sun-Times*, an educator specializing in public-policy issues, and a community activist. Morehouse was an academic, activist, and author or editor of some twenty books dealing with international political affairs.

In November 2004, Oppenheim and Morehouse convened a group of residents at their Holyoke home to form an ad hoc association called Holyoke Citizens for Open Government (HCOG). The group included residents, city leaders, union members, students, teachers, and environmental activists. The carefully chosen name—who could be against open government?—was an attempt to transcend traditional left-right divisions and reach people on the whole political spectrum. HCOG was not so much against privatization as it was in favor of a fair deal for ratepayers. "Even a homeowner would call for several bids before doing any renovation work," said Oppenheim.[17]

HCOG's analysis showed that a municipally run project to end the sewage pollution of the river could be funded by lower rates than a privately run project could. They also wanted to defend the twenty-six jobs at the sewage plant, which, they said in an open letter, "have been livable wage, union, civil service jobs that help anchor the community of Holyoke to a decent standard of living."[18]

Jeremy Smith, a young activist and video editor whose family goes back generations in Holyoke, became HCOG's facilitator. "I wasn't antiprivatization at all costs," said Smith, "because there are plenty of city services that are contracted out to private companies, and it's fine. But this one was definitely worth examining because it was one of the biggest contracts the city ever signed, and I had heard plenty of horror stories about this sort of thing. I compare it to a trial. If there's enough reasonable doubt, why put the city in potential jeopardy?"

An additional factor that played a part in fueling public opposition to privatization was the excellent reputation enjoyed for over a century by the local public power company. According to the company's history, in 1902 the city bought out the private power company because city leaders feared "being held hostage by ever-increasing rate hikes which might eventually bankrupt the City coffers." Since then, Holyoke Gas & Electric has been a city-run power utility known for its reliability and customer service.[19]

The public's confidence in the city's ability to provide power carried over to water. Based on their first-hand experience, a large number of residents subscribed to the "if it ain't broke, why fix it?" school of thought. A corollary was old-fashioned Yankee pride in a long string of local public-works success stories, including the city-run dam on the Connecticut River and the new drinking-water treatment facility, which had won awards from the EPA. With this record, why would anyone think that the city couldn't handle the wastewater upgrade or believe that outsiders could do a better job than the locals? "They're pocketbook issues," Lubold declared. "Holyoke has, in general, good public service, and if they're going to privatize this, then what's next? Our water, our trash, our gas and electric department? I think people are afraid of that because they realize what they have."

HCOG allied itself with the Connecticut River Watershed Council, the leading environmental group focused on cleaning up the Connecticut River, and with Massachusetts Global Action, whose organizing director, Jonathan Leavitt, was a veteran of anti-privatization campaigns throughout the state, including successful efforts in Lawrence and Lee. This new coalition demanded that the mayor open the process to the public and make the contract available to residents. "Democracy, real self-governance, should be the prevailing political culture of the town," said Morehouse. HCOG also demanded a public hearing, calling on the city to notify every ratepayer by postcard of possible changes in a basic city service.

The mayor reluctantly acquiesced, putting some information on the city website. But his willingness to promote active debate had a limit. Even though every city meeting was usually broadcast live on the local public-access channel, no crew was dispatched to record the HCOG-organized public hearing called by the City Council Finance Committee and the Department of Public Works. Hundreds of people gathered in a high school auditorium to discuss and challenge the privatization and proposed sewer-rate increases. The hearing strengthened HCOG's claim to be the legitimate voice of public opinion on the privatization question, but Sullivan ignored the meeting and the recommendations by HCOG and by Lubold to conduct new studies on alternatives to privatization.[20]

Media coverage was, likewise, selective if not outright slanted. The *Springfield Republican* supported the privatization wholeheartedly on its editorial page and in the transparent bias of its reporting. Lubold complained that everything he said was treated skeptically by the paper, while the mayor's statements were assumed to be accurate. HCOG members also felt the paper's coverage was less than balanced, as the reporter on the story consistently refused to write about growing public criticisms of the contract.[21]

In spite of his indignation about the mayor's maneuvers, Lubold was not ideologically opposed to privatization of water services. "In some places it's good, and in some places it's bad," he said. His real worry was that towns like Holyoke don't have the capacity to control big private companies once they get their foot in the door. "Over and over the key is monitor the contracts, monitor the contracts. And smaller cities don't have the in-house capability to do that."

The Conflict Escalates

Since Kelda acquired it in 2000, Aquarion had been on a shopping spree, buying small private water companies in New England. It had operations providing drinking water in more than fifty towns, most of them in Connecticut, and it now wanted to branch into sewage. Its lack of experience with sewer systems raised questions about the company's ability to deal with Holyoke's sewage problems. Aquarion was eager to get into the business because there was consensus in the industry that future growth and profits would come primarily from the downstream end of the water cycle. In addition, the public put up less resistance to private control of wastewater than of drinking water in spite of the fact that treated sewage goes right back into a river to be used by downstream towns for their drinking water. As one environmental attorney put it, "One person's waste is another person's water right."[22]

As Aquarion expanded its operations, it built a controversial track record of laying off or forcing out workers, often in spite of promises not to do so. Indeed, Peter Cook, the lead lobbyist for the private water industry in Washington, D.C., touts the ability of private companies to reduce the workforce as a key advantage of privatization. "The civil service system that exists in most municipalities can create major problems for managers. That's where the private sector company can come in and really reduce some of these overhead burdens. They can break this pattern of inefficiency."[23]

Sure enough, after a profit shortfall in 2004, Kelda ordered Aquarion to cut its total workforce by 20 percent to improve efficiency. Aquarion's rate hikes were also raising hackles across New England. On average, Aquarion charged $557 a year for drinking water in Massachusetts compared with the $321 a year charged by public systems. In Connecticut, where 80 percent of its customers were located, Aquarion requested a 14–25 percent rate hike in 2004. The state attorney general responded by labeling the company "arrogant," and the Connecticut Department of Public Utility Control not only turned down the request as "outlandishly excessive" but ordered a reduction in Aquarion's existing water rates.[24]

By late 2004, members of the Holyoke City Council who opposed the contract fully realized how hamstrung they were because of the special legislation they had approved three years earlier. It was a frustrating time. The Council is normally required to approve city contracts over $3 million dollars, and here they had no say on the largest contract in the city's history, worth over $170 million.

They began plotting a counterattack, a kind of guerilla war against privatization, and the pace of the conflict picked up. In early 2005, they voted fourteen to one to authorize a fresh study of city-run alternatives to the Aquarion contract. They also voted to petition the legislature to modify the special legislation to reinstate the power of the City Council, but the mayor refused to sign the petition. The Council responded by refusing to approve the rate increase needed to fund Aquarion's work.

Because the mayor did not need Council support to approve the deal, he went ahead and signed the contract with Aquarion in July 2005. Attempts by "a small and vocal minority" to block it by derailing a rate increase were "not going to deter me from taking the right steps for the city," he said.[25] But at this point the mayor ran into a snag. He still needed a sewer-rate increase to cover Aquarion's first-year management fee. That increase required the approval of two-thirds of the Council, and the mayor didn't have the votes.

Ultimately, in order to get the contract started, Mayor Sullivan and Aquarion hit upon the kind of plan that shows how easily contracts can be manipulated and changed to enable privatization to proceed. They renegotiated a deal to defer the city's first-year payment to Aquarion and to add the deferred amount to the contract as debt payable at 6 percent interest, well above the rate the city would normally have to pay. As a result of these maneuverings, the contract could commence on October 1, 2005. Council member and privatization critic Helen Norris asked, "How can this happen?" She called the maneuver an "off the books . . . slush fund" with no oversight by either the Council or the city auditor.[26]

Will the Voters Decide?

The City Council, increasingly frustrated by the way it and the public had been shunted aside, placed a nonbinding referendum on the November 2005 ballot that let the citizens weigh in on the Aquarion contract, even though it would already be in effect. The one-sentence initiative read: "Should the City of Holyoke have a 20 year contract with Aquarion Operating Services to operate the city's wastewater system?" A "yes" vote would be for the contract, "no" would be against it. The referendum would carry no legal weight, but many Holyoke residents assumed the mayor would honor the wishes of the voters.

Lubold for one, however, did not believe Sullivan would change course, and after much deliberation he decided to throw his hat in the ring for mayor, ensuring a hot campaign season. Lubold's candidacy was a long shot, and he was starting late for an insurgent. Sullivan's supporters called him a "one issue, overnight candidate," but he presented a different vision of the city's future than did Sullivan. In particular, Lubold believed that the city should focus on developing the river front and rejuvenating downtown, where most of the city's Latino, low-income, and unemployed live, rather than focusing primarily on new development in the more suburban, white, middle-class corridor along the interstate higher up on the hill. As a result, Holyoke's Latino leaders were increasingly drawn into Lubold's campaign, and the former head of the Hispanic Chamber of Commerce became the campaign treasurer. Even so, Lubold was the underdog. "There's a great dividing point between people who live up the hill and people who live down the hill," he said during the campaign, "and the people down the hill don't vote."

Nevertheless, the wastewater privatization was at the heart of Lubold's campaign. The referendum on Aquarion was nonbinding, but a vote for Lubold could have a decisive impact because, if elected, he promised to explore canceling the contract and to move ahead with a plan for the city to expand and operate the wastewater system. "It isn't based on any ideology or perspective or anything," he said. "I saw the facts and the facts don't add up. And it's that simple. I'm not against privatizing per se, but it's got to be right and it's got to benefit the people who are using it. And I came to the conclusion that in Holyoke a private sewer system is not in the best interest of ratepayers." In the runup to the election, Sullivan raised more than twice as much money as Lubold did, while Aquarion spent close to $25,000 urging a yes vote on the referendum.[27]

On election day, it was no surprise that Lubold's underdog mayoral bid was soundly defeated. Sullivan was overwhelmingly reelected, with 67 percent of the vote. As Lubold feared, the inner-city population failed to turn out to vote while the middle class turned out in force for the mayor. But Lubold won a different victory. The nonbinding initiative asking citizens whether they wanted the contract with Aquarion received a resounding "no" from 56 percent of those casting ballots.

During the campaign, Sullivan had said he would listen to the voters and look at alternatives if the initiative failed, but if he did, he apparently gave the alternatives only a glance. He quickly dismissed the initiative's significance, saying that the one-sentence ballot question was unclear. An editorial in *El Dialogo* was stinging. "Would the Mayor be saying the ballot question was unclear if voters supported the Aquarion deal? Of course not. Voters have spoken and elected officials need to follow without delays."[28]

The mayor was also facing a growing challenge from the newly elected City Council, which was much more critical of the Aquarion deal than the previous Council had been and which demanded its right to vote on the issue even though Aquarion was already at work. Sullivan wouldn't budge. "I have no intention of severing the contract at this point in time," he said. "It's incredibly upsetting to see government sabotaged like this." And so began an ongoing war between the mayor and the Council.[29]

In 2006, councilors repeatedly rejected the first sewer-rate increase in sixteen years, but finally a deeply divided council approved a 139 percent rise under pressure from the mayor.

Local opponents of privatization continue to monitor Aquarion's performance and are carrying the conflict statewide, demanding an end to what Morehouse called the "mischievous use" of special legislation that suspends competitive bidding and guts requirements for democratic, public input on water decisions.[30]

HCOG facilitator Smith calls the whole affair "Mayor Sullivan's Iraq. There were no weapons of mass destruction and there were no savings. The City Council is split, and the citizens are skeptical and against it. If you're an elected official, at some point you have to say, 'I haven't been able to make my case, we should not go forward with this.' It's become an abuse of power."

Sullivan has a different take. "That's leadership," he said. "That's what you have to do. You have to make decisions even when they are not palatable."[31]

Corporate Target

The Great Lakes

8

When Nestlé Comes
Wisconsin Dells, Wisconsin

In the United States, bottled water has moved beyond being a fad and a fashion accessory to become an accepted—even pervasive—part of daily life. How pervasive? In 2005, Americans spent well over $10 billion on bottled water, and sales are skyrocketing. The Beverage Marketing Corporation reports that bottled-water sales are increasing nearly 10 percent a year, growth almost unheard of in the food and beverage sector. In a spectacular triumph of marketing, the beverage industry found a replacement for sagging soda sales by convincing great numbers of people that drinking bottled H_2O, rather than plain old tap water, produces miraculous results: youth, good health, vitality, sexiness, affluence, enhanced memory, and general well-being.[1]

Since the mid-1990s, giant food and beverage conglomerates Nestlé, Coke, and Pepsi have rapidly created new water brands or bought out old ones. A host of boutique companies like Fiji, Sylvester Stallone's Sly Pure Glacial Water, Donald Trump Water, and the $38-a-bottle Bling H_2O pocket nice profits from tiny slivers of the market. There is even bottled water for dogs.

Bottling Nature

The campaign to wean Americans from the tap to the bottle has delivered more than extraordinary profits. It has been a driving force in shifting cultural attitudes toward the privatization of water. Once consumers are persuaded that water is a grab-and-go consumer product, water becomes a commodity like any other. In addition, if we get used to paying gas prices for a bottle of water, we might also get used to the idea that private corporations should provide tap water as well—at prices that guarantee a hefty profit. And an even more serious, long term threat is inherent in the bottled-water craze. If we as individuals get used to paying whatever price the market will bear for bottled water as a product, will we slowly give up the collective commitment to clean, affordable water as a public service that must be guaranteed by government?

From California to Maine to Florida, local and state governments are giving water bottlers tax breaks and incentives, in effect paying them to appropriate the natural springs and aquifers we own in common as a people, all in return for the promise of a small number of jobs. Other companies receive similar subsidies for filling their bottles with inexpensive municipal water, slightly filtered or straight from the tap.

Consumers of bottled water pay roughly one thousand, sometimes even ten thousand, times more for bottled water than for tap water. And what do we get? Study after study has concluded that bottled water is neither cleaner nor greener than tap water. The Natural Resources Defense Council discovered that a surprising number of the bottled waters they tested contained contaminants, pesticide residues, and heavy metals. The results shocked most people, who had not realized that bottled water is less regulated than tap water. While the Environmental Protection Agency enforces strict standards on municipal tap water, the Food and Drug Administration oversees bottled water and is concerned more with the accuracy of the label than with the contents of the bottle. Water bottled and sold inside a single state isn't covered by federal regulations at all but by state regulations, which vary from strict to virtually nonexistent.[2]

The industry has avoided direct statements that its products are cleaner or healthier than tap water, but industry advertising clearly leaves that impression with images of alpine streams and snow-covered mountains and claims that their water is pristine and pure. Reporter Gregory Karp of the *Chicago Tribune* concludes "After all, the industry has to find some way to differentiate and sell a liquid that has no color, no smell, virtually no taste and literally falls from the sky."[3]

Although the product that attracts consumers is the water, the industry's real product is the bottle itself. Of the over forty million bottles consumed every day in the United States, more than 88 percent are not recycled. That leaves more than thirty million plastic bottles a day to be dumped into landfills or to float down the rivers where the salmon used to run. In addition, all those plastic bottles are made from oil, and transporting them uses still more oil. However, the bottled-water industry is by no means the biggest contributor to global warming, pollution, littering, landfills, or the waste of water, and that dismal fact has become their major line of defense against environmental critics.[4]

As for the advertisements and conventional wisdom suggesting that bottled water tastes better than tap, taste tests around the country routinely produce surprising results: tap water wins time and again. A 2006 ad campaign by Fiji Water boasted that its product was free of pollutants and "purified by island trade winds." The punch line: "The label says Fiji because it's not bottled in Cleveland." Cleveland water officials took umbrage at the implication that their city water is less than pure. They analyzed Fiji's product and found it contained much higher levels of arsenic than allowed in Cleveland's tap water. When a Cleveland television station followed up with a blind taste test, the subjects preferred the taste of tap. "I thought Cleveland was much more refreshing," said a tennis player who perhaps should have been hired to promote city tap water except that public water agencies do not have advertising budgets.[5]

The drawbacks of bottled water are a new issue even for many veteran environmentalists,[6] and few Americans think about the problems at all until a bottling company arrives in town to pump millions of gallons a day from local springs or aquifers. Few issues command citizens' attention as much as local concerns, and with water-bottling plants the concerns are many—the environmental impact on watersheds; the lowering of real estate values; the noise, dust, and danger of hundreds of trucks rattling to and from the plants every day. In this chapter and the next, we describe how local residents in two rural communities in the Midwest responded to the bottling of their water, but the story is being repeated across North America. Slowly, but surely, the bottled-water industry is facing an increased flow of opposition. Local critics are beginning to see the industry as a harbinger of wider threats, including the commodification of water, the export of water in bulk, and the end of the keystone idea of affordable water as a public trust and human right.

Which brings us to Wisconsin Dells.

The Defenders

Every room of Hiroshi and Arlene Kanno's modest farmhouse in the central Wisconsin hamlet of Newport is crammed with boxes and papers. It resembles a great sprawling office—or the headquarters for a military campaign. In fact this is the residue of a battle, which they barreled into when they heard that the Perrier Group of America planned to locate a water-bottling plant just across the road. The Kannos had raised their eight children a few hours away in Oak Park, Illinois, just three blocks from the Chicago city limits. Hiroshi worked for the federal Department of Health and Human Services in Chicago, while Arlene taught science in public schools.

The Kannos say they never experienced discrimination as an interracial couple, but Hiroshi himself did as a small child when he and his family were exiled to the Japanese-American internment camp at Minidoka, Idaho, during World War II. He remembers his late uncle, a U.S. combat soldier on the European front, returning on leave to visit his family in their squalid barracks. "I regret never asking him how he felt," said Hiroshi. "But we were very proud he was a soldier."[7]

There's an ironic connection between that early experience and the couple's later retirement in rural Wisconsin. Hiroshi had been active in the Japanese American Citizens League's successful effort to win an apology and monetary reparations for internment. When he retired, he used his reparations money to buy the Newport farmhouse. There is clear satisfaction in his deep voice about this journey from the internment camp to a comfortable home surrounded by rolling hills and open fields. The farmhouse is in an area known as the Wisconsin Dells, a family summer-vacation mecca about an hour northwest of the state capitol in Madison. "It's very restful to look at these hills," says Arlene, whose warm laugh is a contrast to Hiroshi's dignified rumble.

The Kannos bought their land from longtime residents Don and Anita Nelson, who own a nearby dairy farm. The area is zoned for agriculture, but, like many new residents in the area, the Kannos had no intention of being farmers. They leased back ten acres to the Nelsons for grazing and started restoring much of the rest to its original state as wetlands populated by sandhill cranes, baby foxes, muskrat, and deer. There's plenty of water for the purpose. The Kannos live near Big Springs, a well-known source that feeds local ponds and streams and ultimately Lake Michigan. They had no idea that their location near Big Springs and their growing friendship with the Nelsons were about to shake up Wisconsin state politics and spark a growing movement against some of the world's largest corporations.

Perrier Arrives

On Valentine's Day 2000, without any warning, Perrier, the bottled-water division of Nestlé, announced plans to draw water from springs in the nearby town of New Haven. Based in Switzerland,

Nestlé is the world's largest food company. It entered the U.S. bottled-water market in 1992 with the purchase of the French company Source Perrier, famous for its green glass bottles and refreshing-looking bubbles. Nestlé's Perrier Group had already established itself in the United States and quickly expanded by acquiring major regional water brands, including Poland Springs in the Northeast, Calistoga in California, Zephyrhills in Florida, Arrowhead in the Southwest, Ozarka in the South, Deer Park in the mid-Atlantic, and then Ice Mountain in the Midwest.

Nestlé's takeover of Perrier was a major step in the company's plan to become the largest bottled-water company in the world. Nestlé Waters sells seventy-two brands in 160 countries. By 2005, its U.S. subsidiary was exploiting 150 water sources to feed over twenty bottling plants. The company's $3.1 billion in 2005 sales accounted for almost one third of the U.S. bottled-water market.[8]

Just after the Kannos and their neighbors learned of Perrier's plans for the area, the company called an open meeting—actually more of an extended lecture—to tell residents how the pumping plan would benefit the community. The turnout was huge given the area's small population, and the company's condescending presentation did not placate fears. After the lecture, there were plenty of questions but only one answer that anyone really remembers anymore. Perrier's Midwest director told the meeting, "We won't even drill a test well if there is opposition. We will leave if we're not wanted."[9]

The response at that meeting, said Hiroshi, was clear: "Leave." But Perrier apparently developed a hearing problem because it chose to hold a second meeting instead. More people showed up, and more people said, "Leave." Perrier dismissed the message, saying that those attending the meeting were not representative of the community.

Perrier's confidence in its plan's ultimate success may have been due in part to the area's recent political history. The little towns in the Wisconsin Dells area had long been strongholds of support for Republican Governor Tommy "The Bull" Thompson, who had developed a national reputation in conservative circles for what many considered to be a punitive welfare-to-work program. The Kannos began digging to uncover the role the Republican governor and his administration had played in bringing Perrier to New Haven's Big Springs source. A pattern slowly emerged of behind-the-scenes dealing, secret meetings, and government complicity. The Kannos discovered that the Wisconsin Department of Commerce had contacted Perrier more than a year earlier, hoping to attract the company to the state. The department followed up by identifying eleven potential water sources and even arranged a free round-trip flight for a Perrier executive to visit the state. Perrier was interested in two possible sites, and company officials eventually met with Governor Thompson's chief of staff in December 1999.

The company's first choice was a water source on government-owned land. No muss, no fuss, if you have the governor on your side. Except that a group called Trout Unlimited, comprised of hard-core, longtime fishermen, objected to a massive pumping project that would threaten some of the best trout streams in the Midwest. Drawing down all that cold water couldn't help but affect spawning patterns. What Perrier didn't count on, however, was that some of those fishermen were heavy contributors to Republican candidates, and therefore their calls were returned a mite faster than the average rod 'n' reeler's. And they got results: Thompson encouraged the company to abandon the plan—and to go instead to New Haven's Big Springs. "They thought that this area would be a pretty good shot because they figured there's nobody important in this area," Arlene says, laughing. "Nobody with a lot of pull." "A bunch of farmers, you know," adds Hiroshi, completing her thought.

Fortunately, some of the folks who opposed Perrier's previous site choice weren't just "not-in-my-backyard" advocates. In particular, the Wisconsin chapter of Trout Unlimited thought Perrier shouldn't be in the Kannos' backyard either. "When they found out that a deal had been cut to get Perrier out of their area and essentially sicced them on us," said Hiroshi, "the Trout Unlimited people said, 'That's not fair.'" They sent one of their experienced grassroots activists to help the Kannos get organized and investigate Perrier's secret negotiations for access to Big Springs.

The information the Kannos uncovered was disturbing. Perrier
had already contacted several local landowners with access to spring
water, offering to negotiate a price for their water if they agreed to
keep the discussions secret—from relatives, neighbors, everyone.
Given the amount of money the landowners stood to receive, their
silence was guaranteed. The private maneuverings echoed those in
one of the most infamous water raids in U.S. history. One hundred
years earlier, William Mulholland and his collaborators in Los
Angeles secretly purchased land from farmers in the Owens Valley
until they controlled enough land and the accompanying water
rights to drain the valley dry. The story is the trigger for environmental paranoia about the secret deals that watered, and still water,
imperial cities and agribusiness kingdoms across the country.

The Kannos didn't blame the landowners for wanting to reap a
windfall. However, they couldn't abide the complicity of state agencies whose mandate was supposedly to protect the public interest—
namely the governor's office and the Wisconsin Department of
Natural Resources (DNR). "They were going to pump about 500
gallons per minute," Hiroshi recalled, "which is 720,000 gallons a
day, about 260 million gallons a year. That's a lot of water out of our
springs. What's the environmental impact of all of this? We have a
wetland here we've created. What's going to happen to it?'" "When
we bought our land," Arlene remembered, "I said, 'What if somebody on the other side of the street decides to put in a factory or
something?'" And that turned out to be Perrier's plan. The company
proposed to build a 250,000-square-foot bottling facility that would
eventually grow to a million square feet directly across from the
Kanno farmhouse. Hundreds of trucks would come and go daily. So
much for the quiet country life the Kannos had dreamed of.

Other longtime residents were also upset. The targeted springs
run through sensitive wetlands and feed Lake Mason, an artificial

body only six feet deep that covers some 850 acres. It's a quiet spot, popular for placid fishing and pontoon boats. "Of course," said Arlene, "around any lake—even a six-foot-deep lake—cottages spring up. Most of them are older and modest. There are no great trophy homes or anything like that. There were real questions about how the withdrawal of water would affect the depth of Lake Mason, and people had some idea because many winters they draw down the lake to prevent the growth of algae or lake weeds. So they know when it's drawn down what the lake looks like. They realized if their properties were made into a mud puddle, it wouldn't be worth anything to themselves or for sale purposes."

Jon Steinhaus, who lives ten minutes away from the Kannos, owned a small resort on the lake as an investment. When he and his wife, Judy, decided to sell it, they ran into a problem. "I had a letter from a realtor that said there's no way people are going to buy this until they understand what this water thing is going to be."[10] In his early sixties and an avid hunter, Steinhaus became a formidable opponent of Perrier's plan. He had plenty of contacts and experience in the political arena, having lobbied politicians for years on behalf of the rural electric cooperative he managed before retiring. Perrier told him not to worry about the lake. "But you know better than that," Steinhaus said. "There's no way you can control them once they get those pipes in the ground."

"We're Going to Be Destroyed"

The Kannos and the Nelsons in their hamlet of Newport and Steinhaus and others in New Haven joined together to form Waterkeepers of Wisconsin. One of the first events it organized was a hearing at the high school with representatives of the DNR. Several hundred people showed up for an emotional confrontation. Some residents feared their wells would dry up. Others were worried about their trout streams, and still others warned about the eight hundred or more truck trips a day on local roads. Some were concerned about their property values. "We're going to be destroyed," Hiroshi testified. "We're going to be devastated."[11]

The residents attacked point after point of the DNR and Nestlé's joint argument for the plant. Perrier had promised forty-five new jobs and more to come as the plant expanded. It's an appeal that works well in the job-starved Midwest, but it didn't work here. Donald Nelson told the meeting that unlike more desperate neighboring states, Wisconsin had a labor shortage: its unemployment rate was the lowest since the 1960s. "Doesn't look like we're in dire straits for jobs," he said. "I don't think so."[12]

People still recount the event as a local legend, particularly the moment when an old farmer came down from the bleachers to testify. He asked how anyone could trust Perrier's reassurances when Perrier's mother company, Nestlé, had been involved in one of the major corporate scandals of the 1980s: the company had refused to stop selling its baby formula in the developing world even after it was clear that many infants died when their mothers stopped breast-feeding and instead mixed the formula using contaminated local water supplies. "If they would allow babies to die from dysentery because of their shareholders, and they are sitting here today saying they are going to protect our wetlands, who are you going to believe?" the old man asked. You could hear a pin drop. "It was sort of like in the *Norma Rae* movie," said one witness. "All of a sudden everybody is applauding, and you could see that the DNR people were thinking, 'Oh, my God, what are we doing here?'"

"They are good people in our administrative agencies," said attorney Melissa Scanlan of Midwest Environmental Advocates in Madison, "but the reality is they spend most of their time talking to the industries they're regulating. And it's easy for them to forget who their real customers are and that they're supposed to be protecting the public, not the private companies."[13] Another ally of the Kannos, attorney Ed Garvey, was less generous about corporate power in government. "Legislators take a look and say, 'Where am I going to get my campaign contributions? Are they going to come from Hiroshi Kanno or from Perrier, its lawyers, hangers-on, and experts?"[14]

The work of the Kannos and the Waterkeepers resonated with deeply rooted Wisconsin traditions of populist democracy, rural rebellion, and labor agitation. Community activists still like to quote the state's fabled populist, Senator Bob La Follette: "The will of the people shall be the law of the land."

Nestlé had a different approach to the law of the land. It was investing directly in the law and lawmakers, spending on average $1.2 million a year lobbying the federal government alone, as well as making substantial "soft-money" contributions to political parties and candidates.[15]

Governor Thompson, however, was at a point in his career when he didn't need campaign contributions. For him, the Perrier battle was generating political heat at an inconvenient time. Already in office fourteen years and still popular, the last thing he wanted was a widening controversy as he angled for the 2000 Republican vice presidential nomination he ultimately did not get. Other than giving some muttered reassurances, Thompson started dodging the Perrier issue, eventually avoiding all comment on the controversy for months on end. "I know him very well," said Steinhaus, "and he was between a rock and a hard place because he had made those promises to Perrier."

Perrier itself had another set of problems. The company was desperate to expand its operations in the Midwest. Business was booming, and the company faced new competition. American soft-drink companies PepsiCo and Coca-Cola had entered the market in the 1990s with Aquafina and Dasani, respectively, national brands using filtered tap water, unlike Perrier's regional spring-water brands. The giant cola companies saw bottled water as an essential source of new profits at a time of soda pop stagnation. To keep its lead against these deep-pocket contenders, Perrier needed to get new water sources and new plants on-line fast.

The small but fierce Waterkeepers of Wisconsin didn't look like a big obstacle, even if it had already demonstrated its ability to turn out supporters. The Waterkeepers, however, now moved to demonstrate the breadth of local opposition to Perrier. The group called for an advisory referendum to prove where public sentiment lay. Although the vote in June 2000 would not be legally binding, Perrier took it seriously, mailing glossy brochures to every home in an effort to reassure residents that Perrier cared for the environment. Nonetheless, the referendum results were decisive. In New Haven, 74 percent of the voters opposed Perrier; in Newport, 81 percent.

Incredibly, the lopsided results were not enough to convince the New Haven town chair, who put up a pro-Perrier sign on his lawn and proclaimed, "Many people still support Perrier."[16] That may sound like a formula for political suicide, and it was. The community circulated a recall petition to oust him from his post, and on Election Day, fittingly, he received the same measure of support as had Perrier—26 percent. An opponent of Perrier became the new town chair.

Activist attorney Garvey believes the referendums were a turning point. "[The referendums showed] there is a commonwealth here," he said. "It's not just individuals who are in charge of raising hell. Because what the Perriers and their lawyers and the Wal-Marts do is to try to categorize anybody who is opposition as being radical troublemakers, out of touch, unrealistic people who don't care about jobs. Here in this community, people spoke up and said, 'We don't care what you're saying, we want you out of here.'"

Strategic Differences: Legal Contests and Public Pressure

Perrier officials were starting to get worried. Perrier's North American CEO and President Kim Jeffery met with Governor Thompson in July 2000 and followed up with a letter asking Thompson to use "political capital" to help the company in its fight.[17] The gov-

ernor, however, remained officially neutral even as a number of
Republican and Democratic state legislators, local county governments, and the state attorney general came out against the pumping unless an environmental-impact report proved there would be
no damage to local water supplies.

Perrier ran its own outreach and media campaign to present a
caring face, but Arlene Kanno was struck by the way that the company's arrogance always seemed to surface in public. "I remember
sitting in the little New Haven town hall that has no indoor bathroom, and Perrier said, 'Well, we have contracts to fill.' We sat
there, and we were thinking, 'So what! You have a problem.' But
they acted like it was their water already. They obviously thought
of it as their water. And they were just panting." In spite of the
angry meetings and the referendums, Perrier public relations director Jane Lazgin still maintained, "Not everyone wants us to leave."
That kind of defense eventually earned Perrier a spot on a California public relations company's "6th Annual List of PR Blunders."[18]

However, another Perrier strategy was more effective than its
public relations denials. Across the country, bottled-water companies have frequently chosen to set up shop close to a county line or
to locate a bottling plant in a different county from the spring. As a
result, opponents have been forced to pursue electoral or zoning
strategies (or both) in two jurisdictions, effectively splitting the
opposition's meager human and financial resources. The New Haven
and Newport groups in Waterkeepers were on opposite sides of a
county line, and other divisions between the two groups were
becoming apparent as well.

Steinhaus and the New Haven group opted to head off Perrier
through restrictions on siting an industrial plant in an area zoned
for agriculture. They also filed objections to Perrier's proposed truck-
ing route because it passed a school and thus posed a potential danger to children. "It was really amazing," said Steinhaus. "Each time
Perrier revised the route, we'd tell people on that route, and the
people would just raise whoopee." But the Kannos and the Nelsons

fretted that route and zoning restrictions could be overruled and the New Haven victories easily erased. "We began to realize," said Hiroshi Kanno, "that there's some different views on how we're going to fight this."

The tactical differences mirrored other differences between the two towns in background and orientation. The Newport area was becoming a bedroom and vacation community for folks employed in the state capital. That orientation brought in young, middle-class urban professionals. "Years ago," said Anita Nelson, "I knew exactly what that guy two miles down the road was doing. If he was polluting, I knew about him. I knew he kicked his wife and he hit the stove and broke his toe. I mean, we knew about each other. But we don't now."[19]

In contrast, the New Haven area had an older, less affluent population with families that had been in the area for decades, even generations. "It was the little old lady that gave us the only twenty-five bucks she had [to fight Perrier] and the old farmer that lived around there," said Steinhaus. "I mean they're the salt of the earth."

The differences came to a head in September 2000, when Perrier received a permit to drill a test well. Opponents in the community had thirty days to challenge the permit, and if the window closed, Perrier's operation would be hard to stop. "I'm the [retired] bureaucrat and I know," Hiroshi says. "Once that wheel starts turning you can't stop it." The thirty-day deadline created a pressure cooker, and the heat started splitting the Waterkeepers at the seams. The Kannos and the Nelsons concluded that they had to go to court to file a complaint within the thirty days, but they couldn't convince Steinhaus and his group in New Haven to join them.

The New Haven group was worried about all the money involved in a lawsuit and wanted to pursue other strategies; it hoped to hire a lobbyist to influence the state legislature against Perrier. "We tried to do it politically," said Steinhaus, who was also reluctant to go up against a popular governor he liked and hoped to convince. "My whole philosophy has always been if you talk to people long enough, you should be able to work something out." The Kannos and the Nelsons were "very much allied with the Democratic Party," Steinhaus proclaimed, "while I don't belong to any party. I vote for who I think is best. [The Newport group] assumed we were very Republican."

The proof of the pudding for Steinhaus was the decision by the Kannos and the Nelsons to work with attorney Garvey, who had recently run unsuccessfully against Thompson for governor as the Democratic candidate. For that reason alone, Garvey wasn't popular among the large number of Republicans and Independents in the anti-Perrier coalition.

These strategic disagreements under the pressure of the deadline to file suit caused a permanent split in the Waterkeepers, what Steinhaus called "the rift" and Hiroshi, "the schism." "The element of distrust between the two factions that were fighting was real," said Hiroshi. "Still is real. And it really was because of that distrust that we had to create another organization, CCN, Concerned Citizens of Newport."

The Kannos and the Nelsons worked out a strategy with Garvey and litigator Glenn Stoddard to challenge the DNR and Perrier on several fronts. "The last thing we wanted to do is a lawsuit," Arlene asserts. "But we had to. We had already tried every other avenue we had. We had done a video, and we had gotten on talk radio. We had gotten on television. We had been in the newspapers repeatedly." They had even organized an outrageous singing group called the "Raging Grannies" to raise funds and spirits. They had been so successful at publicizing their views that the Perrier issue was voted one of the top ten news stories of the year in Wisconsin.

The Kannos and the Nelsons signed on as plaintiffs on the lawsuit, which, among other obligations, meant that they had responsibility for the attorney fees. "I had to mortgage my farm to fight them," said Hiroshi, but that development just seemed to make him more militant than ever. The local Ho-Chunk Indian tribe also filed suit against Perrier, claiming that Big Springs is a sacred site to its people. The two suits were eventually merged into one court challenge to the pumping plan.

Although his firm was working on the suit, Garvey insisted that the citizens not rely on the courts but instead anchor their legal strategy in a larger political-outreach campaign. "We let people know right away," he said, "[that] 'if you want us involved, you've got to be doing the heavy lifting when it comes to community involvement, contact with the media, and organizing' because that puts the pressure on in order to make a legal strategy a possibility." It has become conventional wisdom among lawyers that the law works best when both sides have roughly the same amount of money to spend. Because grassroots groups can't match multinational corporate cash, citizen action and militancy must be the equalizer. "Our approach was totally confrontational," Garvey said. "We told the Department of Natural Resources and the legislators, 'Look, you guys aren't going to help us any. So, we're going to make it obvious to you that you should.'"

On the legal front, Garvey and Stoddard planned to challenge Perrier based on the pumping's negative environmental impact on the area. They asked public-interest attorney Scanlan to be their co-counsel to develop a second front. She pursued the case as a way of formalizing the public trust doctrine, a legal principle that is not explicitly stated on the books but is deeply embedded in legal tradition. For environmentalists, the doctrine has become a kind of El Dorado.

"Since the fourth century we've known, based on Roman law, that there were things people couldn't own, and water was one of those things," Scanlan explained. "Water was considered a commons, it was something that was shared by the public and couldn't be owned by any one person." For Scanlan, having a corporation exploit the commons by bottling the water and selling it back to the populace marks "a very significant departure from hundreds of years of legal history in lots of different cultures."

In Wisconsin, the tradition of the public trust doctrine had been enshrined in a unique institution. Wisconsin had been the only state in the nation to boast an Office of Public Intervenor, an independent agency charged with protecting the environment. Assisted by an autonomous board, the Intervenor would study various proposals and make recommendations, bringing suit if necessary against government officials or private developers. Alas, the position of Intervenor had been cut from the state budget at the behest of Governor Thompson. Scanlan's legal strategy was therefore aimed at formally establishing in law what the Office of Public Intervenor had done in practice. "Privatization of water is the newest frontier," she maintained, "and the laws haven't caught up with it yet. So you're going to see a lot of taking of public property without compensating the public or without being regulated by permit. It's like the timber barons of one hundred years ago."

With Scanlan's participation, the legal team was planning to ask the court not just about a single bottling plant but also about the big issues: When does the public trust become the public trough for private profits? Is business a part of the commons or above it? If climate change means society can no longer afford to allow business to pollute the planet, how can that principle be enshrined in law?

Perrier maintained that its water takings were no different from water use by other companies. Whenever the company has been attacked, it has likened itself to the major brewers, which use large quantities of water to make beer, or to companies that mix water with orange juice concentrate. Scanlan didn't buy the argument. "My rebuttal is that it's different when water itself is the product. We need to draw the line somewhere, and that's where we need to draw it. Water taken from its natural state and not changed in any way shouldn't be a product itself. Once water in its natural state is defined that way, it will be very difficult to stop bulk water exports from the Great Lakes."

In spite of all these arguments, the Concerned Citizens' legal strategy appeared to be a long shot. It wasn't even clear whether the Kannos and the Nelsons would be given legal standing to sue in the case because they were across the street and thus across the county line from the Perrier site.

The Kannos' call for a full environmental-impact study of the pumping was also unprecedented. The secretary of the DNR argued publicly that none of the ninety-four hundred high-capacity well applications his department had approved over the years had required such a study, but the Kannos countered that, of those wells, only "between six and twelve are for spring-water extraction, and none of those pumps more than eighty-seven gallons a minute" compared with Perrier's proposed extraction rate of five hundred gallons a minute.

The Kannos and Nelsons formally filed their suit against the DNR and its permits to Perrier in October 2000. And then a revelation on television cracked the situation wide open. In a televised debate, Stoddard accused the DNR of failing to safeguard the state's groundwater in the Perrier case. A DNR administrator responded by dramatically throwing down a paper, which he said was an agreement between the DNR and Perrier to guarantee protection of the environment. Stoddard was stunned. "Who did this?" he asked. No one had known about the secret deal, which was simply titled "The Agreement." Suddenly, the Kannos and the Nelsons had legitimate legal standing to sue because the public hadn't known or been able to comment on the DNR/Perrier agreement. The document also revealed that the DNR hadn't done its own investigation of possible harm from the pumping, instead depending on Perrier to test for environmental damage.

Meanwhile, the New Haven group kept up the pressure on Perrier in its own way. "We enjoyed fighting them," said Steinhaus, a sentiment that seemed to unite the two groups even as they went their separate ways. Having served for a time in county office himself, he lobbied county board members to block Perrier because "hey, look, this is wrong."

Steinhaus also believed his political connections played a role with Governor Thompson. He had a chance encounter with the governor at the state capitol, and Thompson asked him for information about the Perrier controversy. Steinhaus believed that was

Thompson's attempt to find political cover to come out against Perrier. "I think he realized in the end that he may have made a mistake originally." Garvey had his doubts about that possibility, but the political winds were changing.

In the fall of 2000, the nation was focused on the presidential race, and Wisconsin was too close to call for George W. Bush or Al Gore. Just days before the vote, Governor Thompson finally made a public statement that had the potential to help the Republican candidate. "The community doesn't want the bottling company," he told TV cameras. "I know the county board, and I don't think they're going to make the zoning change. If they don't, Perrier should look elsewhere."[20] If the statement was aimed at swinging undecided Wisconsin voters into the Republican column, it fell just short. Gore won the state by five thousand votes out of two and a half million cast.

Just days after the election, with the final result still hanging on the outcome in Florida, Perrier began test pumping operations near Big Springs, and several local farmers reported they saw immediate changes in their well levels.[21] Soon after, the county board for Big Springs rejected Perrier's application to change the zoning from agricultural to commercial to permit water extraction and bottling. The vote wasn't even close, fourteen to three. With the tide turning, Governor Thompson decided to sever the knot with Perrier, urging the company to find another location. He also acknowledged that perhaps the dispute had revealed some weaknesses in the state's water laws, which did not allow the state to block pumping operations even if they adversely affected the environment or aroused strong local opposition. The only legal reason to stop such pumping was if the extraction of groundwater adversely affected municipal drinking supplies.

The governor also had his sights on a different job. After the Supreme Court ruled in favor of Bush, Thompson was preparing to leave Wisconsin for his soon-to-be-announced appointment as Secretary of Health and Human Services. His replacement was Republican Lieutenant Governor Scott McCallum, who wanted no part of the hot potato called Perrier. "I have never been supportive of Perrier being in the state. There is no place for them in Wisconsin."[22]

However, Perrier was not ready to give up. Even now, the company claimed to have some public support. Perrier's lawyers announced plans to intervene in the Kanno court case on the side of the DNR. But Perrier's options were clearly dwindling, and in May 2001 the company abruptly changed course, announcing a decision to put its Wisconsin plans on hold for at least five years while it focused instead on a bottling plant it was building in Michigan. CEO Jeffery insisted the decision did not mean that Perrier was abandoning the Big Springs site forever. "The company intends to reconsider the site several years into the future depending on market demand," he said in a press release.[23]

"And we said 'Yay!'" said Arlene Kanno, but Hiroshi added, "We never celebrated 'cause none of us believed they are gone." "We couldn't relax," added Arlene. "Perrier treats us like people in India, as someone they can just roll over." The Kannos had no intention of dropping their lawsuit. They wanted to make sure Perrier could never return, and they intensified their long fundraising and media campaign to support the high costs of the case. The Concerned Citizens and the Ho-Chunk Nation intended to establish the principle that the DNR itself must assess the environmental impacts of groundwater extraction and seek public participation in such decisions.

In early December 2001—more than a year later—the Kannos and Nelsons finally got their day in court. Their supporters packed the courtroom. "It's not to pressure anyone," Garvey said, "but it sometimes, I think, helps convince the court this is serious business when the courtroom is filled with citizens who will be impacted directly by the decision."

In court, Scanlan, Garvey, and Stoddard pressed their two major arguments on behalf of the Kannos and the Nelsons. Scanlan argued that the state of Wisconsin was violating the public trust doctrine by issuing a permit to Perrier to take public water. The other lawyers argued that the state was in violation of the Wisconsin Environmental Policy Act because there had been no public input into Perrier's secret agreement with the DNR and no serious environmental assessment of the pumping.

Citizen involvement in the case paid off when an important detail emerged that had been unknown to the attorneys until uncovered by tenacious activists. Doing research in DNR field offices, members of Concerned Citizens discovered that the DNR itself had considered stopping Perrier's test pump in Big Springs out of concern that lower water levels were already harming a local fish population. This proved to be a powerful rebuttal to the DNR's own testimony that the Perrier plant would have no impact.

The exposés of the DNR's behind-the-scenes collusion with Perrier were crucial because the judge eventually denied Scanlan's big-picture arguments for the public trust doctrine. However, evidence that the DNR was not forthcoming about its own actions strongly supported the attorneys' second argument, that the department failed a critical test of democratic input under state environmental law.

On January 30, 2002, Judge Richard Wright issued his preliminary decision. He ruled that Perrier's permits to test the springs were valid, and he dismissed the Ho-Chunk Nation's claims in the case. It looked bad. "As I listened," said Hiroshi, "I remember thinking, we're going to have to appeal and raise more funds." But the judge wasn't done. On several essential points, Judge Wright sided with the Kannos and the Nelsons. He found that "there may be significant environmental impacts" from the pumping, and he ruled that the DNR's decision not to prepare an environmental-impact statement was "unreasonable" and violated state environmental law.[24]

The company decided not to appeal, apparently wanting to put the controversy and the constant negative press behind it. Perrier's image was badly tarnished, and the day after Judge Wright released his final ruling in April Perrier made an announcement of its own. The company said it was changing its name from Perrier to Nestlé Waters North America. In September, Nestlé allowed its pumping permits to lapse without challenge. However, company lobbyists remained active in Madison, working hard to block or limit the impact of proposed legislation on groundwater pumping.

For their part, the Waterkeepers in New Haven hired a lobbyist, and, with the Kannos joining in, the two groups campaigned in the state capital for legislation to make it difficult for Perrier—now Nestlé—to come back. In 2004, Wisconsin's new Democratic governor, James Doyle, who had supported the citizens' demands when he was attorney general, signed new groundwater-protection legislation. But Nestlé's lobbyists had succeeded in limiting the law to cover only the largest springs, and it is still not clear whether Big Springs will qualify for protection; leaving the door ajar for Nestlé to return.

Steinhaus said he was ready for a rematch if necessary. "I believe if they came back we could marshal the forces even stronger than we did last time because people are so much more aware of the problems now. I think that people are starting to realize that we have a tremendous, tremendous resource here, and we have to do everything we can to protect it."

The two groups of anti-Nestlé activists have remained separate but respectful, as if understanding that their different approaches may have been the necessary one-two punch to knock Perrier out of Wisconsin. "We were working for the same goal, the same cause," said Steinhaus. "They pursued their end of it," said Hiroshi, "and they did a good job."

He and Arlene have now become water activists on a larger stage. "We have the time, and we're not afraid of the consequences," said Arlene. They have traveled to international water and trade conferences in Vancouver, Kyoto, and Johannesburg, where news of Perrier's defeat preceded them. "We realized," says Hiroshi, "that our water issue is much broader: privatization not only of water, but of resources. It's a whole new world for us really. We knew absolutely nothing about it, and we began to realize, geez, this water issue is really, really a global problem. And we're part of it." "And people were actually looking to us," adds Arlene, "and we realized we have something to offer, some hope just by people fighting."

In fact, as we will see in the next chapter, not far away, Nestlé had already descended on another unsuspecting community, and the Kannos would waste no time sharing their insights and strategies with a new, ad hoc group of unlikely activists.

9

To Quench a Thirst

Mecosta County, Michigan

Michigan's and Wisconsin's history and identity are defined by the world's largest bodies of fresh water. Most of the earth's surface fresh water is locked up in ice. The Great Lakes account for an astonishing 20 percent of what's left. Their watershed covers a vast area of the United States and Canada and provides water for more than thirty million people.

It took three ice ages and a unique geology to bring the lakes into existence as ice and water alternately gouged and washed away the area's softer soils to create a string of basins. Five million years is quick work geologically, but for the various peoples who eventually arrived to live by them the Great Lakes seemed timeless oceans without limit.

But limits have hit hard and seemingly all at once in the Great Lakes watershed. The industries that grew up to exploit the region's abundant mineral resources, growing immigrant populations, and access to transportation are shrinking or exporting jobs in pursuit of cheap nonunion labor. As thousands of workers saw the end of jobs once passed from generation to generation, they also began to see that the lakes themselves were finite and precious.

Water levels in the lakes have reached record lows. Water quality has declined because of industrial pollution, pesticide runoff from agribusiness, and urban sewage, which overflows into the lakes during heavy rains. Water diversions out of the lakes coupled with climate change are altering the natural balance as human use surpasses the rate of replenishment. Only 1 percent of Great Lakes water is renewed each year, and hydrologists warn that without conservation lake levels could plummet five to ten feet, damaging if not destroying navigation, recreation, hydropower, and fish stocks, the very attributes that enabled the region's past success.

The Battle for the Great Lakes

In December 2005, two Canadian provinces and eight U.S. states announced the completion of a long-negotiated agreement called the Great Lakes Compact to prevent unlimited withdrawals of water from the gigantic watershed.[1] A driving reason for the deal—which needs provincial, state, and Congressional approval—was the growing realization that if the Sunbelt South and Southwest could siphon so many jobs and people from the region, could siphoning water be far behind? How long could the Great Lakes states hold out, given that their combined Congressional delegations had dwindled by forty-two seats in as many years?

Southwest states have already been desperately reaching out for water as their populations grow. Salt Lake City and Las Vegas have proposed building pipelines to suck aquifers from under nearby deserts. These sources will not be nearly enough to make up for the expected long-term decline in the Colorado River system, whose every drop is already used seventeen times over before the river reaches the sea, if it gets there at all. The mighty Colorado—carver of canyons—no longer even gets to the Gulf of California much of the time. If a fabled river can be sucked dry, are vast lakes invulnerable? Proposals had already been made to drain water from the Great Lakes for housing development in the Southwest, irrigation in the plains, and bulk export by tanker to Asia. Water that is used in cities and in agriculture inside the watershed flows back into the water table. Once diverted outside the watershed, it does not return to the aquifers, streams, and rivers that replenish the lakes.

Putting a stop to bulk-water diversions may have been the spark for the multiparty talks, but the National Wildlife Federation and other environmental negotiators at the talks were more concerned with lake cleanup than with water exports. "It's kind of like the Stockholm Syndrome," said Maude Barlow, chair of the Council of Canadians. "You kind of make friends with your hostage takers. In this case, it was a promise by the Great Lakes governors to really do some serious cleanup of the Great Lakes, and a number of the environmental groups went along with it thinking they were getting something."[2] Instead, according to Barlow, they got vague industry and government promises to request federal funds to revive lake habitats. "When it became clear that the price tag for this so-called partial cleanup was going to be the loss of control over new diversions from the Great Lakes, some of us just put up a red flag," said Barlow. "I think it opened up the Great Lakes to huge new water takings."[3]

In December 2005, just as the Compact was being signed, a former U.S. ambassador to Canada, Paul Celluci, confirmed publicly what Great Lakes area residents on both sides of the border feared was the secret agenda all along: "Water is going to be—already is—a very valuable commodity, and I've always found it odd where Canada is so willing to sell oil and natural gas and uranium and coal, which are by their very nature finite. But talking about water is off the table, and water is renewable. It doesn't make any sense to me."[4]

This remark was a sign of bigger battles to come, but in small towns in Wisconsin and Michigan the fight had already started, and the driving issue was related to a major diversion loophole in the Great Lakes Compact. The agreement specifically carved out an exception for bottled water, calling it a "product" that may be exported from the watershed as long as the containers are no larger than 20 liters (5.7 gallons).

The loophole was a clear sign of the lobbying and public relations power of the private water industry, which was eager to expand in the Midwest. Critics of the bottled-water exception saw it as a first leak in the dike. That leak would become a torrent unless local movements fought to protect water as a public trust and to counter the influence of industry giants, compromising politicians, developer lobbies, and Sunbelt pressure. The odds seemed overwhelming, but once Wisconsin Dells showed it could be done, the front line shifted to rural Mecosta County, Michigan.

The Unlikely Activist

While the cluttered Kanno homestead in Wisconsin Dells bears every indication of a grassroots operation, Terry and Gary Swier's neat-as-a-pin lakeside house in central Michigan's Mecosta County gives off nary a vibe that it's the nerve center for an equally ambitious movement. The Swiers live out in the country, twenty minutes from the city of Big Rapids. Cows graze in nearby fields, and the British Petroleum station announces a new baby's measurements on the sign next to the latest gas prices.

Terry Swier is a focused woman with short gray hair and intense blue eyes. Now a grandmother and in her late fifties, she lived in Big Rapids from eighth grade until she was twenty-four, when she married Gary. They lived and worked in Flint for most of the next thirty years. Gary was an executive with General Motors and Delphi, the now-bankrupt auto-parts manufacturer. Terry was a reference librarian at the University of Michigan's Flint campus until the couple decided to return to the house on Mecosta's Horsehead Lake that had been in her family for decades. "It's serene," she said, "a little bit of heaven, and I'm fortunate to have a piece of it."[5]

In the fall of 2000, word trickled out that a bottled-water company was planning to draw water from a nearby private deer-hunting preserve called Sanctuary Springs, which was owned by Pat and Judy Bollman. For Swier, it was a major turning point in her life. "I wasn't active in anything," said Swier. "This is a conservative county."

A Nestlé representative came to answer questions at a meeting of the homeowners' association, which represented people living on several lakes near Sanctuary Springs. Swier went with a group of neighbors and friends, and they weren't shy about asking questions. What kind of chemicals would be used to clean the pipes? How could local roads handle 150 truckloads a day? What would be the effect on the environment of removing large amounts of water? "We're talking about our backyard," said one landowner, "and that's why we're concerned." The company representative responded with vague answers that Swier says boiled down to a mantra: "No harm, no problem. No harm, no problem. No harm, no problem." The residents, however, sensed that something wasn't right—and that they needed to get organized, quickly. A group of about one hundred met the following week in the local elementary school. It was a remarkable turnout, fueled by word of mouth, and it set a pattern from the outset.

Librarians like Swier have been unfairly stereotyped as meek and retiring, the ongoing sexist residue of disdain for a profession long dominated by women. But librarians have led national campaigns against censorship and the privatization of information that had been publicly available in libraries and more recently on the Internet. Swier is part of this new generation of librarians. "The reason I'm a librarian," she said, "is because I thought that I could prove to the world that there are people that are not like your typical librarian."

When Michigan Citizens for Water Conservation (MCWC) was formed by scores of area residents in December 2000 in response to Nestlé's plans for Mecosta County, a friend suggested Swier for president because of her research and communication skills. "She knows how to organize because she's a librarian. You know, A-B-C order type thing." "I don't think there's one person in MCWC that believes that the water belongs to Nestlé to take," said Swier. The group's battle cry became "Whose water is it?"[6]

Nestlé on the Offensive

When MCWC started, its members didn't even know they were going up against the largest food company in the world. The interlopers weren't called Nestlé then. Michigan's largest bottled spring-water brand was Ice Mountain, which had been bought by Great Springs Water of America, a subsidiary of Perrier, which had been bought by, and later changed its name to, Nestlé North America, a subsidiary of the Swiss multinational. "They've gone through four different names since they've been here," Swier says acerbically. "And we've always said that the reason is just to keep throwing us off: 'Oh, is this a different company now?'"

MCWC took the step of establishing itself as a not-for-profit, tax-exempt organization with the help of James Olson, a leading environmental attorney in the state, and its members began to do research. They quickly discovered that a year earlier Nestlé's representatives met with the Republican governor, John Engler, and his staff and won their support for an expansion of the company's bot-tled-water business. "Support" doesn't quite express the relationship however: Nestlé had been offered almost $10 million in state and local tax abatements and other subsidies over ten years.[7]

One of the governor's senior aides apparently felt some pangs of guilt about the giveaway. In a "conscience-clearing" memo to his boss, the aide, Dennis Schornack, wrote, "Michigan won't just be giving away the water; it will be paying a private and foreign-owned firm to take it away." And in a later interview he went further: "The plentifulness and purity of the water that drew them [Nestlé] to Michigan was going to draw them here anyway," he said. "Tax abatements were unnecessary and unwise." Schornack estimated Nestlé could clear up to $1.8 million a day when the plant was up and running, a figure Nestlé disputed.[8]

Not surprisingly, Nestlé was ecstatic about the Michigan deal, especially after the company was forced to pull out of Wisconsin in the spring of 2001. "Wisconsin's loss is Michigan's gain," boasted

Kim Jeffery, president and CEO of Nestlé Waters North America.[9] Nestlé had learned from its public relations disaster in Wisconsin, resolving that it would campaign differently in Michigan.

Nestlé moved quickly to neutralize potential opposition. It hired Bill Rustem, an influential political fixer or "facilitator" as he preferred to call himself. Rustem had been environmental adviser to the liberal Republican governor William Milliken in the 1970s and early 1980s, and he had extensive contacts in the state's environmental movement. He was also well connected to the major funders for conservation issues, and his firm, Public Sector Consultants, managed the Kellogg Foundation's People and Land program, which granted well over a million dollars each year to Michigan environmental groups. Nonprofits might think twice before crossing him.

"Nestlé made a big mistake in Wisconsin by going to the purest trout stream," said Rustem. "They moved to another location, but it was too late. You've built the opposition."[10] To avoid that happening again, Rustem took representatives of several key conservation groups on a tour of the proposed Mecosta County pumping site, winning their support.

"The most influential groups in the state had already been approached and were basically for some reason co-opted," said an exasperated Olson. "When I called some of those groups, they basically said, 'Well, you know, we've talked to Bill Rustem, and we think it's a good thing."[11] Some of the groups eventually backtracked and became neutral or critical of the Nestlé deal, but they didn't join the movement MCWC was spearheading.

At Rustem's urging, Nestlé itself gave directly to environmental groups. The Michigan United Conservation Club thanked the company for underwriting its youth magazine; this expression of gratitude inspired a retort from Swier. "Is MUCC selling out the Great Lakes and our water future?" she asked on her group's website. "Shame on MUCC!"[12] And MUCC wasn't alone. Although Wisconsin's chapter of Trout Unlimited had been a leading opponent of Nestlé's plans there, the Michigan chapter initially supported the bottling plant and received a $50,000 grant from Nestlé. The group eventually gave the money back after criticism from MCWC.[13]

Nestlé also took pains to mute criticism of the huge state subsidy it had been offered. Rustem urged Nestlé to show its appreciation for the state's support, and the company dutifully announced that over the next ten years it would donate a half million dollars to care for the local watershed it was pumping.

The company has also taken the public relations offensive by promoting its "Good Neighbor Policy" in a four-color marketing piece. Topping the list of ten good-neighbor commitments was "open communication—with local regulators, office holders and neighbors."[14] That order was significant. Neighbors were always the last to hear, well after company representatives had won state support, scouted potential sites, and negotiated a deal with a local resident with access to water.

The Michigan battle against Nestlé was shaping up to be much tougher than the one in Wisconsin for another reason. In Wisconsin, Nestlé failed to win the support of local elected officials near the proposed plant site. In Michigan, the company made sure early on to wine and dine local leaders in promising areas for plant construction. The company was successful not only at neutralizing potential opposition but also at luring local politicians to compete with one another for its business.

When MCWC members attended a township-sponsored meeting where the Nestlé project was finally to be discussed in the open, they were astonished to see that the packet prepared and handed out by the local officials contained supposedly objective information that was identical to claims on Nestlé's website. In other words, the town representatives were passing off the company line as their own. They didn't even ask for a traffic study. "That was a real red light right there," Swier recalled.

The news that Nestlé had just signed a ninety-nine-year lease to pump from Sanctuary Springs elicited an immediate response from Swier and her allies. They objected to being presented with a fait accompli and asked the township's elected officials for a moratorium so there could be public input. "It was kind of disheartening," Swier says, "because the township basically told us in no uncertain terms, 'We know what's right for you.' And we went away saying, 'We're not scientists, but there's something that just doesn't feel right.'"

This was just the first of countless times when the citizens of Mecosta County felt betrayed by their representatives. However, no elected official in Michigan can be immune to corporate promises of jobs, even if Nestlé was offering only forty-five jobs to start and over two hundred in a few years. That number was barely a dent in a state that had been devastated by three hundred thousand layoffs in the first five years of the new millennium, a hemorrhage of jobs that continues today with plant closures in the auto industry. MCWC considered Nestlé's promise of jobs a form of economic blackmail, and the Big Rapids township supervisor, Maxine McClelland, a Nestlé supporter, seemed to confirm the desperation at the root of the Nestlé deal. "Those of us who are third and fourth generation here," she said, "want to see a diversified economy where our kids don't have to move away to find jobs."[15]

Even many environmentalists were torn. "It's not an environmental emergency," said Andrew Guy of the Michigan Land Use Institute. "This *is* quickly becoming an economic emergency." Water is plainly one of Michigan's greatest assets, and Guy believed, "We've got to figure out how to use this resource to attract new industries."[16]

Nestlé not only promised jobs but also sweetened the pitch by offering the financially strapped local government a new fire truck as a sign it would be a good corporate citizen. To some the gift was chump change, but the water giant put a different spin on community relations. "I think it would be a mischaracterization to suggest that this company doesn't have strong support in the community. In fact, probably overwhelming support in the community," suggested Deb Muchmore, the Nestlé public relations person in Michigan. But, she added, "I think it may be true that a company's first line of responsibility is to shareholders."[17]

"Whose Water Is It?"

MCWC seemed to face an uphill climb. The population in Mecosta County was divided and still uninformed about the issue. As in Wisconsin, Nestlé representatives promised to leave Mecosta County if local residents didn't want the plant. That gave MCWC an opening to educate the electorate and test Nestlé's real support through an initiative campaign.

The group gathered signatures for referendums to block the rezoning necessary to build the bottling plant. However, Nestlé had not yet named a final plant location, forcing MCWC supporters to collect signatures in two townships and countywide, an exhausting process. "I never expected to retire and be busier than I've ever been in my life," Swier said with a wan smile. Swier believed that Nestlé knew all along that it would build its plant in the town of Stanwood, about eleven miles from Sanctuary Springs. "Now we look back and we say we were very green," Swier mused, "because Nestlé knew exactly what they were doing. They had MCWC running in three different directions. . . . I look back on it now and think, How could we have been so dumb?"

Nevertheless, grassroots democracy at the ballot box was beginning to threaten Nestlé's well-laid plans for a $150 million investment. It was time for hardball, and the target appeared to be Swier herself. As the election drew near, she began to get calls from friends and acquaintances reporting visits from unidentified men. This being a rural area, and people being trusting and friendly, the visitors were able to finagle their way inside homes and sound out the owners about the MCWC leader. "Should I have let them in?" one person asked Swier after the fact. Swier believed the visitors were private investigators hired by Nestlé to gather information for a possible effort to isolate her or position her as a liability to MCWC's campaign.

Nestlé's legal team and its supporters in local government went on the offensive. In one township, the town clerk ruled the zoning referendum invalid on a technicality. In the second location, the township board voted to create a new zoning board in order to moot an expected MCWC victory at the ballot box. Swier believed Nestlé's lawyers were at work in both places to ensure those favorable results. MCWC was getting a quick course in corporate power and influence peddling.

Although the initiatives would no longer carry legal weight, a strong vote against Nestlé would undermine the company's claims of near-universal support and give MCWC legitimacy as the representative of majority public opinion. In August 2001, after the seven-month campaign, the voters rejected Nestlé's proposed rezoning for the bottling plant by a two-to-one margin. It was MCWC's first victory, and it demonstrated the growing opposition to Nestlé's plan to pump local springs.

The referendums may have undermined the credibility of Nestlé's promises to leave if not wanted, but nothing seemed to slow the company's ramp-up toward full bottling operations. The same month as the vote, the company obtained the necessary state permits to begin extraction from four wells with a total maximum pumping capacity of 400 gallons a minute, 576,000 gallons a day. It then started work on an eleven-mile pipeline from Sanctuary Springs to the plant site in the town of Stanwood.

MCWC may have been inexperienced and outmaneuvered at first, but its members didn't waste time bemoaning their situation. They retained Olson as their attorney, and he quickly hired a hydrogeologist to review the results of Nestlé's groundwater and aquifer tests, as state regulators were not doing so. The hydrogeologist quickly found evidence to dispute Nestlé's public claims that bottling would not have a harmful impact on water levels. To the contrary, one pumping test had stopped the flow of water from the springs into the local water system! Another Nestlé test showed a 23 percent drop in the flow of the nearby stream, results the company had failed to disclose.[18]

With this information, Olson filed suit in Mecosta County Circuit Court in September 2001 against the Perrier Group of America, Inc., and Pat Bollman Enterprises, on behalf of MCWC and two couples who faced immediate negative impacts from the pumping. Jeffrey and Shelly Sapp owned property on Thompson Lake abutting the Sanctuary Springs pumping site. R. J. and Barbara Doyle resided on the stream whose flow dropped sharply during Nestlé's tests. A few months later, the local Chippewa Indian tribe also filed suit against Nestlé's pumping, but in federal court. Their case was promptly dismissed when a judge decided that the relevant federal law on the Great Lakes gave only states legal standing to sue, not private groups or even tribes. The Chippewa then became important supporters of MCWC's case.

By this time, Nestlé's opponents were pulling out all the stops and paying the price. Anyone who's done political or social-justice organizing has to deal with momentum, morale, and burnout. In Swier's case, the emotional investment was extraordinary. "There are nights where I am up till one, two o'clock in the morning working on stuff and then getting up at six in the morning. Or waking up in the night and saying, 'Oh, I better go and do such and such.' It has really consumed my life."

Nestlé responded to the MCWC suit by threatening some suits of its own. At least three people in the campaign received letters from an attorney accusing them of making "defamatory statements" against "our client, Nestlé."[19] One of the three was Chris Swier, Terry's thirty-one-year-old son, who had been actively supporting MCWC's campaign efforts.

This was not an idle threat but an example of an increasingly common corporate strategy against pesky opponents known as the SLAPP suit. SLAPP stands for Strategic Lawsuit Against Public Participation, and the aim is to intimidate critics, forcing them to spend most of their time raising money to defend themselves rather than pursuing their opposition efforts. In India, PepsiCo had filed a similar suit when the nation's leading environmental group, the Center for Science and Environment, published a study about pesticide residues in soft drinks and bottled water.[20]

The threat against her son had Swier in tears. "I'm done," she told Olson. "I'm finished. They can do whatever they want to me. But when they start attacking my family, I'm not going to do it. My family means more to me than anything else." The threat almost worked. "But as the day progressed," Swier recalls, "people called, and I got madder, and madder, and madder. And finally I said, 'That's exactly what Nestlé wants me to do, to fold my tent and go away. And you know what? I'm not going to give them that satisfaction.'" Ultimately, nothing developed with the threatened SLAPP suit. But the episode angered Terry's other son, Paul, so much that he turned down a job interview with Ralston-Purina, a Nestlé subsidiary, because he said it would be an insult to his mother.

Meanwhile, Olson had his hands full with a series of motions and responses in the state court system, and as the case moved slowly toward trial, the costs were mounting fast. Every time Nestlé's attorneys filed a motion, MCWC had to respond with counter-motions and testimony from its own experts. With no paid staff and no real budget, MCWC depended on volunteers to pay even the paper and postage costs for its newsletter out of their pockets, while Nestlé coasted on its immense financial resources.

Swier and MCWC launched a constant stream of grassroots fundraising activities: bake sales, raffles, garage sales, beach parties, water tours, silent auctions, and collecting returnable bottles and cans. The newsletter even publicized a volunteer's willingness to make her famous meat pastries in return for contributions. "There were no influential people here at all," said Swier. "It's a true grass-roots movement."

Not a single person was paid to do the work, but almost all the people who came to MCWC's first meeting continued to be actively involved. Olson was in awe. "It's phenomenal what these people have done and what they're doing." And they were doing it largely on their own. "We were out there for a long time all by ourselves," Swier recalled, "and it's a scary thing to be out there and have no one." That situation was about to change in ways that some MCWC members found disconcerting.

Reinforcements Arrive

The statewide Sweetwater Alliance was a grassroots group of a different stripe, rooted in the traditions of student, antiwar, and civil rights protest. Formed in early 2002, its environmentalism was based in a critique of privatization and corporate globalization, and while its members included veteran activists, its core was young people.

Among its leaders in Northern Michigan was Holly Wren Spaulding. In her late twenties and bearing a resemblance to Audrey Hepburn, Spaulding had been inspired by the Seattle antiglobalization protests of 2000, but her focus on water emerged from a childhood connection to springs, wells, and streams. Her parents were homesteaders with the back-to-the-land ethos of the 1960s. Home schooled until the fourth grade, Spaulding was raised in northern Michigan without indoor plumbing. "I grew up living on the land, and we didn't have running water," she remembered. She still gets her water from a well where she lives near Traverse City, ninety miles north of Mecosta County. "Most of us have our own wells, and so people talk about how their water tastes." She laughs, "Like, 'I have really great well water.'"[21]

Returning to Michigan after graduate school, Spaulding joined other young activists to start an independent newspaper linked to the Indymedia movement, which took off after Seattle. In 2002, as Olson was building MCWC's court case, Spaulding interviewed one of his colleagues about Nestlé's plans. "That was how I entered the stream, so to speak, with the issue of water bottling in Michigan."

Sweetwater brought needed energy and a new vocabulary to the existing MCWC campaign against Nestlé. "We introduced the word *privatization* to the whole debate," she said. "Prior to that, I think it's fair to say it was more of a NIMBY [Not In My Back Yard] struggle."

Sweetwater members were media-savvy, eager to break the news blackout imposed by Mecosta County's intensely pro-Nestlé local paper. They also brought a willingness to raise hell and get arrested. "We had interesting, creative political actions that were worthy of news. They *were* news. So that gets you out there, and people started to talk about it. So we improved the level of literacy on the issue," said Spaulding.

Sweetwater entered the scene with a bang, first in Traverse City with a Central Michigan University campus punk-rock fundraiser called "Fuck You, Perrier!" and then with what Spaulding called "a legal picket" in front of the plant site with contingents from all over the state. "We didn't want to stir up trouble, as it were, right away," said Spaulding. "We wanted to give space for the locals to partici-pate." Members of the Chippewa tribe joined the protest dressed in traditional garb. There was even a spectacular sign of good fortune from nature itself when an eagle circled overhead. "That's not what MCWC was organized for," said Swier. Protest and civil disobedi-ence were a far cry from MCWC's culture, which tended toward bake sales and newsletters.

Spaulding agreed, characterizing MCWC members as "middle-class people" concerned about Nestlé's impact on their quality of life. "It was probably initially a little bit of an uneasy alliance," she said. "There were at least some in MCWC who were kind of like, 'Who *are* these kids?' They had never seen anyone like us before." Swier's reaction to "these kids" was different. "Thank goodness for Sweetwater Alliance, because most of the people in Michigan Cit-izens for Water Conservation were all pretty straight."

MCWC and Sweetwater maintained their different perspectives, tactics, and constituencies in their "uneasy alliance," but they shared the same goals. For Spaulding and Sweetwater, water bottling in Michigan is part of a larger issue—namely, increased corporate power at the expense of the human right to water, particularly for poor peo-ple, whether in faraway Bolivia, rural Mecosta County, or urban Detroit.

Sweetwater activists also emphasized making cross-race and cross-class coalitions, especially in Detroit, where they allied with the Michigan Welfare Rights Organization to oppose water cutoffs to thousands of people unable to pay their utility bills. The group asked how the state could offer Nestlé millions in subsidies to take and sell public water at the same time that Detroit was cutting off water for inner-city residents. The Detroit coalition also accused city officials of using the cutoffs as an opening salvo in a campaign to privatize their water system.[22]

For its part, MCWC had had a worldview limited to the local bottling issue. But Swier started seeing a shift as her organization's members outgrew a reactive NIMBY stance. "The whole case started as a very local issue," she said, "but it's not local at all. In the years that we've been [fighting], it has gone from a very local issue to a county issue, to a state issue, to a U.S. issue, to a global issue. We didn't know that when we started. We just believed in what we believed."

Pumping Begins

By May 2002, Nestlé had completed initial construction of its plant and pipeline, and on May 23 the company announced it had begun commercial pumping from Sanctuary Springs to the plant. It was a depressing moment for Swier and Spaulding, but Sweetwater Alliance stepped up a series of morale-boosting mobilizations.

The group set off on a tour of small towns in Michigan to drum up support and bring in volunteers. Young activists started flowing into Mecosta County, camping out at a "water warrior base camp" near the bottling plant. Seven protesters blockaded the plant, locking themselves together at the shipping entrance while supporters picketed. Supportive counselors at a Jewish youth camp brought their kids up to the action as July temperatures rose into the nineties.

The uneasy alliance between MCWC and Sweetwater was beginning to become fun. "The next thing you know we were becoming friends," said Spaulding, "and people who owned big, fancy homes [were] hosting us." To call attention to the potential harm that Nestlé's pumping would do to local lake levels and recreation, Sweetwater organized a "canoe-in." A member of MCWC hosted the Sweetwater boaters at what Spaulding called "a palatial home on the lake." After a potluck picnic, they launched their canoes and kayaks from the front lawn. "You don't get that a lot of times, that mixing of classes and mixing of social backgrounds," Spaulding notes. "The water really did bring diverse people together."

The young activists then paddled toward the lake's headwaters at Nestlé's pumping site. "We wanted to see what the springs looked like," said Spaulding. But as the stream narrowed, they encountered a chain-link fence. It was the hunting-preserve boundary. "If you peer through the fence, you can see the land on which the well is located," Spaulding chuckled. "It's completely defoliated and covered in deer shit," she laughed. "The marketing with this bottled water is that it's this bucolic, pristine, natural spring water. And in fact, it's being pumped from this land that is probably contaminated with animal feces."

But not everything about the campaign was as much fun. The lack of unity inside the environmental movement on the water-bottling issue was a baffling obstacle for MCWC. For the first three years of the struggle, MCWC had support from only a few groups, including Sweetwater, the local homeowners' association, Indian tribes, and several fishing clubs. Swier said turf may have had something to do with it. "No one had heard of Terry Swier or [MCWC Vice-President] Rhonda Huff. We just appeared out of nowhere and started running. So maybe people in the environmental movement thought, 'Who are these people?'"

Cyndi Roper of Michigan Clean Water Action agrees. "They were very much alone because people didn't get it, including me," she said. Environmental groups typically focus on wildlife protection, pollution, and habitat preservation. The issues of the public ownership of water and privatization were a leap. "I hadn't connected the dots between water bottles today and supertankers tomorrow," said Roper. "It's taken two years to open that debate inside the environmental community."[23]

In addition, groups may have been worried about their budgets, as many of the largest environmental funders in the region, including the Joyce and Kellogg foundations, have avoided confronting questions of corporate power, limiting their grant-giving to less controversial issues acceptable to their board members. "They don't want to upset the apple cart," said one environmental activist.

Rustem dismissed that idea and said the split in the environmental movement "had been there all along," but he agreed that the defining issue had become ownership of water and the right to use it. "I don't think you can properly regulate water use," he said. "You get away from resource regulation and move to social regulation. . . . If we go in that direction, you're going to have a regulatory system that makes decisions on lots of reasons and that scares me. Where do you draw the line?"

But drawing a line when it comes to public water resources was exactly what Swier and MCWC were about, and they were doing it by crossing the normal political divisions between Republicans, Democrats, and independents. MCWC's views were rooted in the community and not subject to the compromises of politicians and parties. As a result, they could create a new political alignment. That depth of conviction and local credibility were the essential factors that eventually persuaded other groups to support MCWC on the broad issues of ownership and control of water. A new coalition finally coalesced with the help of Clean Water Action, the Sierra Club, and other organizations. "It's been a struggle," said Swier, "but it's taken off a lot of pressure since this coalition got together."

Meanwhile, MCWC faced a series of legal hurdles in its court case against Nestlé. In Michigan, water is held in common by all, but landowners may pump water from under their land as long as the use is "reasonable"—that is, it does not harm any of their neighbors. As far back as 1874, a Michigan Supreme Court articulated a principle for allocating water among various users: "Water is a movable, wandering thing, and must of necessity continue common by the law of nature."[24]

However, such decisions in the past considered only surface water. The movement of groundwater was little understood by scientists, much less by jurists. "The doctrine of 'reasonable use' did not consider the impact of groundwater pumping on streams and watersheds," wrote law professor Robert Glennon in his book *Water Follies*. "The law is virtually ignorant of hydrological reality."[25] A 2004 study by the U.S. Geological Survey illustrated just how overpumping has started to affect the continuum between groundwater and surface water in the Great Lakes. Cities and industry are pumping so much water from the aquifers under Lake Michigan that they are pulling water in through the bottom of the lake, for the first time reversing a flow that is millions of years old.[26] "Michigan is the only state that is completely surrounded by water, and we are the state [that] does not have strong water legislation," Swier pointed out. "Does that make sense? That's what MCWC figured out not too long into our battle: Where is the legislation? Where are the people who are supposed to be protecting our water so it's public and not private?"

Lurking behind the Nestlé controversy is a much larger issue—diversion of water from the Great Lakes to developers and consumers elsewhere in the United States and abroad. In 1998, the provincial government of Ontario approved a proposal to export fifty tankers of lake water a year to Asia. Citizens of the region were furious, the company was forced to give up its permit, and Great Lakes governors and premiers vowed to prevent such outrages in the future.

However, Nestlé contends the diversion issue is a scare tactic that has nothing to do with water bottling. "Bottled water has gotten linked with the diversion issue, and I think it's a false linkage," Nestlé attorney Michael Haines asserted. "Bottled water does not use that much water compared to other products. It's in distinct packages. People don't buy bottled water to water their lawns or other things. I think people that are against bottled water for other reasons have linked it to the diversion issue to marshal the public concern. I think there is no linkage. A diversion is something where the water goes in bulk, somewhere else, so that they can do something with it there."[27] Nestlé lobbyist Rustem framed this argument more colorfully. "If you start down that path, where do you stop? We can't be in the business of saying if you drink water in Detroit and drive across the Great Lakes Basin, you have to come back to Michigan to go to the bathroom."[28]

Obviously, this debate has a lot to do with the power of images. It is easy to see a supertanker loaded with water as a bulk diversion from the lakes, but an individual twelve-ounce bottle of Nestlé's Ice Mountain brand is an innocuous thirst quencher. It's difficult to extrapolate the long-term consequences of buying bottled water from a six-by-six-foot supermarket display.

However, the original supertanker export proposal was to ship about 160 million gallons a year. That's far less than the 240 million gallons a year Nestlé could pump from the springs in Mecosta County alone, and the company was already developing new sources, including wells in the town of Evart, just fifty miles north of its Stanwood plant in Mecosta County.

Nestlé's attorneys are also working hard to delink water bottling from other issues, such as privatization of municipal water services. "I don't see how bottled water is privatization," said Haines. "I think that the privatization issue is a very legitimate issue in social and public policy. What should be government owned? What should be government run? What services can be privately run? When does that make sense? And we do have a lot of privately owned utilities that are government regulated, and that seems to work. But I don't see what that has to do with bottled water. Water bottlers are a user of water like other companies, like other beverages, like baby formula."

Juxtaposing images has become standard for supporters of the water-bottling industry, and to some extent they have a point:

industry and industrial agriculture have been profligate in their use of water to produce food and other commodities. But Nestlé isn't making anything. It is merely exploiting a substance in the public domain, pasting on its brand name, shipping it out, and marking it up for sale by a factor of a hundred or more.

"Our history," said environmental journalist Guy of the Michigan Land Use Institute, "has been [to] harvest natural resources and use them for our economic benefit, whether it was skinning the fur off of beavers in the frontier days or chopping trees in the lumber era. Our natural resources have always been the underpinnings of our economy and our culture. The reflex in the state was to welcome with open arms a water bottling company that's organized around that same principle of resource extraction and exploitation."

MCWC's campaign and court case were now putting this issue squarely in the center of Michigan politics. As the coalition supporting MCWC grew, environmental and citizens' groups in Michigan began demanding government intervention and action on a number of major water issues. In 2002, the Democratic attorney general, Jennifer Granholm, ran for governor, and the future of water became one of her defining issues. Standing next to Swier in the capitol rotunda, she criticized the Nestlé deal and warned the sitting governor that the precedent could lead to "a massive water grab."[29] In November 2002, she won the election but was faced with a Republican-controlled state legislature that had its own ideas about water legislation. Dozens of water bills were proposed, including one by Granholm herself, but almost all of them languished and stalled in the legislative process.

"It feels like no one listened," said Swier. "So the case of whose water it is has ended up in the courts."

Justice

The case of MCWC, the Doyles, and the Sapps versus Nestlé Waters North America and the Bollmans finally went to trial on May 5, 2003, a full year after commercial pumping began and twenty months after the case was originally filed. Swier was worried about Judge Lawrence Root, a Republican who had a reputation as a conservative jurist. "Many people predicted he would never rule in our favor, and on the first day he was frowning." The merits of their argument notwithstanding, all Swier and her MCWC cohorts could do was hope that he was a fisherman.

The trial itself was as arduous as the long journey to the courtroom. It lasted from May to September with 360 exhibits and 27 witnesses, a vast amount of data for the judge to digest before making his ruling. Swier noticed a slow change in Judge Root's demeanor during the trial, especially after he commented dryly that the testimony by Nestlé's hydrologist "throws a glimmer of light on him in the role of being a 'company man.'"[30] The judge seemed to be frowning less and less, "and then the frowns were gone and I felt, 'He gets it!'" But it may have been only an illusion, born of hope and exhaustion.

The testimony went back and forth. MCWC member and co-plaintiff Shelly Sapp brought into court the snapshots she had taken every day since pumping began. They showed a growing mud flat in the stream, and co-plaintiff R. J. Doyle testified that mud flats had never been as large in the forty years he had lived on the banks. The judge took two trips to the area in dispute, canoeing up the stream with his wife on one occasion. Even after the public testimony, the two sides continued presenting briefs throughout the summer. Judge Root called it "undoubtedly the most extensive and intensive [case] in the history of the 49th Judicial Circuit." Root had a folksy side, sharing life-passage events that had occurred since the suit was filed a year and a half earlier. "My two daughters were married," "I learned of my wife's closest uncle's death," and "Our youngest daughter . . . is expecting our first grandchild."

For MCWC attorney Olson, the lawsuit was turning out to be a financial bath. "It put [my firm] into a tailspin for a few years," he said. "And the only reason we took the case was that I was the guy who started the firm, and I wanted to do it." Olson originally had estimated a legal tab of $150,000, but it eventually topped a million dollars. Swier and MCWC sent out a steady stream of fundraising letters, bringing in hundreds of new members to help fund the legal process.

For Swier, the pressure was enormous. "Gary and I have been married thirty-seven years, and in the last five years we've had more arguments than we have had in our entire marriage," she confided, adding that she's lucky to have a husband who "thinks like I do. . . . I'll be very honest. It's been very stressful. Because I want it all. I want to be a grandmother. I want to be a wife. I want to be a mother. And I want to fight Nestlé."

Final arguments in the court case were presented in September 2003. As both sides hunkered down to await the decision, there was a disturbing report. Nestlé workers found unexploded, homemade firebombs at a pumping station. The FBI launched an investigation of "eco-terrorism" and initially pointed fingers at activists associated with Sweetwater Alliance. Sweetwater angrily denied any involvement by its members and charged it was the victim of a witch-hunt. Ultimately, the FBI investigation went nowhere.

After more than two months, on November 25, 2003, Judge Root handed down his sixty-seven-page decision and commented, "In the words of the Grateful Dead, 'What a long, strange trip it's been.'" Biting their nails, Swier, Olson, and plaintiff Sapp went to the courthouse to pick up the written decision. Swier recalled the moment. "Jim came out of Judge Root's office with the decision, and then he went flat up against the wall and gasped, 'I can't believe we won it all.'"

In his opinion, Judge Root emphasized that the case was not about the bigger issues—unemployment in Michigan, bulk-water transfers, the future of the Great Lakes, or privatization of water. However, Root's decision did establish a series of extraordinary precedents, not the least of which was to recognize that public opposition and the health of streams are important even when "measured against the magnitude of [Nestlé's] operation and investment." The stream and its adjoining wetlands, he wrote, "are beautiful and valuable resources not to be lightly disregarded just because someone wants to remove water from its watershed for a commercial product."

The opinion focused on the specific issue of whether Nestlé's groundwater pumping violated the doctrine of reasonable use because it might harm the surface water sources, and therefore the riparian rights, of residents who lived along nearby lakes and streams. The judge accepted MCWC arguments that there was "adverse impact" to the surface waters and that under common law in Michigan "riparian interests are superior to conflicting groundwater interests." His final conclusion was a vindication for MCWC. "In closing," wrote the judge, "I have ordered the termination of all water withdrawals by the defendants from the well field at the Sanctuary Springs. Such must occur within 21 days." MCWC was ecstatic. Nestlé would have to shut down pumping by December 16, 2003.

Foreseeing objections to the ruling because of Michigan's economic straits, the judge wrote, "The prediction (threat?) that Nestlé employees will lose their jobs and the community lose a valuable corporate citizen and taxpayer is entirely in the control of the decision makers at Nestlé. They can develop alternative water sources that do not present the kind of risks that this one does and, after an initial capital outlay, continue bottling and selling water. They came into this situation aware of the risks and must now regroup to deal with the consequences of losing."

As MCWC members left the courthouse with copies of the decision, they saw Nestlé's lawyers go by in a car, deep in argument about what to do next as they drove the wrong way up a one-way street. In fact, Nestlé immediately launched a public relations and political lobbying offensive against what the company called an "extreme" decision, which it said threatened not only 120 jobs in Mecosta County but potentially many thousands more. The company asked, "What water user—industrial, commercial, golf course, or farmer—would not be in similar violation?"[31]

But Judge Root had disagreed. State law, he ruled, "recognizes the value of water being incorporated into products from Michigan and sold wherever a market can be found. However if water is the product, the rationale loses its logical force in the face of the higher social value of preserving water as water. Given that water is a natural resource on its own, I believe the state has a rational basis on which to limit its removal from the state and/or the Great Lakes Basin."

On December 15, Nestlé asked the Michigan Court of Appeals for a stay of Root's decision pending appeal. That same day, company lawyers reportedly held a private noontime meeting with top officials of Governor Granholm's administration. The result was a shocker. The Granholm administration agreed to support Nestlé's appeal. Michigan environmental leaders were furious. "They're in bed with the wrong folks," said the head of the Michigan Environmental Council, and the Michigan Land Use Institute termed the administration's decision "a slam dunk victory" for the company.[32] With the political establishment falling into line, it was not a great surprise that the Appeals Court granted the stay. Despite MCWC's victory with Judge Root, the pumping continued unabated.

Swier had supported Granholm and met with her numerous times during the gubernatorial campaign, but now MCWC found its access denied. "I've written her letters, and I have never received one response, not had a meeting with her at all," said Swier. It was a disillusioning moment, especially because Swier had convinced a number of MCWC members to vote for a Democrat for the first time in their lives on the basis of the water issue. "I have had people in MCWC come to me and say, 'I will never vote Democrat again.'"

While the appeal was pending, MCWC took on new initiatives. By the summer of 2004, it had raised a total of $350,000 from small donations and fundraising events to support the court action. MCWC then expanded its focus, helping to create a coalition of some forty other organizations to lobby the region's governors, who were negotiating the Great Lakes Compact agreement on water use and diversions.

The Compact would limit bulk-water exports out of the Great Lakes watershed but made an exception for bottled water. Critics contend this is not a minor flaw but instead leaves the Great Lakes open to all kinds of water raids. Once water is defined as a commodity, they warn, it could come under the jurisdiction of global trade agreements that open markets in goods and services. Multinationals have lobbied hard for free trade in water at ongoing trade talks. They have failed to win that concession so far but only because of strong popular opposition from international organizations and state coalitions like the one that MCWC helped create.

"We're now working again to put a finger in this dike," said Swier, who never imagined that she would be taking on international trade issues. It made her realize that she herself was going through changes. "What I have learned! My vocabulary has changed. My friends have changed. It has been such an education!"

In November 2005, almost two years after Nestlé won a stay of Judge Root's decision, the state Court of Appeals issued its ruling. It upheld most of the lower court's findings about harm to the local watershed but established a new test for balancing economic and environmental impacts. In effect, the court said, Yes, there is an impact, but we can ignore it because the jobs and economy are more important. Swier said the ruling "opens the door to Nestlé or any other future users of water to compete against local homeowners. All of us will be forced into competition with giant corporations."

The initial precedent-setting victory had turned into a nightmare. Swier was furious because the Court of Appeals stated that individuals and citizens' groups would have to wait until they had already suffered and documented substantial injury before going to court—if, that is, they could afford to. She said the ruling makes the public trust "stand in line" with private interests that want "to sell our common water for use somewhere else."

In early 2006 Governor Granholm signed legislation giving the state oversight of big water users. But the new law followed the Great Lakes Compact language, allowing water exports as "a product" in containers under twenty liters. Environmentalists called the law "the first legally sanctioned mass diversion of water from the Great Lakes in 100 years."[33]

MCWC wasn't done with its case or with its statewide lobbying efforts to put a moratorium on new and expanded bottling operations. At the start of 2006, at the direction of the Court of Appeals, MCWC and Nestlé negotiated an agreement to reduce Nestlé's pumping during fish spawning, dry seasons, and droughts, but the Court also set a bad legal precedent in overturning the lower court's breakthrough decision. "Michigan is giving away its birthright to its water legacy," Olson said in typically blunt fashion. In March 2006, he appealed the case to the Michigan Supreme Court.[34]

Although citizens' groups like MCWC often try to put a good face on bad turns of political fortune, it would be hard to call their battle with Nestlé a victory. MCWC and Swier's accomplishments, however, go far beyond a column of wins and losses. They've created a team that's very much in the race and a cause that won't be going away. "No matter what the court decision turns out to be," said Swier, "MCWC has opened people's eyes." Sitting in her home office, she looked up at the Margaret Mead quote pinned on her bulletin board: "Never doubt that a small group of thoughtful, committed citizens can change the world. Indeed, it is the only thing that ever has."

Whose Water, Whose World Is It?

The stories we tell in this book are just a few examples of a growing grassroots rebellion that has stunned the private water industry. In the space of a few years, scattered local coalitions to protect water as a public trust have coalesced into the beginnings of a formidable national and international movement. As we have traveled across the United States, we have seen an increasing awareness of, and involvement in this new movement—from groups of college students rallying against the abuses of bottled-water companies, to local citizens' groups challenging privatization, to national consumer, environmental, and labor organizations fighting to protect public resources. This wellspring of energy and depth of commitment signal a remarkable reaffirmation of public participation in our communities and in political life.

The challenge is formidable. In the United States alone, billions of dollars are needed to keep our water safe, clean, and accessible. That financial hurdle, once the chief rationalization for privatizing water, no longer appears insurmountable—in part because the water movement has helped shape a new consensus.

The movement may be young and without the trappings of a political party, celebrity endorsements, or centralized authority. But it has dedicated leadership, astute research and analysis, the power of a popular cause, and, as we've seen, the support of autonomous local groups throughout the country that are increasingly coordinating their efforts and sharing their experiences.

A 2005 national poll shows that an extraordinary 86 percent of Americans support the creation of a federal water trust fund like the existing ones that provide grants for highways and airports.[1] Republican Party pollster Frank Luntz told a House subcommittee in 2005 that he found it hard to believe the level of public support for federal involvement in water. "I have been a professional pollster for almost twenty years," Luntz testified, "and I can tell you from personal experience that such an overwhelming consensus about the role of Washington does not happen often—but it exists here."[2]

What is it about water that creates such consensus even after more than twenty-five years of conservative agitation against government spending? The essential nature of water—our irreducible and undeniable need for it—seems to evoke an almost instinctual conviction that water is about us as a community rather than as a collection of individual consumers. That's a far cry from Stockton Mayor Gary Podesto's call to "think of our citizens as customers." Instead, water inspires us to take collective action as engaged caretakers of the public interest.

The stories in this book show it is possible to win against what seems like overwhelming odds. We have watched local political coalitions battle some of the world's largest corporations to a stalemate and, in some cases, win victories. Several of those corporations have retreated from the conflict, an extraordinary sign of success for disparate and largely unconnected local campaigns. Water-sector investment analyst Debra Coy acknowledged the impact of these local actors. "RWE, Veolia, Kelda, and Suez have all found it a discouraging experience to deal with local American politics, and they have become less enamored of the water business here," she wrote. "Aggressive opposition has clearly had a chilling effect on the PPP [public-private partnership] market."[3]

Perhaps advocates of grassroots action have overestimated the power of the multinationals. Perhaps they are more fragile, more dependent on our passivity than we thought. Studies of labor activism have overturned previous assumptions that citizens must act on the same global scale as the multinationals they confront. Instead, these studies suggest that strategic localism can sometimes defeat the plans of a global corporation.[4]

Water itself helps the cause. Heavy, slippery, and unwieldy to transport, it resists being made into a commodity. Even a multinational company has to deal with the localness of water in our streams, rivers, and springs. Down they must come to our towns and neighborhoods with their public relations people, lawyers, and lobbyists, and there the battle has been joined with a kind of joyful ferocity by impassioned citizens.

Nevertheless, the obstacles to local action against privatization are formidable. With headlines like "There's Money in Thirst" (*New York Times*), "A Pipeline to Profits" (*Business Week*), and "Water Outperforms Oil" (*Bloomberg News*), it's clear that water is in play in the marketplace. A swarm of investors has been convinced that money can be made in water. Once that notion becomes accepted wisdom, it's hard to eradicate.[5]

A huge sea of restless cash now moves globally, the result of tax cuts, high corporate profits, and globalization. Like tides, hundreds of billions of dollars wash up on shores around the world in search of investment vehicles. That cash has driven up not only the stock prices of private water companies but also investor expectations of ever higher returns on dwindling supplies of the resource. Once-staid utilities are now the focus of a speculative market, which represents a real threat to a resource that requires stable, steady, long-term investment in infrastructure. Even the head of the largest U.S.-based water company is worried about the threat posed by the "flipping" of utility stocks based on short-term price moves. "I'm concerned about turning our precious water resources over to any private equity buyers who are highly leveraged, bring short-term investment horizons, and have little or no experience in water quality and utility management," said Aqua America chairman and CEO Nicholas DeBenedictis.[6]

The once-stable water sector has now become a risky, if potentially lucrative, business, especially with the entrance of new players eager to make a bundle. Investment companies, venture capitalists, and leveraged buy-out firms have swept up billions in world-wandering dollars to invest wherever they can find the vehicles. These companies have exactly the kind of history that DeBenedictis is worried about. They buy whole companies using enormous amounts of debt, slash services and staff, and then resell the "streamlined" business through an initial public offering (IPO) to investors seduced by buzz and marketing. RWE, burned by unexpected local conflicts in the water sector, was thrilled to see the hype generate a bidding war for its Thames Water subsidiary in Great Britain. Nowadays, buying and selling a water company is much more profitable than owning and running one.

In this increasingly turbulent market, some old blue-chip industrial firms are viewed as rocks of stability. General Electric, ITT, Dow, and Siemens are buying up smaller technology firms that specialize in filtration and desalination. These appear to be the normal activities of large industrial companies rather than the speculative excesses of new financial players, but they are still premised on the idea that water scarcity will be the source of future profits. As population, pollution, and climate change increase pressure on clean water supplies, investors seek new, potentially profitable technologies to purify contaminated water.

The local political movements working to ensure that water remains a public trust appear to be on the sidelines of these great flows of capital. But ultimately the money flow still has to depend on the real world's flow of actual water to slack a thirst, to grow a plant, or to catch a fish.

The Learning Curve

North American water activists have learned hard lessons not only from bruising fights on their home turf but also from water conflicts in the developing world. Similar and repeated patterns have emerged. In particular, we have seen that successful campaigns against privatization occur when communities organize early and proactively. Once the companies have a foothold at City Hall, they are hard to dislodge.

We have seen community coalitions win support from Republicans and Democrats and make efforts to cross borders of race and culture. The growing movement for environmental justice in minority communities is a natural ally against privatization, as are unions that represent water workers, but only if the specific needs of their constituencies are recognized by the coalition. Faith communities—including conservative church groups—are potential allies because the poor are hardest hit by the increased rates sought by private companies and because of an innate resistance to profiting from a substance that many religions associate with holiness and sanctification.

A number of the struggles described in this book ended up in court, but lawsuits should be a last resort and should be avoided if possible. Stockton activists have had their case tied up in the courts for years. Michigan activists have suffered rulings that compromise the public trust. Community groups, and even their attorneys, have grossly underestimated costs and financial hardships, time frames, and the potential obstacles of an increasingly conservative judiciary. Michigan activist Terry Swier called it "legal strangulation."

Lawsuits rarely bring about social change. As one environmental attorney told us, "Even the most dramatic legal victory of our time, *Brown* v. *Board of Education*, banning segregation, came about only after decades of social action and, even then, would not have been implemented unless the movement took that victory and fought for it in the South and later in the North." Yet, he added,

"Martin Luther King would not have had a moment's pause in asserting the importance of targeted legal actions. Occasionally a judge will do profound justice."[7]

Part of the learning curve for community groups has been grappling with the tendency to avoid becoming entangled in the compromises of political office and elections. However, the choice between taking the high road and playing hardball in politics may be a false dichotomy. A growing number of mayors are fed up with the corporate orientation of the U.S. Conference of Mayors. They have convened the New Cities Project to develop policies for a strong public sector that is not held hostage by contractors.[8] Local control and public accountability are high on their agenda, but it is often hard to find ways for local coalitions to work with such policy-oriented elected officials.

One surprising arena for cooperation is international trade negotiations, which are aimed at stripping both local officials and their communities of authority over water and other services. Media pundits were shocked when World Trade Organization meetings brought out tens of thousands of protesters for the "Battle of Seattle" in the fall of 2000. Trade negotiations are complex, secret, and dominated by corporate lobbyists. How could it be that students, trade unionists, and some local elected officials were even paying attention, much less working together? These coalitions have achieved important successes, but the corporate agenda still drives the negotiations. The multinationals are still pressing for agreements that would permit trade courts—operating in secret sessions—to overrule local government regulations on the environment, health, and worker safety as unfair restraints on trade.

If the private water companies are able to impose their will through internationally-ratified trade treaties, it will be far more difficult for cities like Chattanooga, Peoria, Champaign, Charleston, and Lexington to succeed in their efforts to take control of their water services. We may even see what many fear are the multinationals' ultimate goals: virtually unrestricted privatization, crippling of government regulations that ensure water quality and accessibility, and open season for bulk-water trading.[9]

Corporate Initiatives

The private water industry and various market-oriented entrepreneurs have proposed a series of initiatives to create new water markets for profit-seeking investors. Schemes for private bulk-water storage and transport have become popular among some entrepreneurs, but they have turned out to be tough to implement. Ric Davidge's proposal to ship water in giant bags down the California coast was quickly scuttled by enormous public opposition, as was Keith Brackpool's idea to "bank" water in a Mojave Desert aquifer.[10] However, other water speculators are still in the hunt, including legendary oil entrepreneur T. Boone Pickens, who has spent some $50 million to buy Texas water rights for potential sale to cities and real estate developers.[11] Like the bottled-water companies, these entrepreneurs aim to exploit the weaknesses of current water law and regulation to commandeer vast quantities of public water that they can sell for a windfall profit.

In addition, entrepreneurs, cities, and some farmers have exerted strong pressure to create water markets to facilitate the transfer of agricultural water rights to urban development. Agriculture remains by far the nation's—and the world's—largest consumer of water. In the United States, agriculture accounts for about 70 percent of all water used. Reducing agricultural water use by just 10 percent would double the amount available to cities.[12] But the question is, Who will control that water? Who can afford to pay the price? And will any of that water be returned to the environment?

Other potential areas of privatization are proliferating. The water industry is proposing and lobbying for dozens of water-desalination projects, particularly on the coasts. The late Illinois senator Paul Simon believed that by giving us access to ocean water, desalination would be the Holy Grail of water supply, another technological quick fix for a deeper social and political problem. But even with techno-logical advances, desalination uses enormous amounts of energy at a time of rising prices and fears of global warming. In addition, chemi-cals and the super-salted residues from the process pose a serious threat to local waters, especially to sensitive coastal estuaries. And, ominously and under the radar, desalination also opens the door for private companies to own and sell the flow from the enormously expensive plants they build. A 2006 study by the Pacific Institute con-cludes that desalination may be useful in some circumstances, but other options, especially conservation, should be tried first.[13]

Yet another potential vehicle for privatization is recycled water from sewage-treatment plants. The water returned to a river from some of these plants is cleaner than the water in the river itself. Such water is already being used for landscaping and to water golf courses, where it is affectionately called "pee to tee" or "butt to putt." Real estate developers are using the promise of recycled water to help them justify large-scale development projects to skeptical environmentalists and regulators. A major unanswered question is who will have the rights to recycled water. Will private operators of publicly owned sewage plants have the right to sell recycled water to the highest bidder as if it were another commodity? Or does the treated water remain part of the public domain?

A Return to Public Stewardship

Unlike the more abstruse issues of corporate globalization and trade deals, the right to control affordable, accessible, and sustainable water resources is an emotional touchstone that reaches people in their cities, towns, and homes. As we have seen, the issue inspires people to fight for human rights, local control, and democracy where they live, and to extend solidarity across boundaries of nationality, race, religion, income level, and political affiliation.

Government response to these movements has been mixed. On the local level, mayors and city councils continue to be in desperate need of infrastructure dollars. But an example from New York City shows there is still no replacement for the long-term commitment of the public sector. Five hundred and fifty feet below the streets of Manhattan, construction crews have been boring through bedrock in the dank air and eerie light of one of the largest public-works projects in American history. It's called Water Tunnel #3, and it started more than thirty years ago.[14] In August 2006, the mayor of New York posed for pictures in the tunnel as workers completed a new section. It was an important milestone in the long and ongoing construction project. More important than increasing the potential flow of drinking water to the city, opening this new section will allow city workers to close and inspect the city's two old tunnels, built in 1917 and 1934. The flow in those tunnels has never been interrupted for repairs because some engineers feared the tunnels could collapse without the continuing pressure of the water running through them. Even if the tunnels held, workers weren't sure the old valves would work to shut off the flow. Worse, they weren't sure they could get the valves open again afterward. The risk of cutting off the city's drinking-water supply was simply too great. At the cost of twenty-four workers' lives and $6 billion, Water Tunnel #3 has become a symbol of the long-term commitment needed to assure uninterrupted public water and sewer services for future generations. But where will that kind of commitment to the public come from in future years?

We have seen some positive signs. Even pro-privatization politicians have become wary of the high prices and short-term profit horizon of private water companies. After high-profile disasters like the one in Atlanta, politicians are thinking twice before proposing public-private partnerships (PPPs) for water. When Food & Water Watch researchers asked the editor of *Public Works Financing* magazine why so few PPP contracts had been signed in 2005, he responded simply, "You guys."[15]

But these initial anti-privatization successes and PPP disasters are no guarantee for the future because the problems that sparked the privatization drive are still with us. While the privatization of drinking-water systems has slowed, the number of private contracts for wastewater grows. We are seeing fewer PPPs in large cities, but more in smaller towns. The retreat of RWE and some of the other major multinationals may even make it easier than it has been for investors and smaller private water companies to gain ground under the covering rationale that they are local or U.S.-based rather than "foreign" corporations. Already, large U.S.-based companies like Aqua America and OMI are on shopping sprees to acquire local systems.

The struggle for control of water is also a struggle for access to talent. Corporations, whether multinational or national, are competing for valuable human resources in the water sector. Just as federal, state, and local governments have allowed their infrastructures to decay, they have also abandoned their human infrastructure, their existing corps of experienced employees, by cutting funds and support for training, new experiences, and intergovernmental cooperation. Compare that lack of support in the public sector to the attractive training packages offered by multinational companies. For example, when Intel decided to build a new plant in Israel, it flew hundreds of workers and their families to a training campus in Portland, Oregon, for a year to prepare them for the work they would be doing. Accounting giant KPMG sends a thousand student summer interns to an all-expenses-paid training camp in Orlando, Florida. This isn't just a luxurious perk. These people are learning skills, teamwork, and esprit de corps. They are also seeing that they are valued by a company that treats them well.[16]

Public utilities have not been funded adequately to support and sustain their employees, but good models are emerging. One, a public-*public* partnership, brings together public agencies in different countries. With adequate funding, it could become a kind of Marshall Plan for the 90 percent of world water agencies still in public hands. Public Services International (PSI), a global confederation of public sector unions, has spearheaded this idea, winning support from the United Nations for what PSI's David Boys calls "systematic coordination among public utilities" to share resources and skills across national boundaries. Programs are already under way in Europe, Latin America, and Africa.[17]

Such "reengineering" efforts have been successful in U.S. cities. In San Diego, the Wastewater Department and the union, the American Federation of State, County, and Municipal Employees, collaborated to enhance operational efficiency and ended up saving $37 million, nearly double the target amount. In King County, Washington, a program that targets savings has reduced the need for large rate increases. In Miami, after a successful reengineering program, employees received pay increases while water rates remained the same. In Stockton, the public water department had already slashed costs through a reorganization, but the effort was politically sabotaged by a city government intent on privatization.[18]

Finally, the need to conserve water has become an obstacle to privatization. Private companies have little incentive to conserve water because payments and profits increase with rising water consumption. But cities with public water systems, including Los Angeles, Seattle, Tucson, and Boston, have reduced water use, often dramatically, through consumer-friendly conservation programs. New York City's Department of Environmental Protection recently reported that water use had dropped 28 percent since 1979 in spite of increased population.[19]

Private companies like to sell expensive, high-tech solutions to water problems. Low-tech conservation techniques won't make anyone a profit, but they can be much more efficient means for individuals and society to save money, water, and the environment. One example is rainwater harvesting—collecting rain in tanks, ponds, or aquifers so it can be reused; this technique has been used successfully in rural India and in cities like Berlin, Beijing, and Austin, Texas. In India, long-dry rivers are flowing once again as a rainwater-harvesting revolution has transformed desert landscapes into productive farm fields. The basis of the change is a communal water ethic—a social commitment to future generations. We can learn much by listening to the stories of others around the world.[20]

The 4th World Water Forum, Mexico City

In the spring of 2006, we traveled to Mexico City to meet up with the "water warriors" once again at the World Water Forum. It had been three years since we filmed the protests at the previous Forum in Kyoto, and much had changed.

One of the most jarring differences was the location itself. Unlike Kyoto, Mexico City faces a devastating water crisis. A magnificent metropolis of twenty-four million, the largest in the world, this historic city is sinking into the bed of a bygone lake, an Atlantis in the making. Ancient pyramids and colonial churches crack slowly as the earth settles due to the depletion of the city's aquifers. Water gods with daunting names are legion in this ancient capital of the Aztecs: Tlaloc rules the rain, and Chalchiuhtlicue rules the "horizontal water"—the lakes and rivers—but the gods have seemingly abandoned the city . . . or perhaps they are just waiting for revenge.

Contaminated water and dried-up springs make Mexico the world's third-largest market for bottled-water companies, which see opportunity in the country's failure to adequately invest in a public water supply. Trucks carrying water tanks lumber through Mexico City's cobbled streets at night, and plastic bottles are neatly stacked in the back of every corner bodega, ready to safely quench your thirst—if you can afford it. Even at the World Water Forum, supposedly dedicated to making water accessible and affordable to all, a bottle of water cost $1.50.

The Forum was filled with such contradictions. It welcomed all who paid the price of admission, but it was clearly dominated by the private water industry, which used the event to advance its agenda through direct participation on panels, glossy handouts, and the ubiquitous presence of polished public relations flacks. But here, too, the growing water movement intervened to challenge privatization, and the message started to echo in the press. Forum leader Luc Fauchon of the World Water Council was quickly put on the defensive in press conferences where he clearly expected to deliver lectures rather than to be interrogated. He complained that 95 percent of reporters' questions were about privatization. "Let me repeat," he said in obvious frustration, "privatization in the case of water is *nonexistent*. We will not make progress in financing if we don't repeat this for the media who want to create ambiguities."[21]

The industry's defensiveness grew when tens of thousands of people marched from the city's Independence Monument to the convention complex past thousands of police officers dressed in full body armor. The peaceful protesters, led by peasant women from the Mexican countryside, carried the message of water as a human right for all—hardly a subversive idea. Yet the situation had become so polarized that conference attendee Patrick Cairo, executive vice president of Suez's U.S. subsidiary United Water, described these critics as "a vocal minority of ideological opponents" who "take to the streets in violent protests."[22]

By the end of the conference, the Forum's organizers, in an apparent fit of pique, blocked any reference in the final declaration to water as a human right because doing so would carry certain legal obligations and guarantees under international treaties. Instead, they substituted vague pabulum: water is "a guarantee of life for all of the world's people."[23] The head of UNESCO voiced dismay, contending that signatories to the United Nations Charter have a "moral obligation" to consider water a human right.[24]

Civil-society groups called for access to water to be recognized as "a fundamental and inalienable human right." Their declaration demanded that every human being be allocated the minimum amount necessary for hygiene and good nutrition "free of charge" to ensure that the poorest people in the world have enough water to live.[25]

The civil-society groups spent little time at the Forum itself. Instead, they held their own International Forum in Defense of

Water, a sign that the movement had advanced considerably beyond the protest orientation at the Kyoto Forum three years earlier. This time, the coalition included a larger spectrum of grassroots groups, unions, and indigenous peoples, with access to increasingly sophisticated analytic and research tools and respected international leaders like Oscar Olivera, leader of the uprising against Bechtel in Bolivia. In a Mexican union hall covered with colorful murals, Olivera challenged the international water activists to confront the practical difficulties of delivering community-controlled water in a corporate-controlled world. "Like water, we must be transparent and in movement," he said. "We cannot just complain to governments now—we must move forward to build an alternative."

A clear example of how such a movement can be built comes from a town in an unlikely country. Eighty percent of people in France get their water from private water companies. The world's two largest global water companies, Veolia and Suez, are based in France and are powerful players in national and local politics. Michel Partage hardly seems their match. The gregarious and charming mayor of Varages, a village near the Riviera known for its vineyards and ceramic dinnerware, Partage has sparked a movement that is gathering strength across France.

It started, Partage explained to activists in Mexico City, when he and other residents had had enough of the foul, swimming-pool taste of their drinking water. Being French, he thought that this situation was not only intolerable but unpatriotic. When he looked into the matter, he found that the town's private water provider did so little to maintain the system that it over-chlorinated the water to make sure no one got sick. In addition to this insult to the palate and the insult of poor service, the company said it wanted a 100 percent rate increase because it claimed to be losing money. "So we decided to help them out," said Partage, "by cutting off the contract and re-municipalizing the water supply."[26]

The ensuing battle of Varages pitted a village of two thousand proud *citoyens* against Suez, one of the world's largest corporations.

But democratic, egalitarian tradition runs deep in rural France. Partage and his supporters called for a referendum to take the water back, and won 93 percent of the vote.

"The day that decision was made our stomachs hurt because we were terrified we couldn't do it," recalled Partage. It was an enormous challenge, especially because many French cities have ceded control of their water for so long that they no longer have the skills needed to run their water departments. With its water under public control, Varages found it could hire additional workers, improve service, and increase investment without raising water rates. "Like a little baby that realizes it can breathe on its own, we realized we could do this ourselves," said Partage. The Varages victory was not merely economic but gastronomic. According to Partage, "The water is not only cheaper, it tastes much better!"

In 2005, Partage and supporters, including Danielle Mitterrand, wife of the late president of France, issued "The Call from Varages" for public management of drinking water. "Water, the patrimony of humanity, a responsibility of local citizenry since the French Revolution . . . must be a right and must not be controlled by the rules of the market. . . . We invite all elected officials and the citizens of France to join us in this resistance."[27] The Call has gathered support from mayors around the country. "Many are afraid," said Partage. "The important thing is to not be alone."

Communities in the United States are beginning to realize that they, too, are not alone. Again and again, from Lee, Massachusetts, to Mecosta County, Michigan, from Stockton, California, to Lexington, Kentucky, the efforts we see to preserve or restore water as a public trust and human right have returned to the same themes. The fight for water has inspired citizens to regain confidence in their ability to control their own destiny, to effectively participate in decisions and to recharge not only aquifers but democracies that have fallen under corporate control. "Our thirst," said Bolivia's Olivera, "is not just for water, it is also a thirst for justice."

In the United States, our century-old public water system provides clean, inexpensive, regulated water around the clock to tens of millions of people. It has been a model for and the envy of much of the world. But after years of neglect, public water is weakened and embattled. The outcome of the current conflict between corporations and citizens' movements to control this precious resource will be decided in the years to come. Whether clean and safe water will remain accessible to all, affordable and sustainable into the future, depends on all of us. The stakes could not be higher. The outcome will surely be a measure of our democracy in the twenty-first century.

Notes

Preface

1. We first heard about the water bags from Jill Hannum and Karen Ottoboni of KZYZ-FM Radio in Mendocino County, California. The story has since taken on the quality of an urban legend, like the alligators in the New York City sewers. However, it really did happen: U. Jones and Friends of the Gualala River, "Proposed Water Export from Two Northern California Rivers Faces Opposition," undated, http://www.gualalariver.org/export/ujarticle1.html; M. Geniella, "Alaskan Defends Proposal to Ship Mendocino Water South," Press Democrat, Feb. 11, 2002; E. Bailey, "Plan to Bag Rivers May Not Float," Los Angeles Times, March 2, 2002; R. Davidge, interview on KZYX-FM, Aug. 2, 2002; J. Rossi, "Is the Water Bag Proposal a Trojan Horse?" North Coast Journal, Feb. 6, 2003; World Water, SA, website: http://www.worldwatersa.com/management.html

2. Enron's water unit, Azurix, was broken up and sold in pieces, with its North American operations going to American Water Works, which was later acquired by RWE/Thames; American Water Works, "American Water Works to Acquire Azurix North America," press release, Aug. 6, 2001. Enron's close connections to the Bush family had enabled its expansion. The company used those connections to advance privatization of public services abroad. In 1999, Marvin Bush, the youngest son of former president George H. W. Bush, visited Argentina to lobby on behalf of U.S. companies, including

Azurix, which won the contract for water services in Buenos Aires province in June of that year. Two years later, as Enron collapsed, the administration of George W. Bush intervened in Argentina in support of Azurix. L. Henales, *The Water Sector of the Province of Buenos Aires* (Buenos Aires: unpublished report, Dec. 2002); Inter Press Service, "Enron Used U.S. to Bully Poor Nations," *AlterNet*, June 2, 2003; K. Bayliss and D. Hall, *Enron: A Corporate Contribution to Global Inequality*, Public Services International Research Unit, University of Greenwich, June 2001, www.psiru.org; C. McCarthy, "Enron's Looming Demise Sinks Madera County Water Bank Plan," *Fresno Bee*, Dec. 1, 2001; B. Murphy, "Final Chance to Buy a Vowel," *Houston Chronicle*, Dec. 3, 2002; Canadian Broadcasting Corporation, *The Fifth Estate*, "California: Enron and the Dot Com Bubble That Burst," broadcast Mar. 31, 2004, http://www.cbc.ca/fifth/deadinthewater/california.html.

3. *Thirst*, Snitow-Kaufman Productions, 2004. National broadcast premiere on PBS series *P.O.V.*, July 13, 2004, http://www.pbs.org/pov/thirst. See also http://www.thirstthemovie.org.

4. The World Water Council website is http://www.worldwater council.org. The site also includes information about the World Water Forums.

5. The World Bank loans about $20 billion a year to the less-developed countries of the world. This money is leveraged with billions of dollars of loans from other international financial institutions like the International Monetary Fund and the Asian Development Bank. Together, these institutions control the fate of much of the developing world's economies, their development strategies, and the payments on their soaring national debts. About $3–5 billion of the World Bank's aid is related to water, and much of that is designated for large infrastructure projects like dams and hydroelectric projects, but it also funds municipal water-supply services, particularly through the establishment of public-private partnerships. J. Briscoe, senior water adviser, World Bank Water Resources Management Group, *Water Resources Sector Strategy* (Jan. 1, 2004), http://www.worldbank.org; On World Bank conditionality, see

N. Alexander, *A Critical Analysis of the UN Millennium Project's Approach to MDGs* [Millennium Development Goals] (Citizens' Network on Essential Services [CNES], Sept. 2005), http://www.servicesforall.org, especially p. 3: "The World Bank claims that it has reduced the policy conditions attached to its loans substantially. However, in saying this, the Bank is playing a 'shell game.' For middle-income countries, the Bank has begun issuing 'guidelines for engagement' for borrowers. Like conditions, the 'guidelines' carry threats of reprisal insofar as, when governments do not heed the guidelines, the Bank withdraws financing." Also, N. Alexander, *The Roles of the IMF, the World Bank, and the WTO in Liberalization and Privatization of the Water Services Sector,"* Citizens' Network on Essential Services, Oct. 21, 2005, http://www.servicesforall.org; T. Kessler, *Who's Taking Risks? How the World Bank Pushes Private Infrastructure and Finds Resistance in Some Surprising Places* (Citizens' Network on Essential Services, July 2004), http://www.servicesforall.org; International Consortium of Investigative Journalists, M. Beelman, and others (eds.), *The Water Barons: How a Few Private Companies Are Privatizing Your Water* (Washington, D.C.: Public Integrity Books, 2003), pp. 14–15.

6. On the World Water Forums, see the World Water Council website, http://www.worldwatercouncil.org; M. Barlow and T. Clarke, *Blue Gold: The Fight to Stop the Corporate Theft of the World's Water* (New York: New Press, 2002). On the human right to water, see Blue Planet Project, http://blueplanetproject.net; Food & Water Watch, http://www.fwwatch.org/water/right; United Nations Economic and Social Council, *General Comment No. 15: The Right to Water* (Geneva, Nov. 26, 2002): "The human right to water is indispensable for leading a life in human dignity. It is a prerequisite for the realization of other human rights"(paragraph 1). "The human right to water entitles everyone to sufficient, safe, acceptable, physically accessible and affordable water for personal and domestic uses" (paragraph 2). "State parties have a constant and continuing duty under the Covenant on Economic, Social and Cultural Rights to move as expeditiously and effectively as possible toward the realization of the right to water" (paragraph 18).

7. G. Podesto, Mayor of Stockton, "State of the City, 2003," speech delivered Feb. 19, 2003, Stockton, California.

8. G. Podesto, interview with authors, Feb. 12, 2003.

Chapter One: Water: Commodity or Human Right?

1. A. Garnier, conference speech at "Profiting in the Water Industry: Tapping a Reservoir of Wealth," New York City, June 8, 2006, quoted in "Behind the Lines," blog by Food & Water Watch, June 19, 2006, http://www.foodandwaterwatch.org/blog/archive/ 2006/06/19/behind-the-lines/?searchterm=Garnier; "Water Outperforms Oil, Luring Pickens, GE's Immelt, Guy Hands," *Bloomberg News,* June 26, 2006, http://www.waterindustry.org/New% 20Projects/investment.-4.htm.

2. N. Hundley, *Privatization of Water Utilities in Light of California History and Common Sense,* 2004, http://www.pbs.org/pov/pov2004/ thirst/special_california.html.

3. Aaron Burr's Manhattan Company was like privatization on steroids. The state government gave the company substantial rights to eminent domain, exclusive water rights in the city, and a contract in perpetuity. It could set water rates as it saw fit, and it did not even have to repair streets it tore up for pipe laying. That wasn't a big problem, however, because the company didn't do much pipe laying. In fact, the Manhattan Company was a mere front operation to get government funding to start a bank to compete with Burr's enemy Alexander Hamilton's Bank of New York. The Manhattan Company never supplied significant water to the city, but it did make personal loans to Burr that totaled only slightly less than its spending on water delivery. (At the time, Burr was vice president of the United States.) It took decades for the city to break the Manhattan Company's monopoly on water rights. G. T. Koeppel, *Water for Gotham* (Princeton, N.J.: Princeton University Press, 2000), esp. pp. 70–101.

4. G. Palast, J. Oppenheim, and T. MacGregor, *Democracy and Regulation: How the Public Can Govern Essential Services* (Sterling, Va.: Pluto Press, 2003). The book focuses primarily on energy regula-

tion but also refers to water privatization, especially in Britain. See, in particular, p. 6: "What America has is the toughest, strictest, most elaborate system for regulating private utility corporations found anywhere in the world (with the possible exception of Canada). This may come as a surprise. America, after all, has sent out an army of consultants to every corner of the Earth to extol the virtues of deregulation, free markets, and less government. But this is an export-only philosophy, not applied within the U.S. itself." In India, in the state of Tamil Nadu, a leading public water official told us that he and others had been astonished to learn that U.S. water systems are in public hands after so many Americans (and the World Bank, which they considered to be an extension of U.S. policy) had lobbied them to privatize their troubled water systems; interview with Vibhu Nayar, project director, Tamil Nadu Water Supply and Drainage Board, Feb. 1, 2006. On regulation, Michael A. Cohen, former senior adviser to the World Bank's vice president for environmentally sustainable development and now director of the International Affairs Program at the New School, told us that an effective regulatory system reflected as high a state of economic development as a working water system. "Why assume," he asked us, "that it's easier to regulate a service than provide it directly?" Interview with authors, Dec. 24, 2002.

5. There are about fifty-four thousand drinking-water systems and sixteen thousand wastewater systems in the United States. Private systems serve between 15 and 16 percent of the population. However, most drinking-water systems are extremely small. Of the fifty-four thousand, forty-six thousand serve fewer than one thousand people, and the majority of these are privately owned. However, because the large public systems serve so many more people, they dominate the sector. Environmental Protection Agency, *Community Water System Survey*, 2003, http://www.epa.gov/safewater/cwssvr.html; G. Wolff and E. Hallstein, *Beyond Privatization: Restructuring Water Systems to Improve Performance* (Oakland, Calif.: Pacific Institute for Studies in Development, Environment, and Security, 2005), p. 93, provides a summary of many studies on the impact of private companies on the

delivery of water services. The summary concludes that of the two major forms of privatization, investor-owned utilities and contracting out of service management, "contract operations are serving far fewer people than private, investor-owned utilities" (a little over four million compared with thirty-six million). The large companies profiled in this book all pursue both types of investments, owning water services as well as seeking contracts to manage water services (often called public-private partnerships); for example, RWE/ Thames owned Lexington's Kentucky-American Water but was a contract operator of water service in Stockton, California.

6. American Water Works Association, "Water Industry's Optimism Eroding," press release on State of the Industry report, June 13, 2006, http://www.awwa.org/communications/mainstream/2006/ 0620/Lead13stateofindustry_main06202006.cfm.

7. Urban Water Council, "2005 National City Water Survey," *Urban Water Council Newsletter,* Spring 2006, p. 12.

8. Congressional Budget Office, *Future Investment in Drinking Water and Wastewater Infrastructure,* Nov. 2002, http://www.cbo.gov/ showdoc.cfm?index=3983&sequence=0.

9. M. Barlow, speech at Third World Water Forum in Kyoto, Japan, Mar. 2003, special-features section of DVD *Thirst,* http://www. bullfrogfilms.com.

10. Editorial, "And the Winner Is Bechtel," *New York Times,* Apr. 19, 2003.

11. RWE planned to spin off its United States division, American Water Works, the largest private water company in the country, in a 2007 initial public offering. American Water's assets include California American Water and Kentucky American Water, which are involved in the public battles described in Chapters Three and Five. "RWE Sees IPO of American Water in Second Half of 2007," *Dow Jones International News,* Oct. 23, 2006.

   In October, 2006, RWE announced the sale of its British-based water division, Thames Water, to Macquarie Bank, an Australian investment group, which has become so well-known in financial circles for its purchases of global infrastructure that its deals are called "Macquisitions." In buying Thames, Macquarie traded up, selling its smaller British water property, South West Water, in a move that fits the company's reputation for being "unashamedly and aggressively oriented to making as much as it can as fast as it can." *Guardian* columnist Will Hutton quotes one unnamed Australian executive as saying that Macquarie's approach is to "hollow out what it holds and walk away." As for Macquarie's qualifications for owning and operating a major public utility, Hutton concludes, "Ownership matters profoundly. I find the spectacle of the management and direction of the water supply of 11 million people being auctioned to the highest bidder, in which the character and long-term intentions of the buyer are allegedly of no concern to anyone, close to unbelievable. Yet that is what we are witnessing." Macquarie is already an important water player in the United States, having purchased Aquarion, the largest private water company in the Northeast (see Chapter Seven). E. Conway and B. Harrington, "Macquarie Buys Thames Water in 8 Billion Pound Deal," *Daily Telegraph*, Oct. 17, 2006; N. Chowdhury, "Eyes on the Prize," *Times Asia*, Jul. 2, 2006; W. Hutton, "Old Father Thames Is Being Sold Down the River," *Guardian*, Oct. 22, 2006; D. Reid, "Aquarion Divisions Sold," *Springfield Republican*, Feb. 25, 2006.

12. International Consortium of Investigative Journalists, M. Beelman, and others (eds.), *The Water Barons: How a Few Private Companies Are Privatizing Your Water* (Washington, D.C.: Public Integrity Books, 2003), p. 2.

13. Internal Revenue Service (IRS) Procedure 97–13, 1997. The tax-code change enabled cities to use tax-exempt bonds for capital construction carried out under privatization contracts. Gaining increased access to tax-exempt municipal financing (which is less expensive than private financing) was a major priority for the water industry and its allies, including the Urban Water Council of the U.S. Conference of Mayors, which played a leading role in lobbying the Clinton administration for the IRS rule change. "Contract Operations Continues to Grow Despite Rumblings of Public Doubt," *Environmental Business Journal*, 1(5/6), 2002, 1–12; Wolff and Hallstein, *Beyond Privatization*, p. 93; M. Hudson, "Misconduct

Taints the Water in Some Privatized Systems," *Los Angeles Times*, May 29, 2006.

14. Interview with authors, Dec. 20, 2002.

15. In the United States, wholesale sales for bottled water exceeded $10 billion in 2005, a 9.2 percent increase over the $9.2 billion in 2004. Volume exceeded 7.5 billion gallons. International Bottled Water Association, "Bottled Water: More Than Just a Story About Sales Growth," press release, Apr. 13, 2004; T. Clarke, *Inside the Bottle: An Exposé of the Bottled Water Industry* (Ottawa: Polaris Institute, 2005).

16. M. Barlow and T. Clarke, "Who Owns Water," *The Nation*, Sept. 2/9, 2002.

17. Interview with authors, Dec. 20, 2002.

18. "New Jersey Indicts 2 Ex-United Water Executives," *Asbury Park Press*, June 16, 2006; G. Mulvihill, "Water Executives Accused of Hiding Radium," Associated Press, June 16, 2006, http://www. northjersey.com/page.php?qstr=eXJpcnk3ZjczN2Y3dnFlZUVFeXk 1JmZnYmVsN2Y3dnFlZUVFeXk2OTQ4ODE5JnlyaXJ5N2Y3MT dmN3ZxZWVFRXl5Mg==.

19. M. Hudson, "Misconduct Taints the Water in Some Privatized Systems," *Los Angeles Times*, May 29, 2006. Industry think tanks, lobbying groups, and trade associations provide similar testimonials— for example, Water Partnership Council, *Establishing Public-Private Partnerships for Water and Wastewater Systems: A Blueprint for Success* (Washington, D.C.: author, 2003). Conservative think tanks backing the industry include the National Council for Public Private Partnerships, the Reason Foundation, and the Canadian Council for Public-Private Partnerships.

20. Office of Water Services (OFWAT), "Bigger Is Not Always Better in the Water Industry," press release, Jan. 14, 2004. "[The consultants] found there was no clear evidence of economies of scale for the water service companies. They also found significant diseconomies of scale—unit costs rising as companies get bigger—for water and sewage companies, although these are now declining." The full report is Stone and Webster Consultants, *Investigation into Evidence*

for Economies of Scale in the Water and Sewerage Industry in England and Wales, www.ofwat.gov.uk/./publish.nsf/AttachmentsByTitle/stone_webster_150104.pdf/$FILE/stone_webster_150104.pdf.

21. Quoted in M. Ester, "Dry Hole: Great Expectations for Private Water Fail to Pan Out," *Wall Street Journal,* June 26, 2006.

22. Concerned Citizens Coalition of Stockton, *Annual Service Contract Compliance Review* (Stockton, Calif., Dec. 7, 2004); M. Hudson, "Misconduct Taints the Water in Some Privatized Systems," *Los Angeles Times,* May 29, 2006; Food and Water Watch, *Faulty Pipes: Why Public Funding—Not Privatization—Is the Answer for U.S. Water Systems,* June 2006, p. 17, http://www.foodandwaterwatch.org/publications/reports/faulty-pipes.

23. *Lexington Herald-Leader,* Feb. 4, 1995, sec. B, p. 8; cited in *RWE and Lexington Timelines,* 2004, http://www.lwvky.org/Lexington_LWV/water.htm. S. Pfarrer, "Water for Profit: Should Private Companies Manage Public Supplies," *Daily Hampshire Gazette,* May 5, 2006. Felton, California, was the fifth of six local districts whose water rates were studied in Santa Cruz Local Agency Formation Commission, *Proposed Felton Amendment to San Lorenzo Valley Water District Sphere of Influence* (Santa Cruz, Calif., July 2003), p. 45. Felton's Friends of Locally Owned Water says that with a new rate increase the town's private water company will be charging residents double what they would pay if they received their water from the nearby public water district; http://feltonflow.org/ratecalc. The deputy city manager of Thousand Oaks, California, said residents served by a subsidiary of RWE/Thames are paying one-third higher rates than neighbors across the street, who buy water from the city; S. Skeel, "Who's in Charge of Our Drinking Water?" *California Coast and Ocean,* Winter 2003–2004, p. 31. A survey of eighteen water providers in Ventura County found that Thousand Oaks's Cal Am had the highest rates; G. W. Griggs, "Sale of Thousand Oaks Water Utility to German Corporation Approved," *Los Angeles Times,* Dec. 20, 2002, p. B3, cited in Polaris Institute, *RWE Corporate Profile—Updated August 2003,* http://www.polarisinstitute.org/polaris_project/water_lords/corp_profiles/corp_profile_rwe.html.

24. Interview with authors, Dec. 20, 2002.

25. P. H. Gleick, G. Wolff, E. L. Chalecki, and R. Reyes, *The New Economy of Water: The Risks and Benefits of Globalization and Privatization of Fresh Water* (Oakland, Calif.: Pacific Institute for Studies in Development, Environment and Security, 2002), p. 38.

26. G. Cross, *A Dynasty of Water: The Story of American Water Works Company* (Voorhees, N.J.: American Water Works Company, 1991), p. 175 The utility company's public relations strategies after World War I included programs that trained employees to be "missionaries for private ownership."

27. Cited in M. Hudson, "Misconduct Taints the Water in Some Privatized Systems," *Los Angeles Times*, May 29, 2006. Because water-privatization decisions are made locally, the bulk of private water-company political and lobbying spending is on attempts to influence local or state governments rather than the federal government. In California, the state's ten largest private water companies spent more than $1 million from 2000 to 2005 on state and local political races and ballot initiatives, according to a *Los Angeles Times* study compiled by Maloy Moore; T. Reiterman, "Small Towns Tell a Cautionary Tale About the Private Control of Water," *Los Angeles Times*, May 30, 2006.

28. E-mail message from Peter Gleick to authors, May 5, 2005. For many years, US Filter, then the subsidiary of Veolia, sponsored the Conference of Mayors website, where it was the only company to appear on the masthead.

29. W. Finnegan, "Leasing the Rain," *New Yorker*, Apr. 8, 2002, http://www.newyorker.com/fact/content/?020408fa_FACT1; O. Olivera and T. Lewis, *Cochabamba! Water War in Bolivia* (Boston: South End Press, 2004); J. Shultz, *Bechtel vs. Bolivia: The Bolivian Water Revolt*, a compilation of articles by a writer who has covered Bolivia for many years, http://www.democracyctr.org/bechtel/.

30. International Consortium of Investigative Journalists, Beelman, and others (eds.), *The Water Barons*, p. 2.

31. Cyndi Roper, interview with authors, Jun. 8, 2006. A veteran environmentalist, Roper, along with her organization, Clean Water Action, eventually became deeply involved in opposing commodifi-

cation and privatization of water in Michigan and the Great Lakes. In Roper's view, "I don't think many environmental groups are focused on issues of justice and affordability. They have been focused on habitat and wildlife, but it's not just about having fish, but about having healthy people."

32. Interview with authors, Mar. 8, 2003.

33. M. De Villiers, *Water: The Fate of Our Most Precious Resource* (Boston: Houghton Mifflin, 2001), esp. pp. 246–260; J. Rothfeder, *Every Drop for Sale* (New York: Jeremy P. Tarcher/Putnam, 2001), esp. pp. 128–131; M. Barlow and T. Clarke, *Blue Gold: The Fight to Stop the Corporate Theft of the World's Water* (New York: New Press, 2002), esp. pp. 129–132 and 136–139; J. Opie, *Ogallala: Water for a Dry Land* (Lincoln, NE: University of Nebraska Press, 2000), esp. pp. 274–279.

34. Luntz Research Companies, *New Poll: Americans Overwhelmingly Support Federal Trust Fund to Guarantee Clean and Safe Water* (Alexandria, Va., Mar. 3, 2005). These poll results from a conservative Republican pollster emphasize the nonpartisan nature of the public consensus on water. "Among young and old, male and female, Democrat AND Republican, the demand for clean and safe water is universal. An overwhelming majority of Americans—91%—agree that 'if, as a country, we are willing to invest over $30 billion dollars a year on highways and more than $8 billion a year on our airways, we certainly should be willing to make the necessary investments in our nation's rivers, lakes and oceans.'" Also see *Faulty Pipes: Why Public Funding—Not Privatization—Is the Answer for U.S. Water Systems* (Washington, D.C.: Food & Water Watch, June 2006), pp. 6–8.

35. G. Podesto, presentation at the Urban Water Council session at the U.S. Conference of Mayors annual meeting, June 2003.

Chapter Two: Hardball vs. the High Road

1. Unless otherwise indicated, all quotes in this chapter are from interviews conducted by the authors in 2003 or from City Council or Concerned Citizens Coalition of Stockton (CCCOS) meetings

attended by the authors. These interviews include those with Mayor Gary Podesto; Municipal Utility District Senior Plant Maintenance Supervisor Michael McDonald; former Municipal Utilities District Director Morris Allen; CCCOS Chair Sylvia Kothe; CCCOS members Dale Stocking, Dezaraye Bagalayos, and Bill Loyko; City Councilman Larry Ruhstaller; Vice-President Dreda Gaines, Thames Water America; President Don Evans and Executive Vice-President Gary Miller, OMI.

2. G. H. Wolff, cover letter to Mayor Podesto and Stockton City Council for report *Independent Technical Review of Proposed Water Sector Privatization* (Oakland: Pacific Institute for Studies in Development, Environment and Security), Jan. 22, 2003. The first conclusion stated in the summary in the cover letter reads in full: "The potential savings from privatization in Stockton have been greatly overstated. For example, our analysis found that continued City operations would be less expensive than private contract operations (negative $1.7 million net present dollars)."

3. Podesto's 2002 letter to the *Stockton Record* is cited in D. Siders, "His Days as Mayor Done, Gary Podesto Leaves Stockton with a Window of Opportunity," *Stockton Record*, Dec. 31, 2004. In an interview with the authors, April 3, 2003, Podesto said, "I referred to the group as not being experts in this area, and I called them butcher, baker, and candlestick maker. That probably lingered along the way, and I think probably created more animosity." CCCOS members eventually adopted the characterization as their own inside joke. Their comprehensive annual reviews of the privatization contract have been signed "BBC Consulting."

4. For information on OMI, see the company website, http://www.omiinc.com. The company has focused primarily on wastewater treatment plants, which tend to be less controversial privatizations than drinking water systems, but OMI has had its share of controversy, including charges that it falsified water-quality reports in several small cities where it had contracts. In 2003, federal agents seized documents and computer files from wastewater plants operated by OMI in Santa Paula, California. In June 2006, the company settled the Santa Paula complaint, which had charged it with

"unlawful, unfair, or fraudulent acts," but by that time OMI was long gone, having pulled out of Santa Paula in 2004, leaving the city "up the proverbial creek without a paddle" in the words of the *Santa Paula Times*. P. Kelly, "OMI Pulling Out as Santa Paula Wastewater Treatment Plant Operator," *Santa Paula Times*, Feb. 11, 2004; C. Miller, "Two OMI Plants in Hot Water." *Stockton Record*, Mar. 19, 2003; Press release from County of Ventura District Attorney, http://da.countyofventura.org/06-051.htm, Jun. 29, 2006.

More serious charges were leveled in connection with OMI's winning a contract in East Cleveland, Ohio, in 2002. According to Food & Water Watch, "Federal prosecutors say the company won the contract by bribing [Mayor Emmanuel] Onunwor through a series of intermediaries. Onunwor was sentenced to nine years in prison, and the leader of the plot—who was not connected to OMI or CH2M Hill—was later convicted of bribery. In 2004, OMI pulled out of East Cleveland because the city fell into arrears on payments. Food & Water Watch, *Faulty Pipes: Why Public Funding—Not Privatization—Is the Answer for U.S. Water Systems*, Washington, D.C., June 2006, pp. 19–20.

5. Thames's involvement in Stockton preceded its purchase of American Water Works Company, which was not involved in the consortium with OMI. RWE's English-language website is http://www.rwe.com/generator.aspx/language=en/id=450/home.html. The history of Thames Water can be found on the company's website, http://www.thames-water.com/UK/region/en_gb/content. Less complimentary histories include: Food & Water Watch, *RWE/Thames Water: A Corporate Profile*, Apr. 2006, http://www.foodandwaterwatch.org/water/rwe; Polaris Institute, *RWE Corporate Profile—Updated August 2003*, http://www.polarisinstitute.org/polaris_project/water_lords/corp_profiles/corp_profile_rwe.html; E. Lobina and D. Hall, *UK Water Privatization—a Briefing*, Public Services International Research Unit, Greenwich, U.K., Feb. 2001, http://www.psiru.org/publicationsindex.asp. RWE's *Fortune* Global 500 ranking for revenues dropped steadily from 53rd in 2004 to 78th in 2005 and 105th in 2006; http://money.cnn.com/magazines/fortune/global500/2006/full_list/101_200.html.

6. D. Altan, M. Bentlley, M. Hertsgaard, and C. Van Bebber, "Profit on Tap?" *San Francisco Chronicle Magazine*, Feb. 9, 2003. The purge of Morris Allen followed the shredding of a consultant draft report showing that municipal operation of the utility would be less expensive than privatization. "That version was ordered to be shredded by the assistant city manager, who informed me that he did not want it to fall into the wrong hands," said Allen in an interview with the authors, Feb. 22, 2003. Podesto said that the draft report was in error, and that is why it was shredded; interview with authors, Feb. 12, 2003.

7. G. Podesto, Mayor of Stockton, "State of the City, 2003," speech delivered Feb. 19, 2003, Stockton, California.

8. Office of the City Clerk, City of Stockton, "Save Stockton—No on F," *Late Contribution Report* (Stockton, Calif., undated). The contributions included $10,000 and $25,000 from OMI and $25,000 from Thames.

9. The taped phone message from Mayor Podesto was recorded on a phone machine in the days before the Mar. 2003 vote on Measure F. Podesto later denied implying that his opponents were liars.

10. C. Miller, "Privatization Foes Dealt Setback," *Stockton Record*, Apr. 24, 2003.

11. In the ruling dated Oct. 17, 2003, Superior Court Judge Robert W. McNatt concluded that "substantial evidence" existed "that the transfer of the operation of water, wastewater, and storm water facilities to a private operator will likely have a substantial impact on the environment. Common sense dictates that methods of operation will differ between a government and private sector based on (at a minimum) the profit motive. This is not intended as a criticism, but merely an observation that profit or the lack thereof will necessarily drive determinations made in how certain actions or decision are carried out. . . . There will always be situations in which profits versus environment considerations will militate a decision [which] negatively impacts the public." *Concerned Citizens Coalition of Stockton, League of Women Voters of San Joaquin, and Sierra Club, Case No. CV 020397, Petitioners v. City of Stockton,*

City of Stockton City Council, and Does 1–10, inclusive, ruling on petition for mandamus (C.C.P. 1085; C.C.P. 1096.4), Respondents, OMI/Thames Water Stockton, Inc., Does 11–20, Real Parties in Interest. Court documents by both sides are available at http://www.cccos.org/.

12. B. Loyko and S. Loyko, with S. Kothe and D. Stocking, *2nd Annual Service Contract Compliance Review, period August 1, 2004, through July 31, 2005,* Feb. 2006, http://www.cccos.org/, especially pp. 11 on rates, 20 on staffing, 22 on leakage, and 32 on maintenance backlogs.

13. C. Melanie, "City Fined $125,000 for Water Discharge," *Stockton Record,* Oct. 7, 2004; W. Lutz, "Slow Reaction to Sewage Spill," *Stockton Record,* June 20, 2006; W. Lutz, "State Probes Spill of Sewage in River," *Stockton Record,* July 15, 2006.

14. "Breaking News: Ports Sue City of Stockton," *Stockton Record,* May 10, 2006; S. Smith, "Panel Faults Council for Sitting on Sidelines of Spending Spree," *Stockton Record,* June 14, 2006; D. Siders, "Retired Stockton Finance Chief Faults City Spending Spree," *Stockton Record,* Apr. 28, 2006.

15. S. Quinones, "California's Latest Cutting-Edge City: Stockton?" *Los Angeles Times,* June 26, 2006.

16. Superior Court Judge Elizabeth Humphreys, "Ruling on Petition for Writ of Mandate," Case No. CV 020397, *Concerned Citizens et al. v. City of Stockton, OMI/Thames Water Stockton, Inc.,* Nov. 2, 2006. CCCOS Press Release, "Judge Rejects Stockton Water Privatization Project," Nov. 6, 2006; D. Siders, "Ruling Has Environmentalists Declaring Victory Over Stockton Water, Sewage," *Stockton Record,* Nov. 7, 2006.

17. D. Stocking, e-mail to authors, Nov. 6, 2006.

18. Interviews with authors, July 20 and Nov. 8, 2006.

Chapter Three: Small-Town Surprise for a Corporate Water Giant

1. B. Sprenger, "Delivering Water: A Community Says No to Foreign Corporate Ownership," unpublished master's thesis, Department of

Public Policy, California State University at Monterey Bay, 2005; Friends of Locally Owned Water, *Timeline*, http://www.feltonflow. org/chronology.html. This chapter is based largely on interviews conducted in February 2006 with Friends of Locally Owned Water (FLOW) members Francis Adamson, Frank Adamson, Jim Graham, Michelle Moser, and Barbara Sprenger, as well as on local newspaper coverage, public documents, and websites. Representatives of RWE/Thames subsidiary California American Water Company refused repeated requests for interviews.

2. D. L. Beck, "Groundswell for Local Control," *San Jose Mercury News*, Nov. 3, 2004.

3. Sprenger, "Delivering Water," p. 2.

4. Quoted in S. Halliday, *The Great Stink of London: Sir Joseph Bazalgette and the Cleansing of the Victorian Metropolis* (Thrupp, U.K.: Sutton, 1999), p. 76. The Great Stink of London in the summer of 1858 was the result of hot, dry weather that lowered the level of the Thames River so that it was unable to flush the raw sewage routinely dumped into it. Halliday quotes the *City Press*: "Whoso once inhales the stink can never forget it and count himself lucky if he live to remember it" (p. 72). Political resistance in Parliament and from competing parishes that had blocked centralized planning to create the citywide sewer system was overcome by the stench. Sir Joseph Bazalgette's massive public-works project is widely credited with making the growing city livable, but his underground accomplishments have been largely forgotten. Clare Clark, in the author's notes to her historical novel *The Great Stink* (Orlando: Harcourt Brace, 2005), writes that Bazalgette's only memorial is a small bust "set into a dark corner beneath the railway bridge at Charing Cross" (p. 358).

5. Quoted in M. A. Gaura, "Water a Hot Commodity: U.S. Waterworks Lure Investors," *San Francisco Chronicle*, Dec. 1, 2002.

6. "Thames Water Is UK's 'Biggest Polluter,'" *Daily Mail*, July 26, 2006; C. Moore, "Water Companies Head Polluters' League," *Guardian*, July 26, 2006. Earlier pollution reports can be found

in Food & Water Watch, *RWE/Thames Water: A Corporate Profile*, Apr. 2006, http://www.foodandwaterwatch.org/water/rwe; a company rebuttal to the charges can be found on California American's Felton website: http://www.feltonwaterfacts.com/www/docs/101–14. The race was won by the red BioHaz team as the blue GasHaz team's "faecal floater looked decidedly soggy and was not slipping through the water at all cleanly." Putney Town Rowing Club website: http://www.putneytownrc.co.uk/rats/events.html. RATS has been campaigning for years to get the river cleaned up. Rowers are often warned to wear gloves and wash thoroughly with soap and water after boating on the river because of fecal contamination from sewer overflows. For reports on the river and pictures of the Thames Turd Race, see the group's website: www.thames.sewage.com. The summer of 2006 was a rough one for Thames Water's reputation. Not only is it Britain's largest polluter, but also it failed for the sixth year in a row to reach the regulatory target for reducing leakage, which on a daily basis amounts to 196.6 million gallons, or 298 Olympic-size swimming pools. This would not have been such a scandal in London if the city were not suffering its worst drought in years while Thames was raising water rates, claiming higher profits, being fined for poor customer service, announcing a 25 percent cut in staff, and banning residents from watering their gardens— all while RWE had put the company up for sale. "Thames Water Is UK's 'Biggest Polluter'," *Daily Mail*, Jul. 26, 2006; C. Moore and agencies, "Water Companies Head Polluters' League," *The Guardian*, Jul. 26, 2006; H. Kundnani, "Thames Water Faces Fine of up to 140 Million Pounds," *The Guardian*, Jul. 19, 2006; R. Murray-West, "Water Firm 'Off the Hook' after Failing to Plug Leaks," *Daily Telegraph*, May 7, 2006; "Thames Water to Cut 25% of Jobs," *BBC News*, Aug. 29, 2006.

7. Quoted in J. Gumz, "California-American Water: Felton System Is Not for Sale," *Santa Cruz Sentinel*, Nov. 17, 2002.

8. Felton's water rates were the fifth of six local districts studied by the Santa Cruz Local Agency Formation Commission. The report said the Cal Am rates were 59 percent higher than the San Lorenzo Valley Water District rates. Santa Cruz Local Agency Formation Com-

mission, *Proposed Felton Amendment to San Lorenzo Valley Water District Sphere of Influence* (Santa Cruz, Calif., July 2003), p. 45. Privately owned utilities like Cal Am are regulated by state commissions like the Public Utilities Commission (PUC) in California, which allows investor-owned utilities to reap a potential profit of 10–11 percent a year on capital improvements. If Felton is able to buy its system, rate decisions will be made in the local area by the water district rather than the state PUC, and FLOW estimates that rate cases, which now cost up to a $1 million to fight at the state level, could cost as little as $5,000. J. Gumz, "Water Rate-Hike Expense Hits $1M," *Santa Cruz Sentinel*, July 22, 2005; "Felton FLOW Talking Points for CPUC Hearing," *Felton FLOW*, May 11, 2006.

9. Quoted in G. Cross, *A Dynasty of Water: The Story of American Water Works Company* (Voorhees, N.J.: American Water Works Company, 1991), p. 171. A lot is at stake in these efforts to keep control. The major source of growth for private water utilities is population expansion and suburban sprawl. When Cal Am purchased Citizens Water in Felton, it also picked up Citizens Water customers in the Sacramento area, giving the company a foothold in one of the fastest-growing areas in the state. A *Sacramento News and Review* cover story in 2003 observed, "Cal-Am is hoping to grow as the region grows. Virtually anywhere farm fields and grasslands are being slated for new subdivisions, Cal-Am and its parent companies see the potential for profits. . . . If Cal-Am can tap into Sacramento's growth successfully, Cal-Am, along with its parent companies, soon could be the biggest water purveyor in the region and a powerful player in regional water politics. 'This is a great time to be in the water-resource business,' said Mitch Dion, manager of Cal Am's North Division." C. Garvin, "Gulp," *Sacramento News and Review*, Nov. 10, 2003.

10. L. Chesky, "Won't Back Down: Cal Am Vows to Fight to Keep Felton Water," *Good Times*, July 22, 2004.

11. J. Lopez and P. Boyd, *Capitalizing on Water*, Spring 2006; this documentary video made by University of California at Santa Cruz

students can be viewed on-line at http://www.feltonflow.org/down
loads/FLOWUCSC.mov.

12. Testimony at a meeting of the California Public Utilities Commission, San Francisco, May 11, 2006; interview with authors,
May 11, 2006.

13. Testimony at a meeting of the California Public Utilities Commission, San Francisco, May 11, 2006.

14. Ibid.

15. Sprenger, "Delivering Water," p. 5.

16. Interview with authors, Feb. 7, 2006. Unless otherwise indicated,
all quotes from Jim Graham are from this interview.

17. J. Graham, e-mail message to authors, Sept. 10, 2006.

18. Sprenger, "Delivering Water," p. 6.

19. Moriah Group, *Felton Communication Plan* (Dec. 1, 2003). Moriah
used similar strategies in Lexington, Kentucky (see Chapter Five):
A. Mead and M. Ku, "Water Ownership Battles Playing Out Across
the U.S," *Lexington Herald-Leader*, June 4, 2006; Editorial, "The
'Felton Communication Plan,'" *Lexington Herald-Leader*, June 4,
2006.

20. *Case Study: American Water Works Service Company*, archived pages
available as a PDF at http://www.jgpr.com/Calam/research.html; this
page was removed from the Moriah website.

21. Moriah Group, *Felton Communication Plan*; J. Graham, interview
with authors, Feb. 7, 2006.

22. Moriah Group, *Felton Communication Plan*. For more information on
the Moriah strategy, see http://www.jgpr.com/Calam/research.html.

23. J. Gumz, "Water Bill: $36,800 in Legal Fees," *Santa Cruz Sentinel*,
Jan. 17, 2006; V. Hennessey, "Measure W Whips Up Local Debate,"
Monterey Herald, July 24, 2005; J. Gumz, "Cal-Am Backed Felton
Lawsuit," *Santa Cruz Sentinel*, June 19, 2005; J. Gumz, "Word Up:
Felton Water Ballot OK'd," *Santa Cruz Sentinel*, June 10, 2005.

24. Testimony at a meeting of the California Public Utilities Commission, San Francisco, May 11, 2006.

25. V. Hennessey, "Felton OKs Takeover of Cal Am," *Monterey Herald*, July 27, 2005.

26. Sprenger, "Delivering Water," p. 9.

27. Quoted in M. Thomas, "Felton Voters Authorize $11 Million in Bonds for Water System," *Valley Post*, Aug. 2, 2005.

28. The bill was introduced by freshman Assemblyman Juan Arambula, a Democrat from Fresno, but it was written by the California Water Association, a trade association, which represents forty-two private water companies in California, most of them tiny. The association is dominated by a few large companies, including Cal Am. Assemblyman Arambula told the *Monterey Herald* he felt burned by the controversy that exploded in his face. "I'm learning that there is no such thing as a 'simple, technical amendment without any significant opposition,'" he said, referring to the lobbyist's characterization of the bill. Cal Am's spokesman Kevin Tilden acknowledged that Cal Am had reviewed the draft legislation. A year later, in 2006, conservative legislators and a taxpayers' group proposed initiatives and constitutional amendments to severely limit the government's power to use eminent domain to take over private property. One of those proposals was on the state ballot in November 2006 and lost. Cal Am denied any role in those proposals. V. Hennessey, "Water-System Takeover Legislation Draws Ire," *Monterey Herald*, Mar. 16, 2005; K. Howe, "Threat Seen to Water-System Sale," *Monterey Herald*, Mar. 31, 2006. For additional information on the issues involved in eminent-domain debates across the country, see E. Kancler, "This Land Is Our Land," *Mother Jones*, Mar. 18, 2005, http://www.motherjones.com/news/feature/2005/03/kelo_eminent_domain.html.

29. Quoted in M. Thomas, "Felton Voters Authorize $11 Million in Bonds for Water System," *Valley Post*, Aug. 2, 2005.

Chapter Four: The Price of Incompetence

1. One of the major reasons mayors cite for privatization is the amelioration of risk. Mayors often believe that a public-private partnership transfers the risks of federal and state fines for pollution, sewage

spills, and failures to complete required work on time to private contractors. However, a city must still enforce a contract, and that means the city has taken on the new risk of potential long and expensive litigation against the contractor. There are a host of other risks that come into existence by the very nature of contracting out an essential service, including the potential necessity of taking back control of the operations in the event of nonperformance or bankruptcy. Cities routinely fail to take these risks into consideration. See G. Wolff, *Independent Review of the Proposed Stockton Water Privatization, January 2003*, Pacific Institute for Studies in Development, Environment and Security, Oakland, pp. 11–13.

Another risk of privatization is that private water companies often cut spending on equipment and maintenance, keeping the difference as profit (but calling it "efficiency"). By allowing equipment to "work to failure," the private company may risk service disruption and a fine, but those results may be less costly to the bottom line than a more socially responsible policy of preventive maintenance. John Kidd, the chair of the trade union for Yorkshire Water, a subsidiary of the Kelda private water group in Great Britain, put it this way in a German documentary film about privatization: "What the water industry is about now, it's about profit margins, and profit margins mean one thing: risk. So they've become managers of risk. It's about how much chlorine do you really have to put in the water? How many staff can we really go down to? Companies like ours, they have whole teams that look at risk everyday. Do we really have to visit that sewerage works today? Can we leave it for three days? For five days? So it's all about risk. My problem with risk in an industry like ours, where it's water, I believe, if the risk is taken too far, there will be a major disaster." Quoted from L. Franke and H. Lorenz, *H₂O for Sale: The Privatization of a Human Necessity*," U. Brodbeck, producer; a joint production of Kern TV (public television in Hamburg, Germany) and NDR; Kern Filmproduktion GmBH, 2005, http://www.kernfilmproduktion.de/k01framep.htm.

2. The indictment was the culmination of an almost five-year investigation that resulted in ten criminal convictions, including those

of Campbell's chief operating officer, deputy chief operating offi-
cer, and various friends, business associates, and city contractors.
R. Whitt, "Former Mayor Campbell Indicted—Feds Allege Bribery,
Fraud at City Hall," *Atlanta Journal-Constitution*, Aug. 30, 2004;
B. Torpy, B. Warren, and J. Scott, "Former Atlanta Mayor Cleared
of Corruption, Nailed on Taxes," *Atlanta Journal-Constitution*,
Mar. 11, 2006.

3. B. Torpy, "Campbell Divides Atlantans—Again: Corruption Trial
   Set to Start This Week," *Atlanta Journal-Constitution*, Jan. 15, 2006.

4. C. Seabrook, "River in Peril: How Atlanta's Sewers Threaten the
   Chattahoochee. Part Three: City Creeks Pay the Price for Leaky
   Antiquated Lines," *Atlanta Journal-Constitution*, July 1, 1997;
   C. Seabrook, "Sewer Probe Cites a Sprawling Mess," *Atlanta
   Journal-Constitution*, Oct. 16, 1997.

5. Quoted in Seabrook, "River in Peril," pt. 3.

6. C. Seabrook, "River in Peril: How Atlanta's Sewers Threaten the
   Chattahoochee. Part Four: Storm Water, Sewage Combine into
   Trouble," *Atlanta Journal-Constitution*, July 2, 1997.

7. D. Scroggins, "Sewer and Water Crisis, the Endless Emergency,"
   signed editorial, *Atlanta Journal-Constitution*, Feb. 17, 1997.

8. N. Osborne, interview with authors, Oct. 24, 2005. Privatization
   was not the central issue for African American and other community groups especially in older sections of Atlanta, which still had
   antiquated sewers that combined storm-water runoff and sewage.
   The combined sewers overflowed dozens of times a year into streets,
   backyards, basements, and local streams. Community groups eventually formed the Clean Streams Task Force to lobby for sewer separation in the 15 percent of the city with combined sewers and
   for storm-water greenways to provide open space where rainwater
   could return to the environment. "The intent to keep any sewers
   in a combined system is really completely out of touch with reality," said Rev. Richard Bright of the Good Shepherd Community
   Church. Bright was standing in the muck of a sewer overflow at an
   apartment-complex playground. Among the twenty groups involved
   with the task force were SAFE (Save Atlanta's Fragile Environment), STOP (Safely Treating Our Pollution), the Environmental

Trust, the Sierra Club, the Southern Organizing Committee for Social and Economic Justice, and the West Atlanta Watershed Alliance. The task force has continued to be actively engaged in support for environmentally sound, community-building solutions to Atlanta's water and open space problems. J. Schaffner, "'Stopgap' City Storm Water Tunnel: Timely Relief or Costly Boondoggle?" *The Story*, Apr. 18, 2002; J. Schaffner, "Citizens Challenge City to Solve Flooding with Sewer Separation," *The Story*, Oct. 3, 2002; Clean Streams Task Force, *Full Sewer Separation with Stormwater Greenways: An Opportunity to Revitalize the Face of Atlanta*, prepared for the Mayor's Clean Water Advisory Panel, July 15, 2002, www.georgia.sierraclub.org/atlanta/conservation/mcwapfin.pdf.

9. D. Fears, "Mayoral Hopefuls Bury Sewer Tunnel Saga," *Atlanta Journal-Constitution*, Mar. 23, 1998.

10. S. Bethea, interview with authors, Oct. 24, 2005.

11. Ibid.

12. C. Seabrook, "Atlanta Sewer Deal," *Atlanta Journal-Constitution*, Apr. 14, 1998.

13. C. Helton, "Focus on Privatization," *Atlanta Journal-Constitution*, Feb. 8, 1997; L. Peeples, interview with authors, July 26, 2006.

14. Helton, "Focus on Privatization."

15. B. Bozeman, interview with authors, Aug. 7, 2006.

16. S. Bethea, interview with authors, Oct. 24, 2005.

17. C. Campos and J. B. Hairston, "Campbell Picks Up Support: Privatization Votes Seen," *Atlanta Journal-Constitution*, Feb. 25, 1998; A. Charles, "Water Sewer Privatization Gets Task Force Endorsement," *Atlanta Journal-Constitution*, Jan. 10, 1998; J. B. Hairston, "Conflict over Specialist May Hinder Privatization," *Atlanta Journal-Constitution*, Apr. 25, 1998; "Community: A Guide to Water Privatization Voices," *Atlanta Journal-Constitution*, Aug. 27, 1998; M. Geewax, "Editorial: Though Awash in Errors, Privatization Can Still Work," *Atlanta Journal-Constitution*, Aug. 16, 1998.

18. B. Campbell, "This Is a Bold Initiative," speech excerpted in *Atlanta Journal-Constitution*, Aug. 20, 1998.

19. L. Peeples, interview with authors, July 26, 2006.

20. Ibid.

21. C. Campos and J. B. Hairston, "Wading into Private Waters: Atlanta's Plan for Utility Still Murky," *Atlanta Journal-Constitution*, Mar. 27, 1998.

22. Ibid.

23. N. Osborne, interview with authors, Oct. 24, 2005.

24. B. Bozeman, interview with authors, Aug. 7, 2006.

25. J. Dickerson, "Privatizing Schools: A Worthy Experiment," signed editorial, *Atlanta Journal-Constitution*, Jan. 27, 1999.

26. Quoted in C. Campos, "Water Privatization Spurs Flood of Big Jobs," *Atlanta Journal-Constitution*, Dec. 4, 1998.

27. J. B. Hairston, "Treatment Plant Bidding Could Be Fierce," *Atlanta Journal-Constitution*, Apr. 9, 1999; Quote of Mestrallet in L. Chertoff, "US Private Firms Shrink from Weak Deals," *Global Water Intelligence*, Aug. 2003.

28. C. Campos, "Atlanta Water Flows to United," *Atlanta Journal-Constitution*, Jan. 1, 1999.

29. N. Osborne, interview with authors, Oct. 24, 2005.

30. M. Ippolito, "Dirty Tap Water Stirs Flood of Complaints," *Atlanta Journal-Constitution*, June 8, 2002.

31. L. Peeples, interview with authors, July 26, 2006; K. Griffis, "Oceans Apart: United Water and Atlanta Soon Will Find Out Whether They're Meant to Be Together," *Atlanta Creative Loafing*, Mar. 6, 2002.

32. M. C. Quinn, "French Water Firm to Buy All of Water Provider," *Atlanta Journal-Constitution*, Aug. 25, 1999. Suez's own status has been subject to market turmoil. When the Italian power giant Enel tried to buy Suez in early 2006, the French government swung into action, eager to defend a major French-based multinational and its many secret connections to government officials and political parties. The government maneuvered a separate deal under which the state-owned Gaz de France would take over Suez instead. Enel and the Italian government accused the French of neoprotectionism and violations of European Union rules. Enel also announced that it

would consider a hostile takeover. There was speculation in the
press that Suez's water divisions would be spun off as a separate
entity. "Passions Rampant Among Thwarted Italians," *AKI*,
Feb. 27, 2006; "Suez, Gaz de France to Announce Merger to Repel
Enel," *Bloomberg News*, Feb. 27, 2006; A. Lagorce "Enel Gathers
Financial Backing for Suez Offer," *Dow Jones Business News*,
Mar. 6, 2006.

33. Information about the Grenoble scandal is based on D. Hall and
E. Lobina, *Private to Public: International Lessons of Water Remunici-palisation in Grenoble, France* (Greenwich, U.K.: Public Services
International Research Unit, Aug. 6, 2001); M. Laimé, "In the
Business of Supply," *Le Monde Diplomatique*, Mar. 12, 2005; Inter-national Consortium of Investigative Journalists, M. Beelman, and
others (eds.), *The Water Barons: How a Few Private Companies Are
Privatizing Your Water* (Washington, D.C.: Public Integrity Books,
2003), pp. 25–31; Food & Water Watch, *Suez: A Corporate Pro-file* (Washington, D.C., Feb. 2006); R. Avrillier, "A Return to
the Source—Remunicipalisation of Water Service in Grenoble,
France," in B. Balanya and others (eds.), *Reclaiming Public Water:
Achievements, Struggles and Visions from Around the World* (Amster-dam: Transnational Institute and Corporate Europe Observatory,
2005).

34. Griffis, "Oceans Apart." Four of United Water's executives con-tributed $4,750 to Campbell's reelection committee in 1999, a year
after winning the contract. However, this is only a small part of the
$250,000 Campbell's reelection committee took in during the two
years after his reelection. A. Judd, "Campbell Fund-Raising Is Elec-tion-Free: Mayor Can't Run, Yet Cash Pours In," *Atlanta Journal-Constitution*, Nov. 2, 2000.

35. Interview with a Suez/United Water executive at the 4th World
Water Forum, Mar. 22, 2006; the executive did not want his name
used.

36. G. Podesto, interview with authors, Feb. 12, 2003.

37. C. Campbell, "Leaky Streets Show Atlanta Water System Is All
Wet," *Atlanta Journal-Constitution*, July 18, 2000.

38. C. Campbell, "Something Stinks in Quiet Neighborhood," *Atlanta Journal-Constitution*, Mar. 1, 2001. For more on the boil-water advisories, sewer-line breaks, brown water, and slow service, see J. R. Luoma, "Water for Profit," *Mother Jones*, Dec. 2002; D. Jehl, "As Cities Move to Privatize Water, Atlanta Steps Back," *New York Times*, Feb. 10, 2003; Food & Water Watch, *Faulty Pipes* (Washington, D.C., June 2006). For the pro-privatization perspective on what went wrong in Atlanta, see G. F. Segal, *That Atlanta Water Privatization: What Can We Learn?* (Georgia Public Policy Foundation, Jan. 24, 2003), http://www.gppf.org/article.asp?RT=20&p=pub/Water/atlanta_water.htm.

39. N. Osborne, interview with authors, Oct. 24, 2005.

40. Quoted in D. L. Bennett, "City Water Firm Wants $80 Million," *Atlanta Journal-Constitution*, Dec. 22, 2001.

41. C. Campos and J. B. Hairston, "Water Firms Pour on the Praise for Their Bids to City," *Atlanta Journal-Constitution*, July 30, 1998; International Consortium of Investigative Journalists, M. Beelman, and others, *The Water Barons*, p. 130.

42. Editorial, "Our Opinions: United Water's Demands Would Soak City Residents," *Atlanta Journal-Constitution*, Jan. 9, 2002.

43. S. Rubenstein, "City Blasts United Water," *Atlanta Business Chronicle*, Aug. 9, 2002.

44. S. Rubinstein, "City Finds Pros, Cons for United Water," *Atlanta Business Chronicle*, Sept. 27, 2002.

45. F. Koller, "No Silver Bullet: Water Privatization in Atlanta, Georgia—a Cautionary Tale." CBC Radio, Feb. 5, 2003, http://www.cbc.ca/news/features/water/atlanta.html.

46. City of Atlanta and United Water, "City of Atlanta and United Water Announce Amicable Dissolution of Twenty-Year Water Contract," joint press release, Jan. 24, 2003; M. Ippolito, "Atlanta Takes Over Water System: Huge Utility with Aging Pipes Back Under City Control," *Atlanta Journal-Constitution*, Apr. 30, 2003.

47. Interview with a Suez/United Water executive at the 4th World Water Forum. The executive did not want his name used. K. DeMarrais, "United Water Shakes Up Executive Ranks with

New Leadership," *Bergen County Record*, Mar. 26, 2003; cited in Food & Water Watch, *Faulty Pipes*.

48. R. Whitt, "Experts Contradict Campbell on Water Document Signatures," *Atlanta Journal-Constitution*, Oct. 30, 2002.

49. R. Whitt, "Former Mayor Campbell Indicted—Feds Allege Bribery, Fraud at City Hall," *Atlanta Journal-Constitution*, Aug. 30, 2004; Office of the U.S. Attorney in Atlanta, *Summary of Indictment: United States of America v. William C. Campbell*, Aug. 30, 2004.

50. U.S. Attorney in Atlanta, *Summary of Indictment*; M. Hudson, "Misconduct Taints the Water in Some Privatized Systems," *Los Angeles Times*, May 29, 2006; R. Whitt and B. Rankin, "Federal Probe of Former Atlanta Mayor Bill Campbell Heats Up: Role in United Water Operating Contract Questioned," *Atlanta Journal-Constitution*, Aug. 11, 2004; R. Whitt and A. Judd, "Former Mayor Campbell Indicted—Feds Allege Bribery, Fraud at City Hall," *Atlanta Journal-Constitution*, Aug. 31, 2004; J. Scott and B. Warren, "TV Anchor Tells of Lavish Trips with Campbell," *Atlanta Journal-Constitution*, Feb. 8, 2006.

51. J. Scott and B. Warren, "Campbell Squeaked Past Corruption Charges, Jurors Say," *Atlanta Journal-Constitution*, Mar. 12, 2006. The particular charge referred to was an allegation that Campbell accepted bribes in return for a multimillion-dollar contract to prepare the city's computers for the changeover to the year 2000.

52. B. Torpy, B. Warren, J. Scott, and S. Poole, "Campbell Sentenced to 30 Months in Prison," *Atlanta Journal-Constitution*, June 13, 2006; "Campbell Begins Prison Term," *Atlanta Journal-Constitution*, Aug. 22, 2006.

53. *Q and A with Shirley Franklin*, C-Span, Jan. 26, 2006.

54. Ibid.

55. L. Peeples, interview with authors, July 26, 2006. Ironically, Atlanta suburbs, eager to differentiate from the city itself, have begun to incorporate and outsource virtually all city services to private contractors, in particular Colorado-based CH2M Hill and its water subsidiary OMI, the company involved in the Stockton public-private

partnership. The city of Sandy Springs, north of Atlanta, pioneered such top-to-bottom outsourcing of public and government functions in 2005. Sandy Springs officials who advocated this arrangement say it's working, but problems have seeped into the press. CH2M Hill possesses all city records. What are usually public records are no longer accessible. The company has moved employees at will without consulting city officials. For example, the company removed the city's public works director without informing the City Council, which is still nominally the government of Sandy Springs. An AFSCME union leader claimed this lack of transparency coupled with normal company confidentiality about its own internal finances and profits creates a climate for potential corruption. S. Dewan, "In Georgia County, Divisions of North and South Play Out in Drives to Form New Cities," *New York Times*, Jul. 13, 2006; D. Nurse, "Sandy Springs a Happy Guinea Pig for Outsourcing," *Atlanta Journal-Constitution*, Sep. 27, 2006.

Chapter Five: The Hundred-Year War

1. C. Talwalkar, interview with authors, Oct. 2005. Unless otherwise indicated, quotes in this chapter are from interviews conducted by the authors in 2005 and 2006 with Mayor Teresa Isaac; City Council candidate and FLOW opponent Jay McChord; Bluegrass FLOW leader H. Foster Pettit; Bluegrass FLOW attorney Foster Ockerman Jr.; former Bluegrass FLOW organizer Chetan Talwalkar; Coalition Against a Government Takeover leader Warren P. Rogers; the business manager of the Service Employees International Union Local 320, Bob Gunter; *Lexington Herald Leader* publisher Tim Kelly; *Lexington Herald Leader* reporters Michelle Ku, Jamie Lucke, and Andy Mead; Green Corps organizers Stephanie Chang, Leila Darwish, and Annie Weinberg; and the chair of the Council of Canadians, Maude Barlow.

2. B. A. Mason, "Bluegrass Blues," *New York Times*, June 11, 2006; I. Brown, "A Stud Is Born," *Toronto Globe and Mail*, Mar. 10, 2001.

3. C. Talwalkar, (Ed.). *RWE and Lexington Water Timelines*, an undated chronology of Lexington's water history 1874–2005, http://www.lwvky.org/Lexington_LWV/water.htm.

4. Cited in G. Cross, *A Dynasty of Water: The Story of American Water Works Company* (Voorhees, N.J.: American Water Works Company, 1991), pp. 172–173.

5. E. T. Breathitt, "City Must Seize Chance to Buy Water Company," *Lexington Herald-Leader*, Feb. 10, 2002.

6. Cited in Talwalkar, *RWE and Lexington Timelines;* originally reported in the *Lexington Herald-Leader*, Feb. 4, 1995.

7. W. Young, "Water Company Purchase an Extraordinary Opportunity for City," *Lexington Herald-Leader*, Oct. 11, 2002.

8. Quoted in Public Citizen, "Report Highlights Benefits of Public Ownership of Waterworks," press release, Sept. 17, 2002.

9. Cross, *A Dynasty of Water*, pp. 173–174.

10. Quoted in J. Stamper, "Water Utility's Leader Is in West Virginia," *Lexington Herald-Leader*, May 6, 2004.

11. B. Varallis, "Kentucky American Impenetrable Under RWE," cited in public file of the Kentucky Public Service Commission, http://psc.ky.gov/pscecf/2004–00103/LFUCG_efs/07082004/LFUCG%20No.4.pdf; originally printed in *Lexington Herald-Leader*, June 28, 2004.

12. Material in this section is based on the websites of the four companies: the Public Opinion Strategies website is http://www.pos.org/research/political.cfm; the Moriah Group site is http://www.moriahgroup.com; Preston-Osborne's website is http://www.preston-osborne.com/kyamer.html; the Tactical Edge site is http://www.tacticaledgeltd.com. This section is also based on Moriah Group, *Case Study: American Water Works Service Company*, archived pages available as a PDF at http://www.jgpr.com/Calam/research.html (this page was removed from the Moriah website); Moriah Group, *Felton Communication Plan* (Dec. 1, 2003); A. Mead and M. Ku, "Water Ownership Battles Playing Out Across the U.S," *Lexington Herald-Leader*, June 4, 2006.

13. Editorial, "Manicured Astroturf: Pro-Utility Coalition's Artificial Grass Roots Showing," *Lexington Herald-Leader*, Mar. 30, 2005. The use of "astroturf" groups by industry and public relations firms has become so widespread it's a big business itself, an $800 million

industry. Such groups—often financed entirely by industry—can provide what appears to be independent affirmation of a company's positions in public controversies. This testimony is particularly valuable because skeptical journalists and the public may see a company's own advertising as self-serving. "Put your words in someone else's mouth," one public relations specialist advised companies; S. Beder, "Public Relations' Role in Manufacturing Artificial Grass Roots Coalitions," *Public Relations Quarterly,* Summer 1998, pp. 21–23. See also B. Burton and A. Rowell, "From Patient Activism to Astroturf Marketing," *PR Watch,* 2003, http://www.prwatch.org/prwissues/2003Q1/astroturf.html; "How to Research Front Groups," *Disinfopedia,* http://www.sourcewatch.org/index.php?title=How_to_research_front_groups. Additional information about the use of front groups by corporations and public relations firms can be found at the Center for Media and Democracy, http://www.prwatch.org.

14. *2003 Fayette County Issues Survey,* University of Kentucky Survey Research Center, Dr. Ronald E. Langley, director, http://survey.rgs.uky.edu/issues/watercompany.html.

15. J. Stamper, "Water Firm's Plan: Courts, PR, Politics," *Lexington Herald-Leader,* Aug. 26, 2004; Editorial, "Takeover Target: Now RWE Wants to Buy the City Council," *Lexington Herald-Leader,* Aug. 27, 2004. Kentucky American's president, Nick Rowe, promised that the costs of the campaign against condemnation would not be passed on to ratepayers but would be paid by RWE shareholders. However, the Stamper article points out that Kentucky American's request to charge ratepayers for campaign expenses had already been turned down by state regulators.

16. S. Kay, "Big Money Infecting Council Races," *Lexington Herald-Leader,* Mar. 23, 2005.

17. J. Stamper and M. Ku, "Voters' Message: End Condemnation: Water Company Wins Big in Election," *Lexington Herald-Leader,* Nov. 7, 2004.

18. For more information about McChord, see www.workplacebuzz.com.

19. J. Stamper, "Second Inquiry of Water Firm Is Sought: Advocacy Group Asks Lobbying Be Reviewed," *Lexington Herald-Leader,* Sept. 29, 2004; J. Stamper, "Water Firm Responds to Election Com-

plaint," *Lexington Herald-Leader*, Oct. 16, 2004; A. Mead, "Election Complaint Dismissed," *Lexington Herald-Leader*, Feb. 14, 2006.

20. J. Stamper, "Coordinator Quits FLOW over Sign Flap," *Lexington Herald-Leader*, Oct. 7, 2004.

21. M. Ku, "New Council: Scanlon's Gift to Himself? Vice Mayor Disputes Isaac's Account," *Lexington Herald-Leader*, Nov. 19, 2004.

22. "Ballot Backers Rally in Protest," *Lexington Herald-Leader*, Nov. 9, 2005.

23. M. Ku and J. Jordan, "RWE to Sell Its American Waterworks," *Lexington Herald-Leader*, Nov. 5, 2005; Roels quoted in R. Orange, "RWE Split over Thames Sale," *Water Industry News*, Oct. 30, 2005, ttp://waterindustry.org/New%20Projects/RWE-5.htm. The pending sale of RWE's major water subsidiaries was not good news for other private water companies in the United States. Nicholas DeBenedictis, CEO of Aqua America, the largest of the still-U.S.-owned companies, said in a conference call on November 9, 2005, "It does not bode well with employees to be bought and sold in a five-year period twice. So I think that hurts our industry"; Food & Water Watch, *RWE/Thames Water—A Corporate Profile* (Washington, D.C.), Apr. 2006, p. 5, http://www.foodandwaterwatch.org/water/pubs/profiles/rwe.

24. A. Mead, "Water Company Drops Suit; Referendum on November Ballot," *Lexington Herald-Leader*, May 23, 2006. Bluegrass FLOW made the sale a centerpiece of its campaign appeal to employees of the water company. In September 2006, as FLOW kicked off its door-to-door effort to win the referendum, the group stated that "employees have no idea who they'll be working for next year— UNLESS the referendum passes and the city is able to buy the system. The city is committed to continuing current employees at their current status though they will actually work for a largely independent chartered board," http://www.bluegrassflow.org/.

25. N. Nadel, "Mayor Pursues Tenn Am Takeover," *WDEF News*, Feb. 7, 2006; K. Howe, "Cities Seek to Own Water Utilities," *Monterey Herald*, Apr. 13, 2006; Food and Water Watch, *RWE/Thames—Water*. In April 2006, a coalition of political leaders from Germany and the United States descended on the RWE annual

general meeting to demand that the company allow their cities to
buy back their local water utilities; Food & Water Watch, "RWE:
We Want Our Water Back," press release at RWE annual meeting,
Apr. 5, 2006. Mayor Laurel Prussing of Urbana, Illinois, attended
the meeting to fire "a diplomatic shot across the bow. I was there
to let them know that Americans are offended by foreign interven
tion and corporate bullying. After all, it's our water, not theirs";
E. A. Torriero, "Pressure Turned Up in the War on Water," *Chicago
Tribune*, May 28, 2006. The American Water subsidiary responded
with a not-too-subtle threat. "They'll find out how long it takes and
how expensive it is," said American Water executive Dan Kelleher.
J. Balow, "City Explores Buying Water Company," *Charleston Gazette*, Dec. 28, 2005. RWE/Thames is also facing stiff resistance in
its home territories of Germany and England. Hamburg, Germany,
rejected privatization, and Berlin's government also wants to buy
its water department from a joint venture of Thames and Veolia.
U. Brodbeck, e-mail message to authors, Sept. 12, 2006. In London,
Thames is the subject of constant exposés and angry columns in
newspapers demanding that politicians have the courage to challenge the corporate monopoly over water: "One privatisation will
always stand out as an unequivocal scandal, the privatisation of
water. It is used all over the world as a classic example of what not
to do. Making millions out of an element that falls freely from the
skies—profiteering from rivers, rain and clouds—affronted most citizens. It gifted shareholders an absolute monopoly over a necessity
no one could do without. There was no chance to choose from
another supplier (unless perhaps bathing in Perrier). The price of
water doubled, great profits were made and the public got nothing";
P. Toynbee, "Forget Drought: First We Have to End This Coward-
ice," *Guardian*, May 23, 2006.

26. S. Choe, "American Water Set for Consolidation," *Houston Chronicle*, Nov. 2, 2006.

27. N. Rowe, "Vote No on Forcing Sale of Water Company," *Lexington
Herald-Leader*, Nov. 5, 2006. The company was even successful get-
ting the paper to print a picture of American Water CEO Donald
Correll as he campaigned door to door in Lexington against local

control. A. Mead, "Utility Company's CEO Makes Pitch for 'No' Vote on Referendum," *Lexington Herald-Leader*, Oct. 14, 2006.

28. Interview with authors, Nov. 9, 2006.

29. The ballot measures passed in eight states. Food & Water Watch, "Eminent Domain Concerns Dominate Lexington Water Vote: Questions Posed to Voters in 11 States Could Affect Local Control of Water," Nov. 8, 2006.

30. Editorial, "A Wealth of Wisdom Behind Voting Yes," *Lexington Herald-Leader*, Nov. 5, 2006.

31. http://72.14.253.104/search?q=cache:ykObtkWtS-QJ:www.bluegrass flow.org/+Bluegrass+Flow&hl=en&gl=us&ct=clnk&cd=1.

32. Editorial, "Right Time, Right Place for Newberry," *Lexington Herald-Leader*, Oct. 29, 2006; M. Ku, "Isaac Loses by Nearly 20,000 Votes," *Lexington Herald-Leader*, Nov. 8, 2006.

33. A. Mead, "Vote Puts Likely End to Water Debate," *Lexington Herald-Leader*, Nov. 8, 2006. The article even quotes Rowe's offer to help the city with its sewer overflow problems, a sly suggestion that perhaps a public-private partnership on wastewater might flow from the city's acceptance of private control of its water supply.

34. However, Urbana, Illinois, Mayor Laurel Prussing, who is spearheading a three-city effort to take local control from RWE, said the vote would not affect her efforts. "We will continue to press this as an issue," she said. "RWE caused a lot of problems for us. Our fire hydrants didn't open during fires. We've had a series of boil water orders. They cut back the maintenance people. I called an 800 number, and the woman on the phone didn't know where Urbana was." Interview with authors, Nov. 9, 2006.

35. A. Mead, "Water Supply Debate Intensifies," *Lexington Herald-Leader*, Aug. 24, 2006; A. Mead, "Water Firm Floats Plan for Bigger Plant," *Lexington Herald-Leader*, Sep. 26, 2006.

Chapter Six: Keeping the Companies at Bay

1. Unless otherwise indicated, all quotes from Deidre Consolati are from interviews by the authors on Aug. 25, 2005, May 29, 2006, and June 7, 2006.

2. The legislation, An Act Authorizing the Town of Lee to Enter into Contracts for Construction, Operation and Maintenance, Lease and Modification of Its Water and Wastewater Treatment Facilities, was eventually approved on October 9, 2003. S. Dam, "What Is Special Legislation and Why Do We Need It? Part II," undated article for public information by the chair of the Charlton, Massachusetts, Water and Sewer Commission, http://72.14.253.104/search?q=cache:B6L8DdO1EocJ:www.townofcharlton.net/forms/Water Sewer_CharltonGazette3.pdf+What+Is+Special+Legislation+and+Why+Do+We+Need+It%3F%22&hl=en&gl=us&ct=clnk&cd=1; W. Morehouse, "Statement to the Joint Committee on Environment, Natural Resources & Agriculture Legislative Hearing on Massachusetts House Bill No. 1333 (An Act to Preserve Public Water and Sewer Systems)," Boston, Oct. 24, 2005, http://www.shays2.org/news/2005–10–24-Testimony.html. Morehouse is cofounder of the Western Massachusetts Committee on Corporations and Democracy and of the Program on Corporations, Law and Democracy. For additional information on this kind of "special legislation" in Massachusetts, see Chapter Seven.

3. Quoted in D. Gentile, "Hodgkins Roils Lee Loyalties," *Berkshire Eagle*, Oct. 7, 2004.

4. Massachusetts Global Action, *Our Communities, Our Water* (Boston, 2006), pp. 14–15. For more on Veolia's record in the United States and abroad, see Food & Water Watch, *Veolia: A Corporate Profile* (Washington D.C., 2005).

5. J. Johnson and M. Orange, *The Man Who Tried to Buy the World* (New York: Penguin Books, 2003), p. 22.

6. M. Wolff, "The Big Fix," *New York Magazine*, May 13, 2002; quoted in Johnson and Orange, *The Man Who Tried to Buy the World*, p. 135.

7. Johnson and Orange, *The Man Who Tried to Buy the World*, p. 186.

8. Quoted in S. Freeman, "Small Towns Easy Prey for Water Companies," *Springfield Republican*, Mar. 27, 2005.

9. Unless otherwise indicated, quotes from Christopher Hodgkins are from an interview with the authors on Feb. 21, 2006.

10. Quoted in Gentile, "Hodgkins Roils Lee Loyalties."

11. Quoted in *Veolia Reference Checks*, July 2004. This report is a summary of interviews with people in cities where Veolia already had contracts. There is no author listed. The report was delivered to the Lee committee negotiating with Veolia on a possible contract.

12. P. J. Cronin, "Former Rockland, MA Superintendent of Sewer Dept., US Filter Regional Manager Accused of Embezzlement," *Mariner*, Oct. 3, 2003; Food and Water Watch, *Faulty Pipes* (Washington, D.C., Apr. 2006), p. 20. The Rockland city official was sentenced to eighteen months in prison, and the Veolia employee received five years' probation. The Massachusetts state inspector general's office told Rockland, "It is sound public policy to abandon a contract that you have determined is tainted by scandalous activity, poorly serves the financial interest of your community, and has given rise to an appearance of misfeasance in the use of public funds"; "US Filter Is Reeling from Cascading Problems in Massachusetts," *Global Water Intelligence*, Mar. 2004, cited in Food & Water Watch, *Faulty Pipes*, p. 20.

13. F. Consolati, interview with authors, Aug. 25, 2005.

14. P. Porrini, interview with authors, Aug. 25, 2005.

15. F. Consolati, interview with authors, Aug. 25, 2005.

16. T. Neilson, *When Freedom Is Outlawed, Only Outlaws Will Be Free*, Roaring Jelly Productions, 2005, www.tomneilsonmusic.com. "Have you heard the news? It's coming to your town. It's called privatization of the water in your ground. It's corporate multinational— Veolia's the name. They say they're satisfactional, but payola is their game."

17. D. Gentile, "Plan to Privatize Lee Water System Hard to Swallow for Some Town Reps," *Berkshire Eagle*, Aug. 25, 2004.

18. D. A. Norton, letter to the editor, *Berkshire Eagle*, Sept. 2, 2004.

19. Veolia ad in the *Berkshire Eagle*, Sept. 9, 2004.

20. The description of the meeting is based on: *Lee Special Town Meeting, Sept. 23, 2004, Veolia*, DVD (no producer credit given); R. Caplan, e-mail message to authors, Sept. 25, 2004; D. Consolati, interviews with authors; C. Saldo, "Lee Says No to Veolia," *Berkshire Eagle*, Sept. 24, 2004.

21. P. Porrini, interview with authors, Aug. 25, 2005.

22. D. Consolati, "Breaking Loose in Lee," *Berkshire Eagle*, Oct. 28, 2004.

23. Gentile, "Hodgkins Roils Lee Loyalties."

24. F. Consolati, interview with authors, Aug. 25, 2005; *Lee Special Town Meeting*, videotape, Sept. 23, 2004 (no credits given); Saldo, "Lee Says No to Veolia."

25. Gentile, "Hodgkins Roils Lee Loyalties."

26. Quoted in J. Dew, "Senate Primary Rivals Debate," *Berkshire Eagle*, May 18, 2006. The Lee controversy may have been decisive in the primary. Hodgkins narrowly lost to a twenty-five-year-old first-time candidate who opposed privatization. J. Dew, "Senate: Downing Wins Very Tight Race," *Berkshire Eagle*, Sep. 20, 2006.

27. The invitation and video clips of various mayors are on the U.S. Conference of Mayors website, http://www.usmayors.org/73rd WinterMeeting/usfilter.asp.

Chapter Seven: Cooking the Numbers

1. The EPA issued five orders from 2000 to 2005 for Holyoke "to take immediate action to reduce the sewage now overflowing into the Connecticut River, even during dry weather." Environmental Protection Administration New England, "EPA Announces Order Requiring Holyoke to Fix High-Priority CSO Discharges," press release, Dec. 19, 2000, http://www.epa.gov/ne/pr/2000/121900.html; Environmental Protection Administration, *Public-Private Partnerships (Privatization)*, undated background document, http://www. epa.gov/owmitnet/cwfinance/privatization.htm. The document goes on to say: "The generic term privatization encompasses a broad range of private sector participation in public services. Partnerships between the public and private sectors in the water and wastewater industry range from providing basic services and supplies to the design, construction, operation, and ownership of public utilities. The basic reasons that the public sector historically privatized services were to realize cost savings, utilize expertise, achieve efficiencies in construction and operation, access private capital, and improve the quality of water and wastewater services." In the case

of Holyoke, critics of privatization like Ward Morehouse of the
Holyoke Citizens for Open Government accused the EPA of play-
ing an active role in supporting privatization. "It is egregious of the
EPA to try to threaten us into an ill advised privatization," said
Morehouse. "The EPA has not been helping the community to
identify and compare its alternatives, with its vast expertise and
experiences." Holyoke Citizens for Open Government, press release,
Feb. 16, 2005.

2. For information on Combined Sewer Overflows (CSOs), see the
EPA website: http://cfpub.epa.gov/npdes/home.cfm?program_id=5.
To determine whether your city is one of the 772 cities with CSOs,
see http://cfpub.epa.gov/npdes/cso/demo.cfm?program_id=5.

3. Quoted in M. Turner, "Contract on Water: Why Has Public Participation in Holyoke's Aquarion Water Services Been Kept to a Minimum?" *Valley Advocate*, Nov. 18, 2004. Mayor Sullivan confirmed
the EPA's role in supporting privatization. "The EPA strongly suggested that there might be some cost advantages to looking at contract services, so much so that the EPA was willing to give us an
extra year to meet the consent decree [on cleaning up the sewer
overflows]." M. J. Sullivan, interview with authors, July 7, 2006.

4. Quotes from Jeremy Smith are from an interview with authors,
Aug. 26, 2005.

5. Unless otherwise indicated, quotes from Mark Lubold are from
interviews with the authors on Aug. 26, 2005, and Aug. 13, 2006.

6. In February 2006, Kelda sold most of Aquarion to Macquarie Bank
of Australia, the same firm that was later to buy Thames from RWE.
Although Kelda sold its investor-owned water utilities, it did not
sell the much smaller Aquarion Operating Services, the division
responsible for public-private partnerships like the one at issue in
Holyoke. "Announcement of Conditional Sale of Aquarion Company, Inc.," Kelda Group PLC press release, Feb. 24, 2006; D. Reid,
"Aquarion Divisions Sold," *Springfield Republican*, Feb. 25, 2006.

7. Quoted in Turner, "Contract on Water."

8. Holyoke Taxpayers Association, "What Is a Public/Private Partnership?" *Newsletter*, Dec. 13, 2000. The newsletter also suggested

looking at extending privatization to the city's drinking water and to the Gas and Electric Department. "Testimony of the Honorable Michael Sullivan on Behalf of the U.S. Conference of Mayors before the House Subcommittee on Water Resources and the Environment on the Water Quality Financing Act of 2002," Mar. 19, 2003.

9. D. Reid, "Aquarion Set for Final Holyoke Public Review," *Springfield Republican*, Oct. 19, 2004. For additional information on the role of consultants, see notes 10, 11, and 14 of this chapter.

10. Office of the Inspector General, Commonwealth of Massachusetts, *Privatization of Wastewater Facilities in Lynn, Massachusetts*, June 2001, p. 4, http://www.mass.gov/ig/publ/lynnwwrp.pdf. The inspector general's report concluded that the analysis by one of the consultants, Malcolm Pirnie, was based on invalid cost comparisons (p. 70) and that any savings "will likely translate to increased profits for U.S. Filter rather than lower rates for the [Lynn Water and Sewer] Commission ratepayers" (p. 73). It also warned against long contracts with only a single bidder: "Because the 20-year contract terms effectively insulate U.S. Filter from the threat of potential competition, U.S. Filter will have little incentive to bargain. Without the potential to periodically test the market by seeking competitive prices, the Commission will have little leverage in its future dealings with U.S. Filter" (p. 74). Also see T. Jourgensen, "Lynn Water and Sewer Commission Fires Contractor US Filter," *Daily Item*, Feb. 24, 2004. In an interview with the authors in July 2006, Mayor Sullivan said, "We looked closely at the Lynn project, where there were very strange maneuvers post-contract award, and we avoided those pitfalls." However, almost two years after the inspector general's report, Sullivan told a House subcommittee, "The Lynn, Massachusetts, experience is an example of what can be achieved by using competitive approaches to design, build and operate infrastructure"; "Testimony of the Honorable Michael Sullivan on Behalf of the U.S. Conference of Mayors before the House Subcommittee on Water Resources and the Environment on the Water Quality Financing Act of 2002," Mar. 19, 2003. For a summary of the inspector general's report, see http://water.homestead.com/rhwhite-malcolmpirnie.htm.

11. Holyoke Citizens for Open Government, "Holyoke Citizens for Open Government Call on Mayor to Reverse Decision to Nix Public Bid for CSO's and Hire an Independent Consultant to Counter the Self-Professed 'Quarterback of Privatization,'" press release, Mar. 10, 2005, http://www.water.homestead.com/hcogpressconference3–10–05.html. The press release quotes a letter, released at a City Council meeting, from the "quarterback," John Lyons, on his qualifications to advise on the Holyoke privatization: "Who else in Massachusetts has more successfully performed for over 20 years the 'quarterback' role for privatization procurements?" http://www.water.homestead.com/hcogpressconference3–10–05.html. See also M. Lubold, letter to the editor, *Springfield Republican*, Aug. 10, 2005.

12. L. Santiago, "Editorial: One Holyoke," *El Dialogo*, Oct. 15, 2005.

13. M. J. Sullivan, interview with authors, July 7, 2006. Under state laws, competitive bidding is required for contracts, and under Holyoke's Code of Ordinances, the City Council's approval is required for contracts with a life span of more than three years; "Water, a Vital Source," *El Dialogo*, undated article from late 2004, http://water.homestead.com/wateravitalsource.html. Special legislation permits cities to ignore their normal rules and procedures.

14. "An Act Authorizing the City of Holyoke to Enter into Contracts for a Sewer Works System and Operation," approved Aug. 6, 2002, http://www.mass.gov/legis/laws/seslaw02/sl020214.htm. At a regular meeting of the City Council on November 1, 2005, Lubold offered a resolution ordering consultant John Lyons to appear before the City Council to explain why he told the Council that "Special Legislation he drafted" would not weaken the Council's "ultimate say-so over such contracts" when Lyons was later quoted in the *Springfield Republican* (see below) as telling the mayor that the legislation allowed him "to do whatever he wanted." Resolution available at http://ch.ci.holyoke.ma.us:81/council/council200.nsf/afa50927760 db29f8525649600458f98/456923acd0baac9c852570ca0069ee9a? OpenDocument; Lyons quoted in S. Barry, "Springfield Players Find Holyoke Home," *Springfield Republican*, Oct. 30, 2005. The resolution asked the city to evaluate whether the Council was misled and whether Lyons "had a conflict of interest in promoting this

legislation, because it would lead to a follow-on contract for approximately $100,000 for Advisory Services to the Holyoke [Department of Public Works] to promote privatization."

15. Quoted in Turner, "Contract on Water."

16. C. T. Oppenheim, e-mail message to authors, June 15, 2006. In an article for the *Valley War Bulletin*, Oppenheim wrote that the comment period was being terminated on a contract "that not even the city councilors had ever seen"; C. T. Oppenheim, "Privatizing H_2O in Holyoke: First They Come for Your Sewers, Then They Want the Water," *Valley War Bulletin*, June 2005, www.westernmassafsc.org/vwb/vwb_Jun05.pdf. The charge was echoed by council member Kevin Jourdain: "We haven't even been given a copy of the contract ourselves"; Holyoke Citizens for Open Government, "Holyoke Citizens for Open Government to Hold Public Hearing," press release, Nov. 8, 2004. For background and information on the Holyoke Citizens for Open Government campaign, see http://water.homestead.com/ and http://hcog.homestead.com/. Also see http://www.shays2.org/.

17. C. T. Oppenheim, undated 2005 letter to press..

18. B. Oelberg, "Letter to the Aquarion Company," Dec. 9, 2004, http://water.homestead.com/aquarionletteroelberg.html.

19. F. Hoey, "Introduction," in D. Moore (ed.), *Holyoke Gas and Electric Department 1902–2002: The First One Hundred Years*, p. 2, undated, http://www.hged.com/HGE_History_-_Final_Draft.pdf.

20. HCOG also demanded that an independent consultant be hired "to give us a public bid for cost comparison." Holyoke Citizens for Open Government, "Holyoke Citizens for Open Government Call on Mayor to Reverse Decision to Nix Public Bid for CSO's and Hire an Independent Consultant to Counter the Self-Professed 'Quarterback of Privatization,'" press release, Mar. 10, 2005. HCOG suggested that the city adopt an approach called "public-public partnerships." "Of particular interest is the 'Bid-to-Goal' optimization plan pioneered in San Diego, which has received numerous awards and saved the city more than $90 million over five years." Holyoke Citizens for Open Government, "Holyoke Citizens Group

Offers Alternative Proposal to Privatization of Wastewater Treatment Plant," press release, Dec. 16, 2004.

21. Editorial, "Politics Muddies Water on Holyoke Sewer Deal," *Springfield Republican*, Mar. 14, 2005: "It sounds like a good deal to us . . We think it's time for opponents to stop muddying the waters and move forward with a reasonable proposal to begin the long overdue cleanup of the Connecticut River." The paper's Holyoke city reporter David Reid even went so far as to file a legal complaint against several City Council opponents of the privatization who chatted with members of the public after a Council meeting was canceled. The complaint to the district attorney's office claimed a violation of laws against illegal meetings of city officials. City Council Member Helen Norris responded, "Talking with people after the meeting who had come to City Hall is not a violation of the law." Lubold was one of the Council members talking to college students who were doing a research paper on the controversy. D. Reid, "Mistake Keeps Issue from Open Meeting," *Springfield Republican*, Dec. 9, 2005; J. Appleton, "Councilor Rejects Claim," *Springfield Republican*, Dec. 9, 2005.

22. Quote from John Leshy, environmental attorney and former Interior Department solicitor general, at the Western Knight Center for Specialized Journalism Seminar "Water and the New West," Jun. 25, 2002.

23. P. Cook, interview with authors, Dec. 20, 2002.

24. M. Harrison, "Kelda Mulls Sell-Off of Its Not So Profitable US Subsidiary," *Independent*, May 26, 2005; Massachusetts Global Action, *Our Communities, Our Water* (Boston, 2005), p. 12; S. Pfarrer, "Water for Profit: Should Private Companies Manage Public Supplies?" *Hampshire Gazette*, May 5, 2006. In spite of the layoffs and high water rates, the British water company Kelda later decided it was not making enough from its Aquarion subsidiary and announced its sale in February 2006. However, the deal did not directly affect Holyoke. The sale, to the Australian Macquarie Bank, included only Aquarion's regulated water assets—that is, its wholly owned water companies rather than the division dealing

with public-private partnerships. Aquarion Operating Services remained a Kelda subsidiary. D. Reid, "Aquarion Divisions Sold," *Springfield Republican*, Feb. 25, 2006. *Dow Jones Newservices* quoted an unnamed analyst's view of Kelda's decision: "They bought the asset during the Dot.com period. They thought that there would be more mergers. But it didn't materialize due to [stiff] regulation." "Kelda Got a Good Price for Aquarion," *Dow Jones Newservices*, Feb. 24, 2006. The coverage noted that Kelda did not make any money on the sale but didn't lose any either. However, one report began, "Kelda, the owner of Yorkshire Water, became yesterday the latest British utility to quit America with its tail between its legs"; G. Parkinson and M. Harrison, "Kelda Stages 'Retreat with Honour' from US Market," *Independent*, Feb. 25, 2006.

25. D. Reid, "Company, Holyoke Mayor Sign 20-Year Sewer Contract," *Springfield Republican*, July 16, 2005.

26. Quoted in D. Reid, "Aquarion Contract Vote Hits Stalemate," *Springfield Republican*, Dec. 22, 2005. Public Works Director William Fuqua, an ally of Mayor Sullivan in the effort to privatize, repeatedly came back to a recalcitrant City Council with proposals for larger and larger rate increases to finance the Aquarion contract.

27. D. Reid, "Mayor's Funds Eclipse Challenger's," *Springfield Republican*, Nov. 1, 2005.

28. H. Norris, "Editorial: Sullivan: the Ballot Question Was Clear," *El Dialogo*, Dec. 1, 2005. The *Republican* reported that Sullivan would be "taking another look at the 20-year contract" after the election; M. McAuliffe, "Mayors: Incumbents Easily Elected," *Springfield Republican*, Nov. 8, 2005. Asked in an interview with the authors whether he had promised to abide by the vote, Sullivan responded, "I never said that. I did say that I would be willing to look and I'm still willing to look at any viable alternative as long as it was cost effective and in the timetable allowed"; M. J. Sullivan, interview with authors, July 7, 2006. However, efforts by members of the City Council to develop public alternatives to privatization were opposed by the mayor and his allies on the Council throughout the controversy.

29. D. Reid, "Aquarion Contract Vote Hits Stalemate," *Springfield Republican*, Dec. 22, 2005.

30. D. Reid, "DPW OKs 139% Sewer Rate Hike," *Springfield Republican*, May 9, 2006; D. Reid, "Hefty Sewer Rate Hike OK'd," *Springfield Republican*, Oct. 31, 2006. W. Morehouse, "Statement to the Joint Committee on Environment, Natural Resources & Agriculture Legislative Hearing on Massachusetts House Bill No. 1333 (An Act to Preserve Public Water and Sewer Systems)," Boston, Oct. 24, 2005, http://www.shays2.org/news/2005-10-24-Testimony.html.

31. M. J. Sullivan, interview with authors, July 7, 2006.

Chapter Eight: When Nestlé Comes

1. International Bottled Water Association, "Bottled Water: More Than Just a Story About Sales Growth," press release, Apr. 13, 2006. The $10 billion figure from IBWA is wholesale; consumer retail expenditures are much higher. Bottled water has now surpassed coffee, tea, and beer to take second place behind soda as Americans' favorite beverage. Two important critiques of bottled water are T. Clarke, *Inside the Bottle: An Exposé of the Bottled Water Industry* (Ottawa: Polaris Institute, 2005), http://www.insidethebottle.org/; and B. Howard, "Despite the Hype, Bottled Water Is Neither Cleaner nor Greener Than Tap Water," *E/The Environmental Magazine*, Dec. 9, 2003.

2. E. D. Olson, with D. Poling and G. Solomon, *Bottled Water: Pure Drink or Pure Hype?* Natural Resources Defense Council (NRDC), 1999, http://www.nrdc.org/water/drinking/bw/bwinx.asp. In its "Principal Findings and Recommendations," the NRDC writes, "It is far better from an economic, environmental, and public health point of view to improve public drinking water supplies than it is to have a massive societal shift from consumer use of tap water to use of bottled water. We cannot give up on tap water safety," Finding #6, Chapter One; T. Boldt-Van Rooy, "'Bottling Up' Our Natural Resources: The Fight over Bottled Water Extraction in the United States," *Journal of Land Use*, Spring 2003, pp. 275–277; Clarke, *Inside the Bottle*, pp. 101–102; Berkeley School of Public Health,

University of California, "Bottled Water: Better Than Tap?" *Wellness Letter*, Nov. 2005.

3. G. Karp, "Tap Water Might Fit Your Bill Better Than Bottled," *Chicago Tribune*, Sep. 10, 2006.

4. Estimates of water bottle recycling rates vary from 10 to 12 percent for bottled water. Estimates of the number of plastic water bottles dumped into the environment vary from thirty to forty million a day in the United States. The Container Recycling Institute advocates a national bottle deposit law to create an incentive to recycle and to shift the costs from taxpayers to producers and consumers. Howard, "Despite the Hype, Bottled Water Is Neither Cleaner nor Greener Than Tap Water"; M. Llanos, "Plastic Bottles Pile Up As Mountains of Waste," *MSNBC*, Mar. 2, 2005, http://msnbc.msn.com/id/5279230.

5. O. Perkins, "Don't Tread on Cleveland Water," *Cleveland Plain Dealer*, July 19, 2006; "Bottled Water Ad Slams Cleveland, Joke May Be on Them," *NewsNet5.com*, July 19, 2006, http://www.newsnet5.com/health/9540128/detail.html. Corporate Accountability International (CAI), which wages global campaigns against corporate abuses, has conducted "Tap Water Challenges" in many cities, asking people to take a blindfolded taste test of bottled and tap waters. "Across the board, people can't tell the difference," CAI's Bryan Hirsch told the *Chicago Tribune*. Hirsch quoted in G. Karp, "Tap Water Might Fit Your Bill Better Than Bottled," http://www.stopcorporateabuse.org/cms/page1353.cfm; M. Blanding, "The Bottled Water Lie," *Alternet*, http://www.alternet.org/story/453480/, Oct. 26, 2006.

6. Opposition to bottled water may be new, but it is growing, particularly among religious organizations where there is a strong belief that "water is a sacred gift that connects all life" and that the common good should take priority over commercial interests. Canada's largest Protestant denomination, the United Church of Canada (UCC), has advised its 590,000 members to stop buying bottled water. The UCC's social policy coordinator Richard Chambers said, "We don't want people buying into some subliminal message that

the water in their taps isn't safe." The UCC's website goes further: "The bottled water industry's marketing of 'safe, clean water' undermines citizens' confidence in public water systems, and paves the way for the water companies to take over underfunded public utilities." Other church groups in the United States are considering similar stands. K. Greenaway, "United Church of Canada Opts for Tap Water in Anti-Privatization Campaign," *Ecumenical News International*, Sep. 21, 2006; P. Biggs, "United Church Calls for Ban on Bottled Water," *Canadian Christianity*, undated article from fall 2006 on group's website, http://www.canadianchristianity.com/cgi-bin/na.cgi?nationalupdates/060907water.

7. Unless otherwise indicated, all quotes from Hiroshi Kanno and Arlene Kanno are from interviews with them on Nov. 12, 2005, and June 1, 2006.

8. Nestlé achieved its goal of being the number one bottled-water brand worldwide by volume and value in 2005; C. Mercer, "Nestlé to Re-organize Bottled Water Division," *Beverage Daily*.com, Mar. 3, 2006, http://www.beveragedaily.com/news/ng.asp?n=66347-nestle-bottled-water-soft-drinks. Nestlé's international chair and CEO Peter Brabeck said he still places a priority on growth. "When you stop growing you start dying," he said; "Daring, Defying, to Grow: Special Report, Nestlé," *Economist*, Aug. 7, 2004, p. 55. The story documented a twenty-year Nestlé spending spree aimed at making the company dominant in its many businesses, only one of which is bottled water. However, bottled water accounted for almost 10 percent of the company's global revenues in 2004–2005, and North America accounted for almost half of that total. H. Miller, "Nestlé's Water Unit Springs a Leak as Activists Block New Wells," *Bloomberg News*, July 26, 2006; Nestlé Waters North America, "Doing What Comes Naturally" (brochure), 2002–2003, http://www.nestle-atersna.com/Menu/Community/Our+Economic+Contribution.htm; International Bottled Water Association, "Bottled Water Continues Tradition of Strong Growth in 2005," press release, Apr. 2006.

9. "Did You Know?" *CCNews* (Concerned Citizens of Newport newsletter), Dec. 2000; J. Block, "New Haven Passes Budget,"

Events, undated clipping circa Dec. 2000. Block reports that Perrier's public relations person Jane Lazgin denied the statement was made, but Nestlé critic Myron Byers told *Events* that he had a videotape of Rob Fisher from Perrier stating the company would leave if it was not wanted.

10. Unless otherwise indicated, quotes from Jon Steinhaus are from an interview with the authors, Nov. 12, 2005.

11. H. Kanno, testimony at a public hearing with the Wisconsin Department of Natural Resources, Wisconsin Dells High School, Aug. 1, 2000; video excerpt in Concerned Citizens of Newport, *A Little Town That Could: A Rural Community Fights Perrier*, Capitol Lights Productions, 2000.

12. D. Nelson, testimony at a public hearing with the Wisconsin Department of Natural Resources, Wisconsin Dells High School, Aug. 1, 2000; video excerpt in Concerned Citizens of Newport, *A Little Town That Could*.

13. Unless otherwise indicated, quotes from Melissa Scanlan, Midwest Environment Advocates, are from an interview with the authors, Nov. 11, 2005.

14. Unless otherwise indicated, quotes from Ed Garvey, Garvey McNeil & McGillivray, S.C., are from an interview with the authors, Nov. 12, 2005.

15. Center for Responsive Politics, *Lobbying Database, Client Summary*, 2005, http://www.opensecrets.org/lobbyists. These federal lobbying figures account for only a portion of the total because Nestlé also makes contributions on the state level, such as efforts to block a 2003 California bill to increase bottled-water plant inspections and disclosures and a 2004 Maine ballot initiative, H_2O for Maine, that proposed levying a tax on groundwater extraction for bottling; M. Hays, e-mail message to authors summarizing information compiled by Corporate Accountability International, May 5, 2006. In addition to Nestlé's lobbying expenditures, Nestlé USA Chair Joseph Weller was a "Pioneer" in the Bush 2004 campaign and raised over $100,000 for the president's reelection; R. Girard, *Nestle: Corporate Profile*, Oct. 2005, http://www.polarisinstitute.org/corp_profiles/public_service_gats/corp_profiles_ps_gats.html.

16. Quoted in R. Seely, "Perrier Public Relations Miscue Was Strike One; the Scope of the Operation, Strike Two," *Wisconsin State Journal*, July 22, 2000; E. Garvey, "It Looks Like Team Thompson Is All Washed Up," *Capital Times*, Sept. 19, 2000.

17. T. Vanden Brook, "Perrier President Asked Thompson to Support Plant," *Milwaukee Journal Sentinel*, Aug. 15, 2000.

18. J. Block, "New Haven Passes Budget," *Events*, undated clipping circa Dec. 2000; Fineman PR's "Top 10 Blunders List," cited in "Did You Know?" *CCNews* (Concerned Citizens of Newport newsletter), Apr. 2001.

19. A. Nelson, interview with authors, Nov. 12, 2005.

20. Television quote cited in "Governor Thompson Breaks Silence on the Perrier Issue," *CCNews* (Concerned Citizens of Newport newsletter), Nov. 2000; J. R. Ross, "Perrier Mum on Water Tests," *Wisconsin State Journal*, Nov. 25, 2000.

21. "Testing Shows Impact on Area Wells," *CCNews* (Concerned Citizens of Newport newsletter), Dec. 2000.

22. Quoted in "Governor Scott McCallum Takes a Stand on Perrier Pumping in Wisconsin," *CCNews* (Concerned Citizens of Newport newsletter), Feb. 2001.

23. Quoted in R. Seely, "Perrier Puts State Bottling Plan Back on Shelf," *Wisconsin State Journal*, May 11, 2001.

24. H. Kanno, "Judge Wright Signs Final Order on CCN-Ho Chunk Suit," *CCNews* (Concerned Citizens of Newport newsletter), Apr.-May 2002; Clean Wisconsin, *10th Annual State of the State's Environment Report*, Apr. 22, 2002, http://www.cleanwisconsin.org/publications/stateofthestate2002.html; "Judge Upholds Perrier Well Permit but Orders More Tests," *U.S. Water News Online*, Feb. 2002, 207.57.24.111/archives/arcpolicy/2juduph2.html.

Chapter Nine: To Quench a Thirst

1. Council of Great Lakes Governors, "Great Lakes Water Management Initiative: Annex 2001 Implementing Agreements Approved and Signed," news release, Dec. 13, 2005. For background on Great Lakes issues, see P. Annin, *The Great Lakes Water Wars* (Washington,

D.C.: Island Press, 2006); A. Guy and P. Cantrell, *Liquid Gold Rush: Michigan Opens Its Waters to Global Exploitation,* Michigan Land Use Institute, Oct. 2001, http://mlui.org; D. Dempsey, *On the Brink: The Great Lakes in the 21st Century* (East Lansing: Michigan State University Press and Michigan Environmental Council, 2004); E. May, *The Great Lakes Primer,* Sierra Club of Canada with other organizations, 2005, www.sierraclub.ca/national/great-lakes/primer.html.

2. M. Barlow, interview with authors, Mar. 18, 2006. National Wildlife Federation attorney Mary Erickson, whose organization agreed to the deal, acknowledged that it was a concession but said it was necessary to get a "politically viable" agreement that could win ratification; J. Flesher, "Attorney Warns of Dangers in Water Protection Plan," *Canton Repository,* Dec. 24, 2005. For more on bulk-water diversions and the Compact Agreement, see D. Dempsey, "A Dubious Loophole for Bottled Water," *Minneapolis Star-Tribune,* Aug. 13, 2006; Clean Water Action and Clean Water Fund, *Don't Privatize the Water: Keeping Michigan's Water in Public Hands* (East Lansing, Mich., Oct. 2005); D. Dempsey, "Bottling the Great Lakes: Whose Water Is It, Anyway," *Lansing City Pulse,* Dec. 10, 2003; M. Barlow and T. Clarke, *Blue Gold: The Fight to Stop the Corporate Theft of the World's Water* (New York: New Press, 2002).

3. M. Barlow, interview with authors, Mar. 18, 2006.

4. Quoted in "Pressure to Export Water to U.S. Could Grow," *Canadian Press,* Jan. 2, 2006.

5. Unless otherwise indicated, quotes from Terry Swier are from interviews with the authors, Nov. 14, 2005, and June 16, 2006.

6. For more information on MCWC, see http://www.savemiwater.org.

7. A. Guy, "Michigan's Attorney General Weighs In: Perrier Plan Is a Great Lakes Diversion," *Great Lakes Bulletin News Service,* Oct. 5, 2001.

8. E. White, "Engler Aide Warned Perrier Could Undermine Effort to Save Water," *Grand Rapids Press,* May 15, 2001.

9. Ibid. Nestlé was eager to expand its operations to meet growing competition and demand for bottled water. "The Midwest is the last growth region for bottled water," said Nestlé spokesperson Deb

Muchmore; M. Hawthorne, "War over Bottled Water Could Leave Many Dry," *Chicago Tribune*, June 13, 2003.

10. Unless otherwise indicated, quotes from Bill Rustem are from an interview with the authors, July 21, 2006.

11. Unless otherwise indicated, quotes from Jim Olson of Olson, Bzdok & Howard, PC, are from an interview with the authors, Nov. 14, 2005.

12. T. Swier, "MUCC Sells Out," Michigan Citizens for Water Conservation press release, Jan. 31, 2006, http://www.savemiwater.org/news/Press%20Releases/MUCC%20sells%20out.htm.

13. E. Zebrowski Jr., "TU State Council Rejects Money from Ice Mountain," *Michigan Trout*, Summer 2004; cited in MCWC newsletter, July 2004, http://www.savemiwater.org/MAIN%20PAGES/News%20Letters.htm.

14. See www.nestle-watersna.com/menu/commmunity/neighbor.htm.

15. Quoted in J. Ginsburg, "Where They're Boiling over Water," *Business Week*, May 27, 2002.

16. Quotes from Andrew Guy are from an interview with the authors, Nov. 15, 2005.

17. D. Muchmore, interview with authors, Nov. 16, 2005.

18. J. Olson, interview with authors, Nov. 14, 2005; MCWC newsletter, 2002.

19. Excerpts from the September 24, 2002, letter from attorney William Horn of Mika, Meyers, Beckett & Jones to Jim Olson, MCWC attorney. Horn sent a similar letter dated September 19, 2002, to another MCWC supporter, Ethan Spaulding. That letter cites a newspaper article quoting Spaulding as saying, "Every other place they [Nestlé] are operating in has become a disaster and the aquifers are drying up: Texas, Maine, and now Florida and Pennsylvania are in trouble too." The letter calls the statement "utterly false . . . irresponsible and actionable" and concludes by demanding a public retraction. No further action on the threats was taken.

20. S. Narain, "Editorial: Want to Be Fried?" *CSE News Bulletin* (Centre for Science and Environment, New Delhi, India), June 1, 2006.

The most famous SLAPP suit was the "McLibel case" filed by McDonald's against two activists in Britain who had distributed a leaflet criticizing McDonald's for contributing to heart disease, cancer, and diabetes; see www.mcspotlight.org.

21. Quotes from Holly Wren Spaulding are from an interview with authors, Nov. 13, 2005.

22. At the time of the Mecosta County confrontation with Nestlé, several other political battles involving water were taking place in Michigan. The Michigan Welfare Rights Organization became proponents of a water-affordability program, a socially conscious business model to provide funding for water to Detroit's low-income residents; see www.mwro.org. The group also warned of possible efforts to privatize Detroit's water system. The city's chief water administrator, Victor Mercado, came from the private water sector; he had worked for Thames in Puerto Rico. Maureen Taylor, a leader of the Michigan Welfare Rights Organization, wrote that Detroit's water cutoffs to thousands of residents for nonpayment were "aimed at improving Detroit water service's revenue stream just enough to place it on the auction block for corporate takeover"; M. Taylor, "United States: Refusing to Back Down," in A. Grossman, N. Johnson, and G. Sidhu (eds.), *Diverting the Flow: A Resource Guide to Gender, Rights, and Water Privatization* (New York: Women's Environment and Development Organization, Nov. 2003), p. 9. Meanwhile, at numerous colleges and universities throughout the state, students organized to suspend contracts between Coca-Cola and school administrations because of accusations of Coke's labor abuses in Columbia and egregious water takings in India. The University of Michigan banned Coke from campus as a result, but then in a controversial move reinstated its contract three months later. See www.killercoke.org; www.stopcorporateabuse.org; www.the crimson.com/article.aspx?ref=512658.

23. Quotes from Cyndi Roper are from interviews with the authors, June 8 and June 16, 2006.

24. Quote from Michigan Supreme Court Justice Thomas Cooley is from J. Olson, "Local Comment: Groundwater Regulations Guard Against Overuse, Misuse," *Detroit Free Press*, May 11, 2004.

25. R. Glennon, *Water Follies: Groundwater Pumping and the Fate of America's Fresh Waters* (Washington, D.C.: Island Press, 2002), p.8.

26. A. Guy, "Lake Michigan Springs a Leak," *Great Lakes Bulletin News Service* (Michigan Land Use Institute), Mar. 17, 2004.

27. Quotes from Michael Haines of Mika, Meyers, Beckett & Jones, PLC, are from an interview with authors, Nov. 16, 2005.

28. Quoted in Dempsey, "Bottling the Great Lakes." Rustem has also compared water bottling to the export of air in tires and of eyewash solution that is 98 percent water.

29. J. Granholm, "Attorney General's Letter to Gov. John Engler on Water Diversion," Sept. 13, 2001, http://www.mlui.org/landwater/fullarticle.asp?fileid=11848.

30. Quotes from Judge Lawrence C. Root of the Forty-Ninth Judicial Circuit/Mecosta County Circuit Court are from his written opinion in the case of *Michigan Citizens for Water Conservation et al.* v. *Nestlé Waters North America et al.*, Case No. 01–14563-CE, delivered Nov. 25, 2003.

31. K. Schneider, "Nestlé Decision a Bipartisan Challenge," *Great Lakes Bulletin News Service* (Michigan Land Use Institute), Dec. 4, 2003.

32. H. McDiarmid Jr., "Ice Mountain Gains a Reprieve: State Asks the Court to Side with Water Plant," *Detroit Free Press*, Dec. 17, 2003; K. Schneider, "Granholm Said Yes to Nestlé Diversion After Court Said No," *Great Lakes Bulletin News Service* (Michigan Land Use Institute), Dec. 23, 2003.

33. A. Guy, "New Law Intensifies Water Diversion Debate," *Great Lakes Bulletin News Service* (Michigan Land Use Institute), Mar. 28, 2006.

34. J. Olson, e-mail message to authors, Mar. 3, 2006. For additional information on the public trust doctrine, see Clean Water Action and Clean Water Fund, *Don't Privatize the Water*, pp. 9–10. In spite of the unresolved lawsuit, Nestlé was considering a new bottling plant and two new pumping sites in Michigan, one of them believed to be near the headwaters of a state-protected trout stream. "Water Bottler Eyeing Two More Pumping Sites in Michigan," *Muskegon Chronicle*, Oct. 2, 2006.

Chapter Ten: Whose Water, Whose World Is It?

1. Luntz Research Companies and Penn, Schoen & Berland Associates, *New Poll: Americans Overwhelmingly Support Federal Trust Fund to Guarantee Clean and Safe Water* (Alexandria, Va., March 3, 2005). See also Water Infrastructure Network, www.win-water.org.

2. Testimony of Dr. Frank Luntz, president, Luntz Research Companies, to the House Subcommittee on Water Resources and Environment, Committee on Transportation and Infrastructure, Washington D.C., June 8, 2005. Commenting on the survey findings, Luntz said, "I'll be blunt. . . . This issue is NOT going to go away. This is not simply an environmental issue. It is an issue that is very personal to voters because of the importance of clean and safe water to their daily lives. This is not a local issue because Americans understand that water has no local boundaries. This is one of those areas where Americans demand that Washington take responsibility."

3. D. Coy, e-mail message to authors, Dec. 26, 2005.

4. A. Herod, "Labor Internationalism and the Contradictions of Globalization: Or, Why the Local Is Sometimes Still Important in a Global Economy," *Antipode*, July 2001, p. 407. Herod argues that because a multinational corporation must still operate in local areas, local groups of workers or activists can affect the company's operations—sometimes even on a global level—because particular local events "can be transmitted much further and much faster than ever before." Herod and others call this "strategic localization" (pp. 408–409). See also D. Hall, E. Lobina, and R. de la Motte, "Public Resistance to Privatisation in Water and Energy," *Development in Practice*, June 2005, p. 286, www.psiru.org/reports/2005–06-W-E-resist.pdf. This view is also reflected in the work of law and political science professor Joel Rogers, who leads the Center on Wisconsin Strategy. "In American politics, who controls the states controls the nation"; J. Rogers, "Devolve This," *The Nation*, Aug. 30, 2004, http://www. thenation.com/doc/20040830/rogers. In India, the charismatic leader in battles against water privatization, Rajendra Singh, points to the rapid spread of his and others' ideas about rainwater harvest-

ing as proof that "local action, small local action, can change global thinking in no time"; *Thirst*, Snitow-Kaufman Productions, 2004.

5. C. H. Deutsch, "There's Money in Thirst," *New York Times*, Aug. 10, 2006; D. Foust, "A Pipeline to Profits," *Business Week*, Dec. 26, 2005; "Water Outperforms Oil, Luring Pickens, GE's Immelt, Guy Hands," *Bloomberg News*, June 26, 2006.

6. "Exec Blasts Investor 'Flipping' of Utilities," *Water Tech News Daily*, June 15, 2006. The fire sale of public facilities has become what the *Financial News* calls a "global craze for infrastructure assets," including public toll roads, airports, ports, stock exchanges, and water and electric utilities, all being put on the auction block by government officials eager to get up-front money and let someone else take the flack for rate increases, poor services, and so on. To finance the acquisitions, the buyers are going deep into debt, a fact that worries some critics. For example, Macquarie borrowed billions of dollars to buy Thames Water from RWE, and industry experts predict there will be little spare cash for much-needed investment in fixing leaks and other problems afflicting the London water system. K. Bingham, "*Financial News* Analysis: Rush to Build Infrastructure Funds," *Financial News Online*, Sept. 29, 2006, http://www.financialnews-us.com/?contentid=1045637512; D. Derbyshire, "Buyers May Not Be Flush Enough to Fix Pipe Network, Warn Critics," *Daily Telegraph*, Oct. 18, 2006.

7. A. Ramo, e-mail message to authors, June 7, 2006.

8. The New Cities Project was launched in February 2005 by Madison, Wisconsin, mayor David Cieslewicz and the Madison-based Center on Wisconsin Strategy. Its mission is to put cities on a path toward "inclusiveness, environmental responsibility, sound management, and democratic accountability." See http://www.newcities.us. J. Nichols, "Urban Archipelago," *The Nation*, June 20, 2005. Also see Center on Wisconsin Strategy (http://www.cows.org).

9. C. Deckwirth, *Water Almost out of GATS?* Corporate Europe Observatory, Mar. 2006, www.corporateeurope.org/water/gatswater2006.pdf; *Call for Action: Derail the Deregulation of Services, No to Any Necessity Test* (Ottawa: Polaris Institute, July 5, 2006); N. Alexander

and T. Kessler, *How GATS Jeopardizes Essential Services* (Citizens
Network on Essential Services). Also see Global Trade Watch at
http://www.citizen.org/trade/ and the Forum on Democracy and
Trade at http://www.forumdemocracy.net/trade_topics/water_
services/water_services1.html.

10. For information on Davidge, see Preface, note 1. Brackpool and his
company, Cadiz Inc., were the subject of fierce controversy in California. The plan was killed in 2002, but a reporter who covered it
wrote in 2006 that "Brackpool has never gone away" and hopes to
revive the plan by working his political connections. One of those
is California Governor Arnold Schwarzenegger's chief of staff Susan
Kennedy, who received $120,000 as a "consultant" for Brackpool
in her former job at the Public Utilities Commission. M. Hiltzik,
"Golden State Column: The Many-Tentacled Keith Brackpool," *Los
Angeles Times Blog*, Feb. 13, 2006, http://goldenstateblog.latimes.
com/goldenstate/2006/02/golden_state_co_2.html; A. Bridges,
"California Water Board Kills Huge Desert Storage Project," *San
Francisco Chronicle*, Oct. 8, 2002; D. Kasler and S. Leavenworth,
"Despite Criticism, a Deal Takes Shape to Collect Water Under the
Mojave" and D. Kasler, "Would-Be Water King Awash in Contro-
versy," both in *Sacramento Bee*, Aug. 19, 2002; G. Wolff, "Economic
Evaluation of the Cadiz Groundwater Storage and Dry Year Supply
Project, Metropolitan Water District of Southern California,"
Pacific Institute for Studies in Development, Environment and
Security, July 16, 2001.

11. For information on Pickens' Mesa Water Company, see www.
mesawater.com; E. Souder, "Billionaire Pickens in His Prime—Once
Again," *Dallas Morning News*, Sep. 9, 2006; K. Breslau, "Wildcat-
ting for Water," *Newsweek*, Sept. 2, 2002; J. Leslie, "High Noon at
the Ogallala Aquifer," *Salon.com*, Feb. 1, 2001.

12. Generally, see S. Postel, *Pillar of Sand: Can the Irrigation Miracle
Last?* (New York: Norton, 1999); P. H. Gleick and others (eds.), *The
World's Water 2002–2003* (Washington, D.C.: Island Press, 2002),
Chapter One: "The Soft Path for Water," pp. 3–32.

13. H. Cooley, P. H. Gleick, and G. Wolff, *Desalination, with a Grain
of Salt: A California Perspective* (Oakland, Calif.: Pacific Institute,

2006). The authors conclude, "We do not believe that the economic evaluations of desalination commonly presented to regulators
and the public adequately account for the complicated benefits and
costs associated with issues of reliability, quality, local control, environmental effects, and impacts on development. . . . California
should pursue less costly, less environmentally damaging water-
supply alternatives first" (p. 82).

14. Information presented here about Water Tunnel #3 comes from
S. Chan, "Tunnelers Hit Something Big: A Milestone," *New York
Times*, Aug. 10, 2006; New York City Department of Environmen-
tal Protection, *City Water Tunnel No. 3*, http://www.nyc.gov/dep;
C. Haberman, "A Water Tunnel Is Badly Needed, Goldin Cau-
tions," *New York Times*, Jan. 5, 1981. See also M. Pottenger, *City
Water Tunnel #3*, a one-woman performance piece about the project
and the workers building the tunnel; P. Marks, "Theater Review:
Water World: Love of Plumbing," *New York Times*, June 9, 1998.

15. Food & Water Watch, internal memorandum, Mar. 28, 2006. Citizen action and government regulation were also factors in Kelda's
sale of Aquarion and RWE's planned IPO divestiture of American
Water. The retreat from the developing world has been much more
dramatic, a fact noted at the 4th World Water Forum in Mexico
City in March 2006. E. Malkin, "At World Forum, Support Erodes
for Private Management of Water," *New York Times*, Mar. 20, 2006;
J. Vidal, "Big Water Companies Quit Poor Countries," *Guardian*,
Mar. 22, 2006.

16. Intel employee and KPMG intern, conversations with authors,
2006. There are public sector precedents for attracting leaders. In
the 1930s, during the Great Depression, the action was not on Wall
Street, which was in the doldrums, but on Pennsylvania Avenue
in Washington, D.C., where new experiments were under way to
revive the economy. Young and ambitious lawyers and economists
flowed to the nation's capital and to state capitals to take up the
New Deal's challenges. They spearheaded the creation of new institutions and laws, from the Securities and Exchange Commission
to the Public Utility Holding Company Act and the National
Labor Relations Act. Government was a magnet for the best and

the brightest; public service was the hot place to be. J. P. Lash, *Dealers and Dreamers: A New Look at the New Deal* (New York: Doubleday, 1988).

17. D. Boys, introduction to the Fourth World Water Forum panel "Improving Local Services Through Water Operator Partnerships (WOPS)," Mexico City, Mar. 19, 2006. Public Services International is the sponsor of WOPS. Additional information can be found at html://www.world-psi.org. The project works in conjunction with the U.N. Secretary General's Advisory Board on Water and Sanitation: http://www.unsgab.org/top_page.html. Also see O. Hoedeman, *Public Water for All—the Role of Public-Public Partnerships*, Transnational Institute and Corporate Europe Observatory, Mar. 2006, http://www.tni.org/water-docs/pubwaterforall.pdf.

18. Food and Water Watch. *Faulty Pipes: Why Public Funding—Not Privatization—Is the Answer for U.S. Water Systems*, June 2006, pp. 11–12, http://www.foodandwaterwatch.org/publications/reports/faulty-pipes. Regarding Stockton, see Chapter Two. In general, see G. Wolff and E. Hallstein, *Beyond Privatization: Restructuring Water Systems to Improve Performance* (Oakland, Calif.: Pacific Institute for Studies in Development, Environment, and Security, 2005).

19. S. Roberts, "More Masses Huddling, But They Use Less Water," *New York Times*, Oct. 3, 2006. MacArthur Fellow Peter Gleick, president of the Pacific Institute for Studies in Development, Environment and Security, has produced many studies on water conservation. In testimony before a House committee, Gleick said "Water conservation and efficiency are the greatest untapped sources of water in this nation—cheaper, cleaner, and more politically acceptable than any other alternative." "Testimony of Dr. Peter Gleick Before the Subcommittee on Water Resources and Environment, Hearing: Water: Is It the 'Oil' of the 21st Century?" Jun. 4, 2003. However, politicians often undermine water conservation measures. In California, Governor Arnold Schwarzenegger vetoed legislation to adopt high-efficiency toilets, a decision criticized by Gleick. P. Gleick, "Flushing Water and Money Down the Drain," *San Francisco Chronicle*, Oct. 12, 2006. Also see P. Gleick and oth-

ers, *The World's Water, 2004–5* (Washington, D.C.: Island Press, 2004), Chapter Five. Also see Food & Water Watch, *Faulty Pipes*, pp. 11–12.

20. On rainwater harvesting in general, see F. Pearce, *Keepers of the Spring: Reclaiming Our Water in an Age of Globalization* (Washington, D.C.: Island Press, 2004); F. Pearce, *When the Rivers Run Dry: Water—The Defining Crisis of the Twenty-First Century* (Boston: Beacon Press, 2006). On rainwater harvesting in India, see P. McCully, "Harvesting Rain, Transforming Lives: India's Stellar Water Harvesting Movement Inspires Hope," *World Rivers Review*, Dec. 2002. McCully and the International Rivers Network believe that rainwater harvesting is a much more efficient way of helping the poor than large dams. "In Rajasthan, supplying water costs $2 per person with rainwater harvesting techniques, and approximately $200 per person through the controversial Sardar Sarovar Dam. Irrigating a hectare of land in India costs $3,800 through the Sardar Sarovar Project, and $120 through treadle pumps. Yet governments and financial institutions spend about $20 billion on large dams every year, but have so far mostly ignored the low cost solutions." International Rivers Network, "Small Is Beautiful in Meeting Water and Energy Needs of the Poor," press release, Mar. 13, 2006, http://www.irn.org. Two organizations in India that are leading the way on the nexus between water and democracy are Tarun Bharat Sangh, which has built a rainwater-harvesting movement in Rajasthan (http://www.tarunbharatsangh.org), and the Change Management Group at the Tamil Nadu Water Supply and Drainage Board, which has developed innovative techniques for using consensus building to challenge and change the hierarchical engineering culture of bureaucratic water departments. The process is described in a pamphlet: V. Suresh with V. Nayar, *Democratisation of Water Management—Nurturing Democratic Change*, http://www.twadboard.com/main_public?democratic.html.

21. L. Fauchon, presentation on panel "Financing Water for All" at the Fourth World Water Forum, Mexico City, Mar. 17, 2006.

22. P. Cairo, "Partnerships, Not Protests, Will Secure Water Needs," *San Francisco Chronicle*, Mar. 30, 2006.

23. The official final statement, "4th World Water Forum Ministerial Declaration," Mexico City, Mar. 22, 2006, is available at http://www.worldwatercouncil.org. On the human right to water, John Briscoe, World Bank senior water adviser, has said, "What does it mean to say that water is a human right? Those who proclaim it so would say that it is the obligation of the government of X to provide free water to everybody. Well, that's a fantasy." Interview with authors, Dec. 2002, appearing in *Thirst*, Snitow-Kaufman Productions, 2004.

24. Quoted in D. Cevallos, "Final Declaration Holds Diluted View of Water as a 'Right'," *Inter Press Service News Agency*, Mar. 22, 2006. UNESCO formally recognized the human right to water in a 2002 statement: "The human right to water is indispensable for leading a life in human dignity. It is a prerequisite for the realization of other human rights." UNESCO Committee on Economic, Social and Cultural Rights, "Substantive Issues Arising in the Implementation of the International Covenant on Economic, Social and Cultural Rights, General Comment No. 15 (2002), The Right to Water," Nov. 26, 2002, www.unhchr.ch/html/menu2/6/gc15.doc, Nov. 26, 2002.

25. "Joint Declaration of the Movements in Defense of Water," Mexico City, Mar. 19, 2006.

26. M. Partage, presentation at symposium "Public Water for All—Improving Public Water Delivery" at the International Forum in Defense of Water, Mexico City, Mar. 15, 2006. Unless otherwise indicated, additional quotes from Partage are from this symposium.

27. *Appel de Varages* [The Call from Varages], Varages, France, Oct. 14, 2005. Also see Association pour le Contrat Mondial de l'Eau: http://www.acme-eau.org.

Resources

Books

Annin, P. *The Great Lakes Water Wars*. Washington, D.C.: Island Press, 2006.

Balanya, B., and others (eds.). *Reclaiming Public Water: Achievements, Struggles and Visions from Around the World*. Amsterdam: Transnational Institute and Corporate Europe Observatory, 2005.

Barlow, M., and Clarke, T. *Blue Gold: The Fight to Stop the Corporate Theft of the World's Water*. New York: New Press, 2002.

Burstyn, V. *Water Inc*. New York: Verso, 2005.

Clark, C. *The Great Stink*. Orlando: Harcourt Brace, 2005.

Clarke, T. *Inside the Bottle: An Exposé of the Bottled Water Industry*. Ottawa: Polaris Institute, 2005.

Cooley, H., Gleick, P. H., and Wolff, G. *Desalination, with a Grain of Salt: A California Perspective*. Oakland, Calif.: Pacific Institute, 2006.

Cross, G. *A Dynasty of Water: The Story of American Water Works Company*. Voorhees, N.J.: American Water Works Company, 1991.

Dempsey, D. *On the Brink: The Great Lakes in the 21st Century*. East Lansing: Michigan State University Press and Michigan Environmental Council, 2004.

De Villiers, M. *Water: The Fate of Our Most Precious Resource*. Boston: Houghton Mifflin, 2000.

Gleick, P. H., Wolff, G., Chalecki, E. L., and Reyes, R. *The New Economy of Water: The Risks and Benefits of Globalization and Privatization of Fresh Water*. Oakland, Calif.: Pacific Institute, 2002.

Gleick, P. H., and others (eds.). *The World's Water 2006–2007*. Washington, D.C.: Island Press, 2006.

Glennon, R. *Water Follies: Groundwater Pumping and the Fate of America's Fresh Waters*. Washington, D.C.: Island Press, 2002.

Hundley, N. *The Great Thirst: Californians and Water: A History*. Berkeley: University of California Press, 2001.

International Consortium of Investigative Journalists, Beelman, M., and others (eds.). *The Water Barons: How a Few Private Companies Are Privatizing Your Water*. Washington, D.C.: Public Integrity Books, 2003.

Koeppel, G. T. *Water for Gotham*. Princeton, N.J.: Princeton University Press, 2000.

Lenglet, R., and Touly, J.-L. *L'eau des multinationals: Les vérités inavouables*. Paris: Fayard, 2006.

Leslie, J. *Deep Water: The Epic Struggle over Dams, Displaced People, and the Environment*. New York: Farrar, Straus & Giroux, 2005.

McCully, P. *Silenced Rivers: The Ecology and Politics of Large Dams*. London: Zed Books, 2001.

Olivera, O., and Lewis, T. *Cochabamba! Water War in Bolivia*. Boston: South End Press, 2004.

Palast, G., Oppenheim, J., and MacGregor, T. *Democracy and Regulation: How the Public Can Govern Essential Services*. Sterling, Va.: Pluto Press, 2003.

Pearce, F. *Keepers of the Spring: Reclaiming Our Water in an Age of Globalization*. Washington, D.C.: Island Press, 2004.

Pearce, F. *When the Rivers Run Dry: Water—The Defining Crisis of the Twenty-First Century*. Boston: Beacon Press, 2006.

Petrella, R. *The Water Manifesto: Arguments for a World Water Contract*. London: Zed Books, 2001.

Postel, S. *Pillar of Sand: Can the Irrigation Miracle Last?* New York: Norton, 1999.

Postel, S., and Richter, B. *Rivers for Life: Managing Water for People and Nature*. Washington, D.C.: Island Press, 2003.

Reisner, M. *Cadillac Desert: The American West and Its Disappearing Water*. New York: Penguin Books, 1986.

Rothfeder, J. *Every Drop for Sale: Our Desperate Battle over Water in a World About to Run Out*. New York: Penguin, 2001.

Shiva, V. *Water Wars: Privatization, Pollution, and Profit*. Boston: South End Press, 2002.

Simon, P. *Tapped Out: The Coming World Crisis in Water and What We Can Do About It*. New York: Welcome Rain, 1998.

Wolff, G., and Hallstein, E. *Beyond Privatization: Restructuring Water Systems to Improve Performance*. Oakland, Calif.: Pacific Institute for Studies in Development, Environment, and Security, 2005.

Film and Media

"Bolivia—Leasing the Rain." *PBS/Frontline World* and *NOW with Bill Moyers*,
    2002.

Cadillac Desert. PBS/KTEH, 1997.

Chinatown. Paramount Pictures, 1974.

Crapshoot: The Gamble with our Wastes. National Film Board of Canada, 2004.

Drowned Out. Spanner Films, 2003.

H₂O for Sale: The Privatization of a Human Necessity. Kern TV and NDR (Germany), 2005.

An Inconvenient Truth. Paramount Classics and Participant Productions, 2006.

Lewis Black: Black on Broadway. HBO, 2004.

The Never Never Water. KENZIsrl-Italy, 2002.

"Penn and Teller: Bullshit, Episode 7—Feng Shui and Bottled Water." *Showtime*,
    2003.

Rising Waters: Global Warming and the Fate of the Pacific Islands. Independent
    Television Service and Pacific Islanders in Communications, 2000.

Tales of the San Joaquin. Christopher Beaver Films, 2004.

Thirst. Snitow-Kaufman Productions, 2004.

The Water Is Ours, Damn It! 1World Production, 2000.

Websites

American Water Works Association: www.awwa.org

Blue Planet Project of the Council of Canadians: www.blueplanetproject.net

Citizens Network for Essential Services: www.servicesforall.org

Clean Water Action: www.cleanwateraction.org

Corporate Accountability International: www.stopcorporateabuse.org

The Democracy Center: www.democracyctr.org

Environmental Justice Coalition for Water: www.ejcw.org

Felton—Felton FLOW (Friends of Locally Owned Water): www.feltonflow.org

Food and Water Watch: www.foodandwaterwatch.org

Green Corps Field School for Environmental Organizing: www.greencorps.org

Holyoke—Holyoke Citizens for Open Government: http://hcog.homestead.com
    and www.water.homestead.com

Lexington—Bluegrass FLOW (For Local Ownership of Water): www.blue
    grassflow.org

Michigan—Michigan Citizens for Water Conservation: www.savemiwater.org

Michigan Land Use Institute: www.mlui.org

National Association of Water Companies: www.nawc.org

Natural Resources Defense Council: www.nrdc.org

Pacific Institute for Studies in Development, Environment and Security:
     www.pacinst.org and www.worldwater.org

Polaris Institute: www.polarisinstitute.org and www.insidethebottle.org

Presbyterian Church (USA) Responses to Trade Agreements: www.pcusa.org/
     trade/thirst

Public Services International Research Unit: www.psiru.org

Red Vida: www.laredvida.org

Sierra Club: www.sierraclub.org/cac/water

Stockton—Concerned Citizens Coalition of Stockton: www.cccos.org

Sweetwater Alliance: www.waterissweet.org

Thirst—the Movie: www.pbs.org/pov/thirst and www.thirstthemovie.org

United Church of Canada Water Focus: www.united-church.ca/waterfocus

U.S. Conference of Mayors—Urban Water Council: www.usmayors.org/
     urbanwater

Water Business News: www.waterwebster.com

Water Industry News: www.waterindustry.org

Water Infrastructure Network: www.win-water.org

Water Partnership Council: www.waterpartnership.org

Water Tech OnLine: www.waternet.com

World Bank: www.worldbank.org

World Water Council: www.worldwatercouncil.org

Index

The Authors

Alan Snitow is an award-winning documentary filmmaker and journalist. His films include *Thirst, Secrets of Silicon Valley,* and *Blacks and Jews.* Prior to founding Snitow-Kaufman Productions, he was a news producer for Bay Area Fox affiliate KTVU-TV for twelve years. As news director at the Bay Area Pacifica Radio station KPFA-FM, he won a Corporation for Public Broadcasting Gold Award for Best Local Newscast. He is a graduate of Cornell University and lives in the San Francisco Bay Area.

Deborah Kaufman is a film producer and director whose documentaries *Thirst, Secrets of Silicon Valley,* and *Blacks and Jews* have been broadcast on PBS and throughout Europe and Asia. She founded and was for fourteen years director of the San Francisco Jewish Film Festival, the first and largest festival of its kind. A noted activist for human rights and social justice, Kaufman is an attorney and member of the California State Bar.

Michael Fox is a San Francisco journalist, film critic, and lecturer. He has written for more than fifty regional and national publications, including *San Francisco Magazine,* the *San Francisco Chronicle,* and *PBS.org.* He curates and hosts a weekly screening series at the Mechanics' Institute in San Francisco and teaches documentary film at San Francisco State University's College of Extended Learning. A member of the San Francisco Film Critics Circle, Fox has an MBA from Loyola University, Chicago.